**W9-CKQ-437**

# The Devil

'The Devil has hardly lacked for biographers in the past forty years, but Philip Almond's new book represents a valuable addition to the list of such studies. It is comprehensive, spanning the whole range of time, amounting to two and a half millennia, in which Satan has been a figure in the Western imagination. It is lucid, explaining often quite complex theology in a manner which can be understood by, and makes the material genuinely interesting and exciting to, any readers. It will have an especial appeal to those in the English-speaking world, as, following a first half which concentrates on the development of the standard concept of the Devil in Christian theology, it examines how the implications of it worked out in England in particular; but it still keeps a hold on Continental European texts and events. All told, this is probably the best scholarly book on the subject currently available to a general audience.'

Ronald Hutton, Professor of History, University of Bristol

'Philip Almond's new book is a triumph of the simple exposition of complex concepts. With humour and charm, it proceeds accessibly from the earliest Jewish writings on demons to eighteenth-century attempts to challenge the belief that Satan was active in human affairs. Angels, giants, demoniacs, witches and divines fill its pages, and the breadth of research informing the book is impressively broad. Yet the text is informal and readable. Almond has made theology and demonology approachable and his account rips along. Readers will find a wealth of great stories recounted here. The book also provokes serious thought about the process of demonising groupings belonging to despised sects or social groups, and the terrible consequences of regarding other people as agents of the Devil. This is an entertaining and informative read.'

Marion Gibson, Associate Professor of Renaissance and Magical Literatures, University of Exeter

'This fascinating – and tragic – account of his influence through history will be a real eye-opener to anyone who supposes that the inconvenience of his not existing would limit the damage the Devil could do. Fundamentally, the Devil owes his powers to the problem of reconciling God's goodness with God's omnipotence. Following with deep learning a trail of confusion, dogmatism and persecution, Philip Almond in his vivid biography convincingly demonstrates that the Devil was, and is, a very bad idea.'

Jill Paton Walsh, author of *Knowledge of Angels*, shortlisted for the Booker Prize

# the Devil

## a new biography

Philip C. Almond

**CORNELL UNIVERSITY PRESS**
**ITHACA, NEW YORK**

Copyright © 2014 by Philip C. Almond

First published in the United Kingdom in 2014 by I.B.Tauris & Co Ltd

First published in the United States of America in 2014 by Cornell
University Press

Typeset in 11.25/13.75pt Palatino by JCS Publishing Services Ltd,
www.jcs-publishing.co.uk

Printed and bound in Great Britain by T.J. International, Padstow,
Cornwall
Librarians: A full CIP record is available from the Library of Congress.

ISBN: 978-0-8014-5337-3

Cornell University Press strives to use environmentally responsible
suppliers and materials to the fullest extent possible in the publishing
of its books. Such materials include vegetable-based, low-VOC inks
and acid-free papers that are recycled, totally chlorine-free, or partly
composed of nonwood fibers. For further information, visit our
website at www.cornellpress.cornell.edu.

Cloth printing   10 9 8 7 6 5 4 3 2 1

Bad as he is, the Devil may be abus'd,
Be falsly charg'd, and causelessly accus'd,
When Men, unwilling to be blam'd alone,
Shift off these Crimes on Him which are their Own.

Daniel Defoe, *The History of the Devil* (1727)

*To Lotus*

# Contents

*List of Illustrations*                                    ix
*Acknowledgements*                                         xii

**Prologue**                                              xiii

**Chapter One: The Devil is Born**                           1
   Angels and Demons, Sons and Lovers          1
   'The Book of the Watchers'                   3
   Angels, Arising and Falling                  6
   The Birth of 'Satan'                        15
   The Archdemon Belial                         19
   Satan and Jesus                              22
   The Fall of the Dragon                       28

**Chapter Two: The Fall of the Devil**                      31
   The Fall of Man                              31
   The Satanic Serpent                          34
   Pride Cometh before a Fall                   39
   Lucifer Descending                           42
   The Battleground of History                  47

**Chapter Three: Hell's Angel**                             49
   Paying off the Devil                         49
   The Demonic Paradox                          53
   The Harrowing of Hades                       56
   In Hell, and in the Air                      61

**Chapter Four: The Devil Rides Out**                       68
   A Pope Bewitched                             68
   Cathars, Moderate and Extreme                70
   Angels and Demons                            75
   The Demonisation of Magic                    77
   Magic Defined, Damned and Defended           82
   Conjuring Demons and Conversing with Angels  87

**Chapter Five: Devilish Bodies**     94
The Demonisation of Popular Magic     94
Errors Not Cathartic but Satanic     97
The Devil, Sex and Sexuality     100
Embodied Demons     111

**Chapter Six: The Devil and the Witch**     118
Infanticide and Cannibalism     118
Travels Sabbatical     121
The Satanic Pact     128
The Devil's Mark     135

**Chapter Seven: A Very Possessing Devil**     141
The Possessed Body     141
Possession, Medicine and Sceptics     144
Forensic Demonology     150
Beyond the Borders of the Human     156
Exorcising the Devil     160

**Chapter Eight: The Devil Defeated**     168
The Binding and Loosing of Satan     168
The Antichrist     172
Adso and the Antichrist     176
The Future Binding of Satan     179
Apocalypse Now     183
Satan and the Fires of Hell     191

**Chapter Nine: The 'Death' of the Devil**     196
Satan and Superstition     196
The Cessation of Miracles     199
The Devil De-skilled     202
The Devil Disembodied     206
Bodies, Platonic and Demonic     213
Disenchanting the World     216

**Epilogue**     220

*Notes*     223
*Bibliography*     250
*Index*     265

# Illustrations

1 The three archangels drive Lucifer from heaven into hell. *The Three Archangels* by Marco d'Oggiono (sixteenth century). By permission of The Picture-Desk.

2 Adam and Eve are tempted by Satan in the form of a four-legged, virgin-headed serpent. *The Fall of Man and the Lamentation* by Hugo van der Goes (1470–5). Public domain.

3 The angel of the Lord, described as a 'satan' ('adversary'), is called out by God to stop Balaam from cursing the people of Israel. 'Balaam and the Angel' from *The Mirror of Human Salvation* (fifteenth century). By permission of l'Agence photographique de la Réunion des musées nationaux.

4 Job, covered in boils, is assailed by God's emissary the Satan. 'Job and the Devil' from *The Mirror of Human Salvation* (fifteenth century). By permission of l'Agence photographique de la Réunion des musées nationaux.

5 Christ is tempted by the Devil. 'The Temptation of Christ' from *The Mirror of Human Salvation* (fifteenth century). By permission of l'Agence photographique de la Réunion des musées nationaux.

6 Demons delighting in tempting Saint Anthony in the desert. *The Temptation of St Anthony of Egypt* by Hieronymus Bosch (1450–1516). By permission of The Picture-Desk.

7 The Devil presents Saint Augustine with the *Book of Vices*. *St Augustine and the Devil* by Michael Pacher (*c.*1480). By permission of l'Agence photographique de la Réunion des musées nationaux.

8 The Angel, holding the keys of hell, enchains the Devil in the shape of a dragon who is then bound in the pit. 'The Angel Enchains the Devil' from a commentary on the book of Revelation by Beatus of Liebana (*c.*776). By permission of Bridgeman Art.

9 Christ harrows hell between his death and resurrection, rescuing those held captive. 'Christ Harrows Hell' from a northern English manuscript (fifteenth century). Public domain.

10 At the request of Saint Peter, the demons enabling Simon Magus to fly allow him to fall to his death. *The Fall of Simon Magus* by Lorenzo Lotto (fifteenth century). By permission of The Picture-Desk.

11 In the top panel, Theophilus makes the first written pact with the Devil. In the second panel, regretting his deal with the Devil, Theophilus begs the Virgin Mary to intercede with God on his behalf. 'Theophilus and the Devil' from the Ingeborg Psalter (twelfth century). By permission of l'Agence photographique de la Réunion des musées nationaux.

12 Faust makes a circle in the dust with a wand. Then he begins to call on Mephostophiles the spirit, and to charge him in the name of Beelzebub to appear there. 'Dr Faustus in a Magic Circle' from *The Historie of the Damnable Life and Deserved Death of Doctor John Faustus* (1648). By permission of Bridgeman Art.

13 The Devil attempts to seize a magician who has formed a pact with him but is prevented by a monk. 'The Devil and the Magician' from *Chroniques de Saint-Denis* (thirteenth century). By permission of Bridgeman Art.

14 The Devil appears as the sin of vanity. The lady looks in the mirror but all she sees is Vanity's backside. 'The Devil and the Coquette' from *Der Ritter von Turm* (1493). By permission of Bridgeman Art.

15 A witch rides backwards on a goat. While referencing the canon *Episcopi* in which women ride on beasts at night with the goddess Diana, it invokes the tradition of witches flying to the Sabbath. *Witch Riding a Goat* by Albrecht Dürer (*c*.1500–1). Public domain.

16 Witches gather at the Sabbath to worship the Devil depicted as a goat. The witch is about to kiss the goat's backside. 'The Witches' Sabbath at Vaudois' from *The Book of Occult Sciences* (fifteenth century). By permission of The Picture-Desk.

17  The ritual kiss of the Devil's backside. 'The Infamous Kiss' from Francesco Guazzo's *Compendium Maleficarum* (1626). By permission of The Picture-Desk.

18  The Devil explains his terms to the novice witches in the *Compendium Maleficarum*. 'The Devil Demands a Pact' from Francesco Guazzo's *Compendium Maleficarum* (1626). By permission of The Picture-Desk.

19  The Antichrist with Christ-like features preaches. But it is Satan, whispering in his ear, who tells him what to say. *Preaching of the Antichrist* by Luca Signorelli (1499–1504). By permission of Bridgeman Art.

20  The Antichrist supported by demons at the top is attacked by an angel. In the centre left, the Antichrist beguiles his listeners while the Devil whispers in his ear. 'The Reign of Antichrist' from the *Liber Chronicarum* (1493). By permission of Bridgeman Art.

21  The Antichrist with three heads that represent the Pope (wearing the triple tiara), the Turk (wearing the turban), and the Jew. 'The Three-headed Antichrist' (seventeenth century). By permission of Bridgeman Art.

22  The angel and the demon weigh the good and the evil in the balance. 'The Last Judgement' by the Master of Soriguela (late thirteenth century). By permission of The Picture-Desk.

23  One of the damned riding on a demon on the way to hell. *The Damned Taken to Hell* by Luca Signorelli (1499–1502). Public domain.

24  The damned are tormented by demons in the mansions of hell. 'Vision of Hell' from Vincent of Beauvais's *Miroir Historial* (fifteenth century). By permission of l'Agence photographique de la Réunion des musées nationaux.

25  Satan, tortured by demons in the fires of hell, presides over the punishments of the damned. 'Satan Confined to Hell' from *Les Très Riches Heures du Duc de Berry* (fifteenth century). By permission of l'Agence photographique de la Réunion des musées nationaux.

26  William Hogarth's 1762 portrayal of witches and demons as the stuff of superstition. *Credulity, Superstition and Fanaticism* by William Hogarth (1762). Public domain.

# Acknowledgements

This book was written in the Centre for the History of European Discourses at the University of Queensland in Australia. I am privileged to have been a member of this Centre for the past eight years. It has continued to provide a congenial, stimulating and, more often than one can hope to expect, an exciting context in which to work. For this I am indebted in particular to Professor Peter Harrison, the Director of the Centre, Professors Peter Cryle, Ian Hunter and Simon During, and Dr Elizabeth Stephens, Australian Research Fellow. I am grateful also to the Postdoctoral Fellows of the Centre, all of whose dedication to their work has provided so much encouragement to my own.

A wide-ranging book such as this is inevitably indebted to those scholars who have previously laboured in this demonic domain. Without their often groundbreaking work, this book would not have been possible. In particular, I want to acknowledge the works of Jeffrey Burton Russell, Henry Ansgar Kelly, Stuart Clark, Claire Fanger, Richard Kieckhefer, Walter Stephens, Bernard McGinn and Michael Bailey. I take the opportunity once again to thank Alex Wright, my editor at I.B.Tauris, for his support and encouragement of this work. I am indebted to Bec Stafford for the indexing of this book. I am grateful too to my partner Patricia Lee. She has again put up with my reading the text to her as it progressed, and she has offered much helpful advice. This book is dedicated to my granddaughter Lotus Linde, more angel than demon.

# Prologue

The Priest: 'Well then let's introduce ourselves, I'm Damien Karras.'

The Demon: 'And I'm the Devil! Now kindly undo these straps!'

The Priest: 'If you're the Devil, why not make the straps disappear?'

The Demon: 'That's much too vulgar a display of power, Karras.'

The Priest: 'Where's Regan?'

The Demon: 'In here. With us.'

*The Exorcist* (1973)

With these words, the Devil re-emerged in late twentieth-century Western culture. *The Exorcist* was a film that reminded audiences of the numinous Other that had been present in Western consciousness for more than two thousand years. It told of a being that represented the dark side of the Holy, one that had been personified as the evil one, the Devil. The girl in whom the Devil had taken up residence spoke with a deep contralto voice, screamed obscenities, vomited and levitated, rotated her head 180 degrees, masturbated with a crucifix and walked like a spider. Audiences were horrified and appalled, yet captivated and fascinated.

It was the beginning of a re-engagement with the demonic in film, television, literature and music that has lasted into the twenty-first century. It caused an increase in apparent demonic possessions in the conservative mainstream Christian churches, both Catholic and Protestant, and provoked the growth in exorcisms and deliverance ministries. It influenced the moral panic about the imagined sexual abuse of children within Satanic cults. It also contributed to increased (though unwarranted) suspicions among conservative Christians of demonic influence in the growing New Age movements, particularly modern witchcraft (Wicca) and neo-Paganism.

The re-emergence of the Devil in popular, if not in elite, Western culture is part of a new Western engagement with the imaginary enchanted world of preternatural beings both good and evil – of vampires and fairies, witches and wizards, werewolves and wraiths, shape-shifters and superheroes, angels and demons, ghosts and dragons, elves and aliens, succubi and incubi, hobbits and the inhabitants of Hogwarts, and zombies. It is embedded in the reappearance of a set of esoteric and occult technologies of the self (both from the East and the early modern West) that serve to enhance meaning where neither science nor matter-of-fact knowledge are useful – astrology, magical and spiritual healing, divination, ancient prophecies, meditation, dietary practices, complementary medicines, and so on. The modern enchanted world is one of multiple meanings where the spiritual occupies a space between reality and unreality. It is a domain where belief is a matter of choice and disbelief willingly and happily suspended.

Whether we believe in the Devil or not is now a matter of choice. It was not always so. For the better part of the last two thousand years in the West, it was as impossible not to believe in the Devil as it was impossible not to believe in God. To be a Christian was not only to believe in the salvation that was available through Christ, but also to expect the punishments inflicted by Satan and his demons in the eternal fires of hell for those not among the chosen. The history of God in the West is also the history of the Devil, and the history of theology also the history of demonology.

The Christian story is an historical one. It begins with God's creation of the angels, the world, the animals, man and woman. It tells of the cataclysmic event of the fall of man after the creation when Adam and Eve were tempted by the serpent in the Garden of Eden, disobeyed God and were expelled from their Paradisal realm. Man's alienation from God as a consequence of the fall was the motivation for God's becoming man in Jesus Christ, which led to a reconciliation between God and man as a result of Christ's life, death and resurrection. Finally, the Christian story tells of the culmination and end of history, when God comes to judge the living and the resurrected dead, to consign the saved to eternal happiness in heaven, and the damned to eternal punishment in the fires of hell.

This Christian story cannot be told without the Devil. Within Christian history, he plays, next to God himself, the most important part. He is first and chief among the angels created at the beginning. He is the first to disobey God and, along with his fellow fallen angels, to be expelled from heaven. From this moment on, history is a record of the conflict between God and his angelic forces, and the Devil and his demonic army. It is the Devil who soon after his own fall, in the form of a serpent, brings about the fall of man. He it is who is ultimately responsible for God's having to become man in Jesus Christ, and it is he whom Christ must overcome. It is the preliminary if not ultimate defeat of the Devil through Christ's life, death and resurrection that is at the centre of the resulting reconciliation between God and man. It is the Devil who, undaunted by his apparent defeat, remains the source of cosmic evil and human suffering. And it is the Devil and his demonic allies who are finally defeated in the great cosmic battle between good and evil at the end of history, as a result of which he and his demons are consigned to eternal punishment in the fires of hell.

Yet this is a story that is deeply paradoxical. The Devil is God's most implacable enemy and beyond God's control – the result of his having been given by God the freedom to rebel against him. Yet he is also God's faithful servant, acting only at God's command, or at least with his endorsement. The Devil literally and metaphorically personifies the paradox at the heart of Christian theism. For, on the one hand, to the extent that the Devil is God's implacable enemy and beyond his control, the responsibility for evil can be laid upon the Devil. God's love is ensured, albeit at the cost of his no longer being all-powerful. On the other hand, to the extent that the Devil is God's servant and the enforcer of his will, the responsibility for the evil that the Devil does is God's. God's all-powerfulness has been guaranteed, but at the expense of his love. This 'demonic paradox' of the Devil as both God's enforcer and his enemy is at the centre of the Christian story.

This book is a new 'life' of the Devil, one that locates his life within the broader Christian story of which it is inextricably a part. Chapter Two, 'The Fall of the Devil', traces his life from his 'birth' just after creation to his fall from heaven along with his fellow angels, to his involvement in the fall of man. Chapter Three, 'Hell's Angel', examines his place in the redemptive work of Jesus Christ, his apparent preliminary though not final defeat and his activity in hell, in history and in the world after Christ's 'victory' over him. Chapter Seven, 'A Very Possessing Devil', investigates the increase in his activities in the bodies of men and women as the end of history and the time of his final defeat draws near. Chapter Eight, 'The Devil Defeated', explores his 'incarnation' as the Antichrist, his final defeat by God at the end of history and his consignment to hell on the Day of Judgement, where, paradoxically, he is both torturer and tortured, both the punisher of the damned and one of them.

At the same time, this book tells another story. Woven throughout the account of the Christian history of the Devil there is another complex and complicated history, one that precedes, parallels, intersects and overlaps with the Christian story – that of the 'idea' of the Devil in Western thought. The Christian history of the Devil is one that only begins to take shape in the first centuries of the Christian era. But the history of the 'idea' of the Devil is one that begins some five hundred or more years earlier.

# Prologue

Thus, Chapter One ('The Devil is Born') investigates how the idea of the Devil begins in Jewish Biblical and extra-Biblical sources, variously evolves and is embellished and elaborated in the Dead Sea Scrolls and the New Testament. The next chapter, 'The Fall of the Devil' analyses the construction of the Christian story of the Devil in the first five centuries of the Christian era and the origins of the demonic paradox. Chapter Three, 'Hells Angel', examines the dominant account during the first millennium of the Christian era of Christ's victory over Satan – the so-called Ransom theory of the Atonement. It is the ambivalent nature of Christ's victory over the Devil, it is suggested, that leads to another 'demonic paradox' within Christian history – that the Devil is both defeated by Christ and yet remains free to roam the world.

The idea of the Devil in Western intellectual history reaches its high point in the first half of the second millennium. Chapter Four, 'The Devil Rides Out', analyses the expansion of 'elite' magic in the West from the eleventh century onwards and the resulting increasing demonisation of it. The next chapter, 'Devilish Bodies', investigates the ever-increasing centrality of 'the Devil' in the demonisation of 'popular' magic and sorcery within the classical demonology of the period from the fifteenth century onwards. Chapter Six, 'The Devil and the Witch', continues the analysis of how classical demonology drove the witchcraft persecutions of the fifteenth, sixteenth and seventeenth centuries.

Chapter Seven, 'A Very Possessing Devil', explores the golden age of demonic possession from 1550 to 1700, when the Devil was seen to be as active within the body of the individual as within nature and history more generally. The surge in demonic possession was read at the time as an indication that the Devil's ultimate defeat was near and that the end of history was at hand. Thus, Chapter Eight, 'The Devil Defeated', analyses Christian theorising about the role of the Devil and his henchman the Antichrist in the final days, within both Catholicism and the newly emerging Protestantism of the sixteenth and seventeenth centuries.

In Christian history, as an immortal spirit, the Devil cannot die. At the end of history, he lives on, albeit confined to hell. But ideas do die, or at least they vanish from the intellectual landscape. Chapter Nine, 'The "Death" of the Devil', investigates the decline of the idea of the Devil in Western thought. While in 1550 it was impossible not to believe in the Devil, this chapter examines the changing intellectual conditions, during the period from the late sixteenth century to the middle of the eighteenth century, that led at least some among the 'literate' elite to contemplate the non-existence of the Devil, or at the very least to question whether he any longer had a role in nature, in history or in human lives. From that time on, it is suggested, there is the possibility that the Devil exists only 'spiritually' or even merely 'metaphorically' within human hearts and minds.

Although the Devil still 'lives' in modern popular culture, for the past two hundred and fifty years he has become marginal to the dominant concerns of Western intellectual thought. That life could not be thought or imagined without him, that he was a part of the everyday, continually present in nature and history and active at the depths of our selves, has been all but forgotten. It is the aim of this work to bring modern readers to a deeper appreciation of how, from the early centuries of the Christian period through to the recent beginnings of the modern world, the human story could not be told and human life could not be lived apart from the 'life' of the Devil. With that comes the deeper recognition that, for the better part of the last two thousand years, the battle between good and evil in the hearts and minds of men and women was but the reflection of a cosmic battle between God and Satan, the divine and the diabolic, that was at the heart of history itself.

CHAPTER ONE

# The Devil is Born

When people began to multiply on the face of the ground, and daughters were born to them, the sons of God saw that they were fair; and they took wives for themselves of all that they chose. Then the Lord said, 'My spirit shall not abide in mortals forever, for they are flesh; their days shall be one hundred twenty years.' The Nephilim were on the earth in those days – and also afterward – when the sons of God went into the daughters of humans, who bore children to them. These were the heroes that were of old, warriors of renown.

Genesis 6.1–4[1]

## Angels and Demons, Sons and Lovers

In the first book of the Bible, Genesis, tucked away between the story of the murder of Abel by Cain and the decision of God to destroy all humankind except for Noah and his family, is the strange story of the sons of God and the daughters of men. In later Jewish and early Christian traditions, these four verses are elaborated into a complex account of the origin of evil in the world as the result of the lust of God's angels for the daughters of men, together with the fall of the angels from God's heavenly council and the populating of the world with demons and evil spirits. From that time on, when the sons of God became lovers of women, there were angels *and* demons.

1

In its original context in the book of Genesis, the meaning of the text is reasonably clear. The sons of God were members of God's heavenly court, divine beings who, since they were to 'mate' with women and produce children, were construed as male. There is no suggestion in this first sentence that their actions in taking the daughters of men as their wives, nor the women's action in letting themselves be so taken, were sinful ones, or matters of guilt or shame.

But the second sentence would lead us to think so. For, although God does not refer to the activities of the sons of God or the daughters of men, it would appear that human beings are punished for the actions of the sons of God and the daughters of men. Prior to this, men lived to a great age – Adam for 930 years, Seth for 912, Enosh for 905, Jared for 962 years and Enoch for 365 years, and so on. Now, though, God's spirit was withdrawn from humankind, and a lifespan of 120 years was fixed as a punishment for this mingling of the divine and the human.

The third sentence tells us that the daughters of men bore children to the sons of God. This is not the sentence's primary purpose. Rather, its main concern is to tell us that, in those days when the sons of God fathered children with the daughters of men, there were Nephilim on the earth. Who were these Nephilim? We get a clue from the fourth book of the Bible, the book of Numbers. There we read that Moses sent spies to reconnoitre the Promised Land. After their journey, they reported to Moses that, 'all the people that we saw in it are of great size. There we saw the Nephilim [...] and to ourselves we seemed like grass hoppers, and so we seemed to them' (Numbers 13.32–3). So the Nephilim who were on the earth before the Flood, 'the heroes that were of old, warriors of renown', were identical to the giant aboriginal inhabitants of Canaan, the Promised Land.

Following this identification of the Nephilim of Genesis and Numbers, the Greek version of the Hebrew Bible, the Septuagint, translated the Hebrew 'Nephilim' as γιγαντες (giants). St Jerome's Latin version of the Bible in the fourth century,[2] the Vulgate, followed suit with 'gigantes'. Thus was initiated the tradition of giants before the Flood. As the King James Version put it in 1611, 'There were giants on the earth in those days' (Genesis 6.4).

The verses that followed the story of the sons of God mating with the daughters of men and producing offspring pointed to the meaning that was later to be found in it. 'The Lord saw that the wickedness of humankind was great in the earth, and that every inclination of the thoughts of their hearts was only evil continually. And the Lord was sorry that he had made humankind upon the earth, and it grieved him to his heart' (Genesis 6.5–6). Hence, God decided to destroy all mankind 'together with animals and creeping things and birds of the air' (Genesis 6.7), with the exception of Noah and his family, and the birds and animals that Noah took into the ark.

If the original Genesis story suggested, albeit inchoately, that the mating of the sons of God with the daughters of men was the final act of cosmic wickedness that determined God to begin creation anew, it only remained for 'the sons of God' later to be identified with the term ἀγγελοι (angels), and the giants before the Flood to be identified as the children who were born of the mating of the sons of God with the daughters of men. The stage was then set for the fall of the angels, the birth of evil spirits and the supernatural origin of evil in the world. And for this we must turn to *The First Book of Enoch*.[3]

## 'The Book of the Watchers'

The traditions contained within *The First Book of Enoch* were written between the fourth century BC and the beginning of the Christian era. Contained within this collection is a set of narrative traditions known as 'The Book of the

Watchers' (chapters 1–36) that was completed by the middle of the third century BC. It is these chapters that are, in the words of Elaine Pagels, 'the first great landmark in Jewish demonology'.[4]

'The Book of the Watchers' interweaves two versions of the fall of the watchers. The first of these is an elaboration of Genesis 6.1–4. In contrast to the Genesis story, in *Enoch* the act of the sons of God, the watchers, becomes an act of rebellion against God that stems from their lust and results in the production of 'bastards' and 'half breeds' (*Enoch* 10.9). According to this, two hundred watchers, under the command of their chief Shemihazah, took wives for themselves from among the daughters of the sons of men and defiled themselves through them. They taught the women sorcery and charms, and revealed to them the cutting of roots and plants. The women bore them giants who begat the Nephilim. Unlike in Genesis, the giants in *Enoch* were ruthless. They devoured the labour of men, began to kill and eat them and drink their blood, and to eat one another's flesh.

The second version of this story has the watcher Asael teaching men metallurgy – how to make all the instruments of war, jewellery and personal ornamentation for women – together with magic and divination. Where the first version of the story has the watchers leading men astray, here it is men who make weapons for themselves and ornaments for their women, and lead astray the watchers (*Enoch* 8.1–3).

Men then cry out to the four archangels – Michael, Sariel, Raphael and Gabriel, who have seen the blood shed upon the earth, and they relay to God the message from the men:

> You see what Asael has done, who has taught all iniquity upon the earth, and has revealed the eternal mysteries that are in heaven, which the sons of men were striving to learn. And [what] Shemihazah [has done] to whom you gave authority to rule over them who are with him. They

4

have gone in to the daughters of the men of earth, and they have lain with them, and have defiled themselves with the women. And they have revealed to them all sins, and have taught them to make hate-producing charms. And now behold, the daughters of men have born sons from them, giants, half-breeds. And the blood of men is shed upon the earth. And the whole earth is filled with iniquity (*Enoch* 9.6–9).

God now acts as a judge and commissions the archangel Sariel to instruct Noah that the end is coming, Raphael to imprison Asael under the earth, Gabriel to destroy the giants and Michael to bind Shemihazah and the others who united themselves with the daughters of men and imprison them under the earth. Thus for the first time in Western thought, dark places beneath the earth become the abode of evil spirits. But not for eternity. For there is also – again, for the first time in Western thought – the announcement of a great day of judgement coming. Then Asael will be 'led away to the burning conflagration' (*Enoch* 10.7).

The imprisoning of the fallen watchers beneath the earth and the destruction of the giants was not, however, the end of evil upon the earth. After the giants were dead, their spirits emerged from their corpses to exercise as demons an ongoing persecution of humanity:

But now the giants who were begotten by the spirits and flesh – they will call them evil spirits upon the earth, for their dwelling will be upon the earth. The spirits that have gone forth from the body of their flesh are evil spirits, for from humans they came into being, and from the holy watchers was the origin of their creation. Evil spirits they will be on the earth, and evil spirits they will be called [...]. And the spirits of the giants [...] will rise up against the sons of men and against the women, for they have come forth from them (*Enoch* 15.8–9, 12).

As disembodied spirits, they escaped the Flood that God sent that destroyed all except for those on the ark of Noah. At the end of time, however, the spirits of the giants too would be destroyed. Michael was charged by God with destroying all the spirits of the sons of the watchers at the time of the judgement. If God had not at this time lost control of evil spirits, it was nonetheless the case that they continued to operate in the world as enemies of the divine, although they would be finally defeated by God at the end of history.

## Angels, Arising and Falling

From *The First Book of Enoch* we know when the angels first sinned, and we know when they will ultimately be defeated. But we are yet to discover when they were first created. For the birth of the angels, we must look to another Jewish text from the middle of the second century BC, the book of *Jubilees*.[5] It retells the books of Genesis and the first half of Exodus. In contrast to these, however, it has an elaborate angelology and demonology.

According to *Jubilees*, the angels were created on the first day, as the fourth in seven acts of creation. There is a hierarchy of groups of heavenly angels, presence and holiness – 'these two great kinds' (*Jubilees* 2.18). Like the watchers in *The First Book of Enoch*, the higher groups were sexed, for they were created circumcised. The role of the lower orders was to oversee the natural world (*Jubilees* 2.2).

In the book of *Jubilees*, the angels played a significant role in the lives of Adam and Eve. They brought the animals to Adam to be named, they assisted in the creation of Eve, they took Adam into the Garden of Eden 40 days after he had been created and later, after 80 days, they also brought Eve into the garden. They taught Adam how to work. But they played no role in the fall of Adam and Eve and their expulsion from the garden. After seven years in the garden, we are told, it was the serpent that approached the woman. She and Adam ate of the fruit of the forbidden tree in the middle of the garden, and God expelled them from it. In spite of the elaborate angelogy, the serpent is just that. We are a long way from the identification of the serpent with a spiritual being such as Satan. Indeed, at the time of the fall, the angels of presence and holiness are still benevolent beings in the celestial court.

As in *The First Book of Enoch*, so also in the book of *Jubilees*: the fall of the angels only happened after the death of Adam and during the time of Noah. Like *The First Book of Enoch*, the story of the evil spirits in *Jubilees* was developed around the story of the sons of God marrying the daughters of men. The progeny of these marriages were the giants: 'When mankind began to multiply on the surface of the entire earth and daughters were born to them, the angels of the Lord [...] saw that they were beautiful to look at. So they married of them whomever they chose. They gave birth to children for them and they were giants' (*Jubilees* 5.10).

In *The First Book of Enoch*, the Flood was announced following the descriptions of the atrocities of the giants and the petitioning of God by the angels on behalf of oppressed humanity. In *Jubilees*, by contrast, the Flood was primarily the consequence of human wickedness (*Jubilees* 5.3–4). God was, nevertheless, angry with the lower orders of angels that had been sent to earth. He ordered the heavenly angels 'to tie them up in the depths of the earth; now they are tied up and are alone' (*Jubilees* 5.6). There they were to remain 'until the great day of judgment when there will be condemnation on all who have corrupted their ways and their actions before the Lord (*Jubilees* 5.10). As for the giants, God 'sent his sword among them so that they would kill one another', and 'they began to kill each other until all of them fell by the sword and were obliterated from the earth' (*Jubilees* 5.9). The punishment of Genesis 6.3, that the days of mankind were to be no more than 120 years, was here applied to the giants.

Nevertheless, as in *The First Book of Enoch*, the giants – or at least their spirits – survived the Flood, for we soon hear of 'impure demons' who began to mislead, blind and kill the grandchildren of Noah. Told about their actions by his sons, Noah beseeches God: 'You know how your Watchers, the fathers of these spirits, have acted during my lifetime. As for these spirits who have remained alive, imprison them and hold them captive in the place of judgment' (*Jubilees* 10.5). As a result, God ordered the angels to tie them up.

Unlike Shemihazah in *The First Book of Enoch* who had played a role in the fall of the angels, Mastema, or the prince of Mastema, the leader of the evil spirits, now entered the scene for the first time. He asked God not to bind all of the spirits 'because if none is left for me I shall not be able to exercise the authority of my will among mankind. For they are meant for [the purposes of] destroying and misleading before my [final] punishment because the evil of mankind is great' (*Jubilees* 10.8). As Mastema's request suggests, God had maintained ultimate authority over the evil spirit of the giants, but he 'outsourced' his capacity to punish mankind for their sins to the evil spirits by allowing one-tenth of them to remain active in the world, 'while he would make nine parts descend to the place of judgment' (*Jubilees* 10.9). With God's allowing the evil spirits, or at least some of them, to remain active in the world until the Day of Judgement, the key relationship between God and the demons in Western demonology is established – evil spirits are active in the world only with the permission of God and, although God could control them, he chooses not to.

The angels that remained in the heavenly court then acted in accord with God's command. They tied up all the evil ones in the place of judgement beneath the earth, and left a tenth of them to exercise power on the earth. Because the evil spirits were the cause of diseases in the world, the angels gave Noah all the medicines he needed to cure these through the earth's plants. In the glorious future, Mastema would be destroyed. Mastema, we read, is *a satan*. But on the final day of judgement, 'There will be neither a satan nor any evil one who will destroy' (*Jubilees* 23.29).

Resonances of this story of the fall of the angels as recounted in *The First Book of Enoch* can be found in the New Testament. Thus, for example, in the first epistle of Peter, which we can date somewhere between the years 60 and 100, we read,

> He [Christ] was put to death in the flesh, but made alive in the spirit, in which also he went and made a proclamation to the spirits in prison, who in former times did not obey, when God waited patiently in the days of Noah, during the building of the ark, in which a few, that is, eight persons were saved through water (1 Peter 3.18–20).

As we will see later, this is a text that would provide the Biblical basis for the later doctrine of the 'harrowing of hell', that Christ between his death and his resurrection preached to those who had died before they had had the chance to gain salvation through Christ. In its original context, 'the spirits in prison' referred to the angels who had erred by having mated with the daughters of men and had been imprisoned beneath the earth as a consequence. Similarly, in the epistle of Jude, the author invoked *The First Book of Enoch* to remind his readers how, in the past, God punished those whom once he had cherished: 'And the angels who did not keep their own position, but left their proper dwelling, he has kept in eternal chains in deepest darkness for the judgment of the great Day' (Jude 6).

The same motif can be found in the second epistle of Peter. Composed around the end of the first century, its author warned his readers of false teachers who would arise, just as false prophets had arisen in times past. He reminded them of past judgements: 'For if God did not spare the angels when they sinned, but cast them into hell and committed them to chains of deepest darkness, to be kept until the judgment [...] then the Lord knows how to rescue the godly from trial, and to keep the unrighteous under punishment until the day of judgment' (2 Peter 2.4, 9).

Outside of the New Testament, the first reference in Christian literature that we find to the Genesis story of the fall of the angels is in the writings of Justin Martyr (second century). In his *First Apology* for Christianity, Justin was responding to the charge that Christians were atheists. He argued that those who made such claims did so under the guidance of the evil demons that lay behind Greco-Roman religion. Since of old, he declared, such demons have terrified men to such an extent that, 'not knowing that these were demons, they called them gods, and gave to each the name which each of the demons chose for himself [...]. We not only deny that they who did such things as these are gods [δαίμωνες, *daimones*], but assert that they are wicked and impious demons.'[6] That the religions that were in opposition to Christianity – the Greco-Roman traditions as well as Judaism – were demonic was a common theme in early Christian apologetics. Who were these demons? As we discover in Justin's *Second Apology*, they were none other than the fallen angels of Genesis 6.1–4, seen through *The First Book of Enoch*. God had entrusted the care of all things under heaven to angels whom he had appointed over them. However,

> The angels transgressed this appointment, and were captivated by love of women, and begat children who are those that are called demons; and besides, they afterwards subdued the human race to themselves, partly by magical writings, and partly by fears and the punishments they

occasioned, and partly by teaching them to offer sacrifices, and incense and libations, of which things they were in need after they were enslaved by lustful passions; and among men they sowed murders, wars, adulteries, intemperate deeds, and all wickedness.[7]

In blaming the evil spirits behind pagan religion and culture for the persecution of Christians, Justin was inaugurating the Christian tradition of demonising those it perceived as its opponents, regardless of their merits or demerits. In so doing, he was also warning his Christian readers that 'they still live in a world ruled by the proxies of the fallen angels and their sons – a world in which evil spirits lurk everywhere, hiding behind every statue and inside every temple, whispering lies into the ears of their pagan neighbours.'[8]

The second-century apologist Athenagoras, an Athenian philosopher who had converted to Christianity, used the story of the fall of the angels to the same end as Justin, namely, to explain the origin of idolatry and false religion. It is clear from his 'A Plea for the Christians' (c.177) that he is familiar with the tradition of the fall of the watchers. According to this work, the angels, like men, were created with freedom of choice as to both virtue and vice. Some continued in their government of things to which God had entrusted them. But some – including their chief, whom Athenagoras calls 'this ruler of matter' – outraged both the constitution of their nature and the government entrusted to them. These, he wrote, fell into impure love of virgins and were subjugated by the flesh. Of these lovers of virgins were begotten those who are called giants. Thus, he declared,

> These angels, then, who have fallen from heaven, and haunt the air and the earth, and are no longer able to rise to heavenly things, and the souls of the giants, which are

the demons who wander about the world, perform actions similar, the one (that is, the demons) to the nature they have received, the other (that is, the angels) to the appetites they have indulged.[9]

The Latin apologist Lactantius in his *Divine Institutes* in the early fourth century may well have been familiar with the Enochian tradition, but his version of the fall of the angels has some significantly different nuances.[10] Differing from all earlier accounts, his fall of the angels took place after the Flood. Unlike those too, the angels were sent to earth by God to look after humanity. Their need so to do was the result of God having foreseen that 'the devil' (*diabolus*), to whom he had given control of the earth at the start, might corrupt or destroy man with his deceptions. God told the angels that, above all else, they must avoid allowing contact with the earth to stain them. In spite of this,

As they continued to spend time with humans, that treacherous lord of the earth little by little habituated them to the lure of wickedness, and sullied them by unions with women. Then, when they were not acceptable in heaven because of the sins in which they had plunged themselves, they fell to earth, and thus out of the angels of God the devil made them henchmen and servants of his own. Because their offspring were neither angels nor men, but had a half and half nature, they were more acceptable below than their parents were above. So two sorts of demon were created, one celestial and one earthly. The earthly ones are the unclean spirits, authors of all wickedness that occurs, and the devil is their chief.[11]

From these demons originated magic and the divinatory arts, astrology, entrail inspection and augury, together with the pagan religions.[12] And because demons have bodies made of very thin air that are 'slender and hard to grasp', they can possess people: 'they work themselves into people's bodies and secretly get at their guts, wrecking their health, causing illness, scaring their wits with dreams, unsettling their minds with madness, till people are forced to run for help to them in troubles of their making.'[13]

In Lactantius then, the origins of evil were not to be found in the fall of the angels around the time of Noah. Rather, as we will see in more detail later, in Lactantius' *Divine Institutes* there was, even before the creation of the world, a spirit created by God who was liable to corruption and who as the result of his own free will turned to evil. The Greeks, Lactantius declared, called this one 'διάβολος' – 'devil'.[14] Thus, for Lactantius, with the origin of evil located before the creation of the world, the angels of Genesis 6.1–4 were not the cause of evil in the world. They, like humanity, were the victims of (the) Devil.

Lactantius was in fact the last major Christian writer to give an angelic reading of Genesis 6.1–4. Eventually, the angelic reading was considered heretical. The fifth-century bishop of Cyrrhus Theodoret even considered it 'stupid'. Others had also claimed that the evil originated before the creation of man but, rather than revise the story of the sons of God and the daughters of men as Lactantius had, they looked to a non-angelic reading. As much as a century before Lactantius, the non-angelic reading had been preferred by the founder of Christian chronography Julius Africanus (c.160–240). Julius was familiar with the angelic reading of the story of Genesis 6.1–4 but, as a chronographer, preferred a reading that more mundanely saw the sons of God as the descendants of Adam's son Seth and the daughters of men as the descendants of his son Cain. Thus, he declared,

What is meant by the Spirit, in my opinion, is that the descendants of Seth are called the sons of God on account of the righteous men and patriarchs who have sprung from him, even down to the Saviour Himself; but that the descendants of Cain are named the seed of men, as having nothing divine in them, on account of the wickedness of their race and the inequality of their nature, being a mixed people, and having stirred the indignation of God.[15]

The fate of the angelic reading of Genesis 6.1–4 was sealed by St Augustine of Hippo in his *The City of God* (413–27), in which 'the sons of God' and 'the daughters of men' denoted the heavenly and the earthly cities respectively. It was the mixing of these two cities that produced evil. Crucially, Augustine gave a non-angelic allegorical reading of the story:

And by these two names [sons of God and daughters of men] the two cities are sufficiently distinguished. For though the former were by nature children of men, they had come into possession of another name by grace. For in the same Scripture in which the sons of God are said to have loved the daughters of men, they are also called angels of God; whence many suppose that they were not men but angels.[16]

For Augustine, the issue was to turn on whether angels were the kinds of beings who had bodies and therefore could have sex with women (see Plate 7). It is a possibility that he did not rule out, not least because there were scriptural references to embodied angels. He was aware too of the well-founded rumour 'that sylvans and fauns, who are commonly called "incubi," had often made wicked assaults upon women, and satisfied their lust upon them'.[17] But he was not convinced that the fall of the angels of God was being described in Genesis 6.1-4, nor that it was of these angels that the second epistle of Peter was speaking in 'God did not spare the angels when they sinned, but cast them into hell and committed them to chains of deepest darkness to be kept until the judgment' (2 Peter 2.4). For Augustine, the fall of the angels did not occur at the time of the Flood, but rather before the creation of Adam and Eve. And thus, the First Epistle of Peter was describing 'those who first apostatized from God, along with their chief the devil, who enviously deceived the first man under the form of a serpent'.[18]

For Lactantius, the fall of the angels after the Flood was the result of their progressive seduction by the Devil, who had himself been created and had fallen before the creation of the world. Evil thus *pre-dated* creation. For Augustine, too, the origins of evil were located in the time before the creation of man, but in contrast to Lactantius, Augustine believed that the angels and their chief the Devil fell at that time. With the relocation of the fall of the angels to a period before the creation of man, the reading of Genesis 6.1–4 as a story about the fall of the angels and an account of the origin of evil became theologically redundant. As a consequence, with the demise of the angelic reading of Genesis 6.1-4, the threefold division into the Devil, fallen angels and demons (the progeny of the sons of God and the daughters of men) collapsed into a twofold one of the Devil and the fallen angels only. It was this twofold division that was to become the dominant motif in the Christian story.

## The Birth of 'Satan'

We have already seen that there was a variety of names for the chief of the evil spirits – Shemihazah, Asael and Mastema. And, as we will see, the chief of the demons will also be known as Beelzebul, Lucifer and Belial. But it was the name Satan or its Greek form διάβολος and Latin form *diabolos*, rendered in English as 'Devil' (French as *Diable*, German as *Teufel*) that came to predominate. Thus, although there were many demons, there was but one Satan. Later, although there were several devils, their chief remained the Devil or even on occasion the Demon. Still, as we noted earlier, in the book of *Jubilees*, 'satan' was not so much a proper name as a description of Mastema's role on behalf of God as the accuser or the adversary. So how did the term 'Satan' transition from describing a role or function to becoming the personal name of the prince of demons?

The proper name 'Satan' comes from the Hebrew common noun *śātān*. This use of the term 'satan' to describe a role rather than a particular being is common in the Hebrew Bible.[19] There it occurs nine times. On five occasions, it refers to human beings and denotes a role as an adversary or accuser. On four occasions, it refers to celestial beings. In the first of these, which dates from around the tenth century BC, it denotes a celestial being sent by God to do his bidding. It arises in the story of Balaam and his ass – which is, apart from the serpent in the Garden of Eden, the only animal in the Bible that speaks (Numbers 22.22–35).

In this story, the angel of the Lord who is described as a 'satan' ('adversary') is called out by God to stop Balaam, a non-Israelite, from cursing the people of Israel (see Plate 3). Three times Balaam's donkey, seeing the angel of the Lord who was invisible to Balaam, refused to go on. Balaam struck it on each occasion. God opened the mouth of the donkey, which said to Balaam, 'What have I done to you that you have struck me these three times?' Balaam replied, 'Because you have made a fool of me! I wish I had a sword in my hand! I would kill you right now.' But the donkey said to Balaam, 'Am I not your donkey, which you have ridden all your life to this day? Have I been in the habit of treating you this way?' And Balaam replied, 'No' (Numbers 22.28–30). At that point God opened Balaam's eyes, enabling him to see the angel, who declared, 'I have come out as an adversary [*śātān*], because your way is perverse before me' (Numbers 22.32). The angel tells Balaam that, had the donkey not turned away, he would have killed Balaam and let the donkey live. Balaam was allowed to continue, although instructed by God to say what God told him to.

In this story in the book of Numbers, the satan functioned only as God's emissary. In the book of Job – written no later than 400–300 BC – Satan was a member of the heavenly council. He fulfilled the function of a tempter of the righteous on earth and their accuser in the divine council. As such, although he remained subordinate to God, he was neither God's faithful servant nor the enemy of God and all goodness in the world. He *was* oppositional, manipulative and contemptuous. In the book of Job, God had ceded responsibility for the sufferings of humankind to the Devil. God's goodness was maintained, although at the cost of a diminution in his wisdom and power.

In the book of Job, the setting is the heavenly court, where the heavenly beings presented themselves before God. Among them was the satan. God asked the satan if he had considered his servant Job 'a blameless and upright man,' said the Lord, 'who fears God and turns away from evil'. The satan declared to God that Job's piety and morality was nothing but the consequence of his having been divinely favoured. 'But stretch out your hand now,' said the satan, 'and touch all that he has, and he will curse you to your face' (Job 1.11).

The satan thus placed God in a difficult position. Should he refuse to test Job, it might appear that he was afraid that there was a basis to the satan's claim. Accept the satan's suggestion, and he would appear as the perpetrator of evil upon a good man. So God laid the responsibility upon the satan: 'Very well,' he said to the satan, 'all that he has is in your power; only do not stretch out your hand against him' (Job 1.12). Unlike the reader, Job and his friends were unaware of the deal struck between God and the satan, and believed that the misfortunes that befell Job and his family proceeded from God. Only thus could Job be presented as a model of faith in the face of calamitous misfortunes.

The satan then inflicted a series of disasters on Job. His livestock was stolen or destroyed and his servants died, along with his sons and daughters. But Job's faith in God remained firm, as God pointedly reminded the satan: 'He still persists in his integrity, although you incited me against him, to destroy him for no reason' (Job 2.3). The satan then raised the stakes: 'All that people have they will give to save their lives. But stretch out your hand now and touch his bone and his flesh, and he will curse you to your face' (Job 2.5). With God's permission, the satan then inflicted loathsome sores all over Job's body (see Plate 4). 'Curse God, and die,' said Job's wife, serving as the satan's earthly mouthpiece (Job 2.9). But Job refused: 'You speak as any foolish woman would speak. Shall we receive the good at the hand of God, and not receive the bad?' (Job 2.10). Job knew nothing of the cause of his sufferings, the battle of wills between the satan and God. He attributed them to God, but his faith in God did not waver.

In the book of Zechariah, written around the year 500 BC, the scene is again that of a tribunal in the heavenly court. The high priest of Jerusalem, Joshua, was standing before the angel of the Lord, with the satan (*haśśātān*) on his right in the role of the accuser. The angel rebuked the satan for his rejection of Jerusalem as the city of God. He declared Joshua free of guilt by replacing the filthy garments in which he appeared with clean ones, appropriate for rituals. The angel then assured Joshua that, were he to walk in God's ways and keep his requirements, he would have a long rule over the house of God (Zechariah 3.1–7). The text is a turning point in the history of the Devil; as Elaine Pagels remarks, the passage depicts the satan 'on the verge of deviating from his role as God's agent to become his enemy'.[20]

This developing role of the satan as God's enemy rather than his emissary becomes even clearer in the first book of Chronicles: 'Satan stood up against Israel, and incited David to count the people of Israel' (1 Chronicles 21.1). We get a clear sense of the significance of this passage when we compare it to the earlier parallel section in the second book of Samuel, in which it was God and not Satan who, angry with Israel, incited King David to take a census of the people (2 Samuel 24.1). We can see that the author of the Chronicles has taken the responsibility for initiating the sinful act of taking a census away from God and laid it upon an intermediary, thus absolving the deity. Here we have the beginnings of a cosmic dualism – of Satan representing evil and God representing good.

## The Archdemon Belial

This distancing of evil from God, albeit in a different way, is also found in two of the first scrolls discovered in 1947 at Qumran on the western shore of the Dead Sea, *The Rule of the Community* (100–150 BC) and the *War Scroll* (second century BC).[21] They were the product of a strict Jewish sect connected to the Essenes that had a strong sense of community identity. The community viewed world history in terms of an ongoing struggle between the forces of light and the forces of darkness.

The writers of *The Rule of the Community* and the *War Scroll* may well have known the books of *Enoch* and *Jubilees*, for they formed part of the library of the Qumran community. Their view of the archdemon Belial, leader of the angels of darkness, was not especially influenced by them, however.[22] Indeed, the story of the origin of evil in these works bears no relation to the story of the fall of the watchers in the books of *Enoch* and *Jubilees*; in the scrolls, God created evil from the beginning. As the *War Scroll*

19

puts it, 'you created Belial for the pit, angel of enmity; his domain is darkness, his counsel is for evil and wickedness' (1QM 13.11).

The origin of evil was presented in more elaborate form in *The Rule of the Community*. Here, all that is and will be came from the God of knowledge. He established the design of all things, and when things came into being, they were in accord with his design. God created the spirits of light and darkness. He loved the spirit of light and took pleasure in all his deeds. But he hated the spirit of darkness. Thus, reality was determined from the beginning by the opposition between spirit and matter, light and darkness, justice and evil, truth and falsehood, the present age and one that is to come, within an overarching pattern predetermined by God.

This cosmic dualism was, however, relative and not absolute. God was not opposed by a being, Belial, who was his equal. As with Christian demonology, Jewish demonology remained committed to the absolute sovereignty of God alone. In both Jewish and Christian demonologies, God was ultimately responsible for the existence of evil, and in control of history from its beginning to its end. God was nevertheless aligned with the good. Thus, in *The Rule of the Community*, there is God with his group – the sons of light, together with the prince of lights (probably Michael) and his angels (including the angels of destruction) – and the prince of darkness (Belial) and his cohorts – the evil angels and the sons of deceit.

God also created man to govern the world. In him, God placed the two spirits, the spirits of truth and falsehood: 'In the hand of the Prince of Lights is dominion over all the sons of justice; they walk on the paths of light. And in the hand of the Angel of Darkness is total dominion over the sons of deceit; they walk on paths of darkness' (1QS 3.20–1). The 'sons of justice' referred to the sect members; the 'sons of deceit' or the 'sons of darkness' referred to those outside the community. The prince of lights had dominion over the sons of justice, but the Angel of Darkness nonetheless caused them to stray. However, the God of Israel, together with the angel of his truth, assisted all the sons of light. Within the hearts of all men, truth and injustice feud, and the men walk in wisdom or in folly: 'In agreement with man's birthright in justice and in truth, so he abhors injustice; and according to his share in the lot of injustice he acts irreverently in it and so abhors the truth' (1QS 4.23–5). Thus is explained evil within the community itself, the struggle between good and evil in the hearts of all men.

However that may be, God had determined that injustice would end, and he would obliterate it forever when he eventually intervened directly in cosmic affairs. For the sons of truth, there would finally be eternal enjoyment with endless life, and 'a crown of glory with majestic raiment in eternal light' (1QS 4.7–8). For the sons of deceit, there would be eternal punishments in the fires of the dark regions at the hands of all the angels of destruction, God's obedient servants exacting his revenge. And 'all the ages of their generations they shall spend in bitter weeping and harsh evils in the abysses of darkness until their destruction, without there being a remnant or a survivor among them' (1QS 4.13–14). Truth would rise up in a world defiled by wickedness. Then God would refine, by his truth, all men's deeds and purify them, 'ripping out all spirit of injustice from the innermost part of the flesh, and cleansing him with the spirit of holiness from every irreverent deed' (1QS 4.20–1).

The final future battle between the sons of light and the sons of darkness, elaborated in *The War Scroll*, was determined by God from the beginning. The first attack would be by the sons of light, against the sons of darkness, 'the army of Belial' (1QM 1.1). It would involve both earthly and heavenly forces. Thus, in the great battle against the Kittim, 'the assembly of the gods and the congregation

21

of men shall confront each other for great destruction' (1QM 1.10). The battle would consist of seven stages, in three of which the sons of light would prevail, while in another three the sons of darkness would force the sons of light to retreat. In the seventh and final stage, God would decisively intervene and subdue Belial, his angels and his men. There would be everlasting destruction for all Belial's supporters. A new age would follow in which there would be salvation for the people of God and a period of rule for all his men: 'the sons of justice shall shine in all the edges of the earth, they shall go on illuminating, up to the end of all the periods of darkness; and in the time of God, his exalted greatness will shine for all the [eternal] times, for peace and blessing, glory and joy, and long days for all the sons of light' (1QM 1.8–9). What are to become the final days of the Devil in the Christian story were taking shape in these Dead Sea Scrolls.

## Satan and Jesus

The prince of demons went by many different names – Shemihazah, Asael, Mastema, and now Belial. There was one office, though it was occupied by many different persons. His name was also Satan, and he appeared as such in a text mentioned above: 'Satan stood up against Israel, and incited David to count the people of Israel' (1 Chronicles 21.1). Here, for the first time, the definite article 'the' has been omitted from the Hebrew text, and 'Satan' has become in the Hebrew Bible a personal name. As the *persona* became a person and the role a name, Satan was 'born'. The date of this text is much debated. But if it is the case that it comes from the period around 100 BC, then already at that time 'Satan' denoted a person and not a role, and he was an accuser (against Israel), a tempter (of King David) and an enemy of God.[23] Satan has been 'baptised'.

The Greek version of the Old Testament, the Septuagint, translated *śātān* as διάβολος, whence *diabolus* in Latin and 'Devil' in English. Crucially, the translator of 1 Chronicles in the Septuagint, noting the absence of the definite article in the Hebrew, read *śātān* as a proper name, translating it as διάβολος and omitting the Greek definite article. Thus, *śātān* (Satan) and διάβολος (Devil) are alternative personal names. There is no definite article in Latin, so whether the Latin term for *śātān*, namely *diabolus*, should be read as denoting a role and translated as 'the Devil' or as signifying a proper name and translated 'Devil' is uncertain.

In the New Testament period, from the years around 50–100, the terms were flexible. Thus, for example, in the book of Revelation, the last book of the Christian New Testament (*c*.100), the reverse usage was in play: 'The one who is called Devil [διάβολος] and the satan [ὁσατανας]' (Revelation 12.9). Within the New Testament more generally, 'Devil' (διάβολος), 'the Devil' (ὁ διάβολος), Satan (σατανας), and the Satan (ὁ σατανας) are used interchangeably, along with a number of other terms that designate his roles – 'the tempter', 'the evil one', 'the enemy', 'the ruler of the demons' and the proper names 'Beliar' (2 Corinthians 6.15) and 'Beelzebul' (Mark 3.22–7, Matthew 10.25, 12.24–8, Luke 11.15–20).

Nevertheless, within the history of Western theology, the convention has become to use 'Satan' (or sometimes 'Lucifer') rather than 'Devil' as the proper name of the leader of the demons, and 'the Devil' to describe his role as the adversary of both man and God. Regardless, whether as Satan or the Devil, by a century before the beginning of the Christian era, he has emerged into the historical light as the prince of demons.

It would be wrong to seek a unified view of the Devil in the varied collection of works that make up the New Testament (*c*.50–100). Nevertheless, there are a number of common themes that range across it. Above all, the

Devil in the New Testament has become God's implacable enemy.[24] He rules the Kingdom of Darkness that opposes the Kingdom of God. The Kingdom of Darkness embraces the whole world: 'The whole world lies under the power of the evil one' (1 John 5.19). The Devil is 'the ruler of this world' (John 12.31) and 'the god of this world' (2 Corinthians 4.4). Human beings are therefore under 'the power of Satan' (Acts 26.18) and 'the power of darkness' (Colossians 1.13), for Satan is 'the deceiver of the whole world' (Revelation 12.9).

The Devil has at his disposal a host of demons to oppose the angels of God and to deprave humankind. Among these are the lesser spirits that cause disease, disability and insanity, often through entering human bodies and possessing them. The story of the Gerasene demoniac, as told in the Gospel of Mark (5.1–20),[25] is emblematic. Jesus and his disciples, we read, had crossed the Lake of Galilee to the country of the Gerasenes. When Jesus stepped out of the boat, he was confronted by a man with an unclean spirit who lived among the tombs. He demonstrated the sort of extraordinary strength that those possessed by spirits were often claimed to show. However often he was restrained with shackles and chains, he was able to break them. He was self-destructive, beating himself with stones and howling among the tombs and on the mountains. Jesus told the spirit to depart. The spirit, recognising Jesus, replied, 'What have you to do with me, Jesus, Son of the Most High God? I adjure by God, do not torment me.' When Jesus asked the spirit his name, he replied, 'My name is Legion; for we are many.' And the spirit begged Jesus not to send them out of the country, but to 'Send us into the swine; let us enter them.' When Jesus allowed it, the spirits came out of the man and entered the pigs. The herd, numbering about two thousand, rushed down the steep bank into the sea and were drowned. The spirit(s) presumably were confined in the waters of the lake.

The swineherds ran off and told the story far and wide, and a crowd came together to see Jesus talking to the demoniac, now clothed and in his right mind. Afraid of the power of Jesus, the locals begged him to leave the region. The former demoniac begged to be allowed to stay with Jesus, but Jesus refused, telling him to go to his friends and tell them what God had done for him.[26]

The Devil had at his disposal not only lesser local demons, but also 'the cosmic powers of this present darkness', 'great world powers of this darkness', 'the spiritual forces of evil in the heavenly places' (Ephesians 6.5). The Devil and his angels ruled the stars and could access the heavens; like the spirits of the giants in the *First Book of Enoch*, the Devil ruled over the spirits who lived in the air (Ephesians 2.2).

As the story of the Gerasene demoniac suggests, a central part of the work of Jesus was to represent the Kingdom of God and oppose the Kingdom of Darkness: 'The Son of God was revealed for this purpose, to destroy the works of the Devil' (1 John 3.8). First, Jesus had to overcome the temptation of Satan. According to the Gospel of Matthew (4.1–11), after he had been baptised by John, Jesus was led by the spirit of God into the desert to be tempted by the Devil.[27] At the end of a 40-day fast, 'the tester' or 'the tempter' came to him. Like the satan in Job and like Mastema in *Jubilees*, here he has a speaking part. His aim was to tempt Jesus to demonstrate that, like him, he was a heavenly being. 'If you are the Son of God,' the Devil said, 'command these stones to become loaves of bread' (see Plate 5). Jesus responded with a quotation from the Hebrew Bible, 'One does not live by bread alone, but by every word that comes from the mouth of God' (Deuteronomy 8.3). For his next test, the Devil took him to the pinnacle of the temple in Jerusalem, and quoted the Hebrew Bible at him: 'If you are the Son of God, throw yourself down; for it is written, "He will command his angels concerning you" and "On their hands they will bear you up, so that you will not dash your foot against a stone"' (Psalms 91.11, 12). Jesus replied with another passage from the book of Deuteronomy (6.16): 'Do not put the Lord your God to the test.' The Devil then took Jesus to a high mountain and showed him all the kingdoms of the world, offering them all to Jesus if he would fall down and worship him. 'Away with you, Satan!' declared Jesus. 'For it is written, "Worship the Lord your God, and serve only him"' (Deuteronomy 6.13).

From that time on, the Devil was the implacable enemy of Jesus, and the work of Jesus in casting out demons was emblematic of the ongoing struggle between him and the Devil, and the kingdoms of good and evil. Moreover, Jesus' exorcisms marked the beginning of the Kingdom of God. Thus, when the Pharisees heard of his works of exorcism, they said that it was 'by Beelzebul, the ruler of the demons that this fellow casts out the demons'. Knowing what they were thinking, Jesus said to them,

> Every kingdom divided by itself is laid waste, and no city or house divided against itself will stand. If [the] Satan casts out [the] Satan, he is divided against himself; how then will his kingdom stand? If I cast out demons by Beelzebul, by whom do your own exorcists cast them out? But if it is by the spirit of God that I cast out demons, then the Kingdom of God has come to you. Or how can one enter the house of the strong man and plunder his property, without first tying up the strong man? Then indeed the house can be plundered (Matthew 12.25–9).[28]

It is clear from the New Testament Gospels that exorcisms continued as part of the ministry of the early Church after the time of Jesus. In a number of passages produced in the early Church, we read of Jesus giving his disciples power and authority over demons and unclean spirits (Matthew 10.1, Mark 6.7, Luke 9.1). They met with success.

Thus, in the Gospel of Luke (10.17–20), for example, the 70 disciples whom Jesus sent out in his name returned to Jesus and reported joyfully that 'in your name, even the demons submit to us.' And Jesus saw this as a sign, as clear as a lightning flash, that Satan was in the process of being defeated and that the Kingdom of God had begun: 'I watched Satan fall from heaven like a flash of lightning.'

Defeated the Devil may have been, but he was not destroyed. He was able to continue using people as his instruments. When the apostle Peter rebuked Jesus for saying that he would be killed, Jesus saw it as the Devil within Peter that was speaking: 'Get behind me, Satan!' (Mark 8.33). He told the Jewish authorities who claimed Abraham as their father, 'You are from your father the Devil' (John 8.44). And it was the Devil who entered Judas Iscariot in order to betray Jesus. The setting was the Last Supper. Jesus was aware that the time had come for him to depart from the world. With the supper taking place, the Devil decided in his heart that Judas Iscariot should betray Jesus.[29] Jesus arose from supper and, putting aside his garments, tied a towel around himself and washed his disciples' feet. Jesus knew who was to betray him and later, when he and his disciples had resumed their meal, he told one of the disciples that his betrayer was he to whom he would give a piece of bread. He gave it to Judas, the son of Simon Iscariot. At that time, 'Satan entered into him' (John 13.27). Jesus told him to do what he had to do; Judas immediately went out and betrayed him to the Jewish authorities.

Jesus himself had not expected his death to signal the defeat of Satan. During the Last Supper, Jesus had prayed to God to 'protect them from the evil one' (John 17.15). He had also taught his disciples themselves to pray to God to 'rescue us from the evil one' (Matthew 6.13). Like a roaring lion, the Devil still 'prowls around, looking for someone to devour' (1 Peter 5.8). He was the cause of the persecution and imprisonment of Christians, having raised external enemies against Christianity. When the magician Elymas opposed Paul and Barnabas and attempted to turn the Roman proconsul Sergius Paulus against them, Paul recognised him as an agent of the Devil (Acts 13.10). The Devil also inspired false teachers within the Church who opposed the teaching of Paul: 'Even Satan disguises himself as an angel of light. So it is not strange if his ministers also disguise themselves as ministers of righteousness' (2 Corinthians 11.14). Nevertheless, resistance was possible: 'Submit yourselves therefore to God,' James told his readers. 'Resist the Devil, and he will flee from you' (James 4.7).

## The Fall of the Dragon

> And war broke out in heaven; Michael and his angels fought against the dragon. The dragon and his angels fought back, but they were defeated, and there was no longer any place for them in heaven. The great dragon was thrown down, that ancient serpent, who is called Devil and [the] Satan, the deceiver of the whole world – he was thrown down to the earth, and his angels were thrown down with him (Revelation 12.7–9).

The story of the fall of the dragon and his angels from heaven is in the final book of the New Testament, and the last to be written – the book of Revelation – ascribed to a John of Patmos. This story of the fall of the dragon and his angels has traditionally been read as referring to the fall of Satan before the time of the creation, and the 'ancient serpent, who is called Devil and the Satan' as referring to the serpent in the Garden of Eden. But Revelation, like the Bible as a whole, knows nothing of a pre-creation fall of Satan. Rather, a close reading of the text of Revelation indicates that the fall of the dragon and his angels occurred, not before the creation of Adam, but after the death of Christ (see Plate 1). It also suggests that, as in Job and in Zechariah, Satan has continued his role in the heavenly court as the accuser until he is defeated, first in a battle with Michael and his angels, and then by the blood of the Lamb – that is, Christ – and by his loss in the heavenly court as a consequence of the testimony of the martyrs: 'for the accuser of our comrades has been thrown down, who accuses them day and night before our God' (Revelation 12.10). Thus did Satan lose his heavenly position as the prosecutor. His work continued at the terrestrial level: 'Rejoice then, you heavens, and those who dwell in them! But woe to the earth and the sea, for the Devil has come down to you with great wrath, because he knows that his time is short!' (Revelation 12.12).

The vehemence of the Devil's actions in the world was increased by his fall, and only mitigated by the brief time that was to follow before his final defeat. The Christian community out of which the book of Revelation came was an apocalyptic one, wedged between present persecution and hoped-for bliss, living in expectation of a decisive intervention from God, and the coming of a new heaven and a new earth. For this community, the ultimate defeat of Satan was a necessary prelude to the Kingdom of God that was to come. An angel came down from heaven, we read, holding in his hand a great chain and the key to the bottomless pit. He seized the dragon: 'that ancient serpent who is the Devil and Satan, and bound him for a thousand years, and threw him into the pit, and locked it and sealed it over him, so that he would deceive the nations no more, until the thousand years were ended' (Revelation 20.2–3).

When the millennium had ended, Satan would be released from prison for a brief time in order to deceive the nations at the four corners of the earth. These nations, described as Gog and Magog, gathered their forces to do battle against the saints. They were destroyed by a fire that came down from heaven. The Devil was thrown 'into the lake of fire and sulfur, where the beast and the false prophet were, and they will be tormented for ever and ever' (Revelation 20.10).

It would then be time for the Last Judgement. The book of Revelation speaks of a great white throne and an awesome figure upon it, from whom the earth and the heaven fled. Death, the sea and Hades gave up the dead that were in them. These stood before the throne to be judged according to their deeds as they had been recorded in the record books. Anyone whose name was not found written in the book of life 'was thrown into the lake of fire' (Revelation 20.15), there to join Satan in eternal torment.

# CHAPTER TWO

# The Fall of the Devil

How art thou fallen from heaven, O Lucifer, son of the morning! How art thou cut down to the ground, which didst weaken the nations! For thou hast said in thine heart, I will ascend into heaven, I will exalt my throne above the stars of God: I will sit also upon the mount of the congregation, in the sides of the north: I will ascend above the heights of the clouds; I will be like the Most High. Yet thou shalt be brought down to hell, to the sides of the pit.

Isaiah 14.12–15 (KJV)

## The Fall of Man

Surprisingly, by the year 100 and the end of the New Testament period, although we know of the end of Satan from the book of Revelation, we know little about his beginnings. There is nothing in the Biblical record about the fall of Satan or the angels before the creation of man. Nor do we find in the Bible any connection between Satan and the serpent in the Garden of Eden.[1] To be sure, as we saw above, Revelation (12. 9) refers to 'that ancient serpent who is called Devil and the Satan'. But there is nothing within the text to suggest that it is the Edenic serpent to which reference is being made. So accustomed are we to the identification of the Edenic serpent with the Devil in the history of the post-Biblical Christian interpretation of the fall of Adam and Eve that we consciously need to put it aside when we read the story in Genesis.

It is common within the critical literature on Genesis to distinguish two different creation stories, dating from two distinct periods, in the early chapters of this book (Genesis 1.1–2.4a and Genesis 2.4.b–3.24). Against the cosmic perspective of the first of these, the second – which tells the story of Adam and Eve – is a myth of origins that explains the state of things now by what occurred in primeval times: the presence of death, the existence of pain and why snakes crawl on their bellies. It was probably written in the tenth or ninth century BC.

In the beginning, we are told, there was a pre-existent earth, though no plant or vegetation. It had not yet rained, though there was a source of ground water that rose up and watered the earth. In contrast to the first creation story (Genesis 1.27), in which the creation of humanity is the last act of creation ('in the image of God he created them, male and female he created them'), here the creation of man is the first: 'then the Lord God formed man from the dust of the ground, and breathed into his nostrils the breath of life; and the man became a living being' (Genesis 2.7).

The man was created as an adult male of uncertain age. The Jewish commentators had him at around the age of 20 (*Genesis Rabbah* 14.7).[2] The dominant Christian view was that he was around the perfect age of 30 years, no doubt by virtue of its being thought that this was the age of Jesus at the time of his ministry.[3] At this stage the garden had not been created, for God then went on to plant a garden in Eden in the East. It was not so much in Eden as close by, for a river, we are told shortly after, flowed out of Eden to water the garden. At any rate, God then placed man in the garden. The river that flowed out of Eden to water the garden divided there into four – Pishon, Gihon, Tigris and Euphrates. From there it flowed out into the four quarters of the world. Although much Christian ink and non-Christian blood was to be spilt in trying to locate the Garden of Eden, this is not a geographical place so much as a mythical one: a cosmic centre, and the closest point between heaven and earth.[4]

God made everything pleasant to the sight and good to eat, together with two trees – the tree of life in the middle of the garden and the tree of the knowledge of good and evil. The fruit of the tree of life conferred immortality, though the man was not aware of this at the time (Genesis 3.22). The location of the tree of the knowledge of good and evil is not initially stated, though it is said later by Eve (Genesis 3.3) to be also in the centre of the garden.

The man's role in the garden was to till it and keep it. God told Adam that he could eat of any tree in the garden with one exception: 'but of the tree of the knowledge of good and evil you shall not eat, for in the day that you eat of it you shall die' (Genesis 2.17). Adam was mortal, but kept alive by the breath of God. He was alone, but also lonely. So God created the birds and animals (including the serpent) as companions for the man. Adam had control over and dominance of them, signalled by his having the responsibility for naming the animals. The creatures were not satisfactory as partners for the man, so God put the man into a deep sleep and created a woman from one of his ribs, and then closed up the place. The man said, 'This at last is bone of my bones and flesh of my flesh; this one shall be called Woman, for out of Man this one was taken' (Genesis 2.23). Thus, the woman was much closer to him than any of the animals. And, unlike him, she was created in the garden.

The key moment in the story then followed: the snake, one of the animals created by God, came on the scene. He was said to be more crafty than any of the others. The snake asked Eve if God forbade them eating from any tree in the garden. She said that they could eat of any except the tree of the knowledge of good and evil. Even to touch it would result in death. The serpent then said to Eve that she would not die but her eyes would be opened, and she would be like God, knowing good and evil. So the woman ate of the tree and gave some to her husband, who was with her (see Plate 2). And the eyes of both were opened, though not perhaps as they might have expected – for they knew they were naked. They sewed fig leaves together and made loincloths for themselves.

Hearing God walking in the garden, they hid themselves from him among the trees. God realised that they had eaten from the forbidden tree. The man blamed the woman for having given him the fruit, and she in turn blamed the serpent. God cursed the serpent, removing its legs, thus allowing it only a diet of dirt. He instituted enmity between snakes and people, increased the pains of childbirth, established the rule of men over women, declared that labour would now be arduous and declared that the man would return to the dust whence he came. Because God knew that the man and the woman would also have come to know that the eating of the fruit of the tree of life would confer immortality, he drove them out of the garden.

## The Satanic Serpent

If the story of the fall of Adam and Eve as told in the book of Genesis originally involved only a created earthly animal rather than a supernatural being, this was soon to change in the second century of the Christian era in the writings of Justin Martyr. He was the first to identify the serpent in the Garden of Eden with Satan.

Justin saw Satan as the chief of the fallen angels.[5] As we noted earlier, for Justin, the fall of the angels occurred at the time of Noah as the result of the lust of the angels for the daughter of men. From that time, not only the fallen angels but also their progeny the demons were active in the world. But, according to Justin, the fall of the prince of demons, Satan, had occurred much earlier.

Like men, all the angels – including Satan – were created with free will although, unlike men, they would never die. God committed the care of men and of all things under heaven to them. Though it is never clear why God created such beings as the angels with the potential to misuse their free will, Satan was the first of them to breach God's trust in that way. For reasons that are not clear, Satan in the form of a serpent tempted Eve and was cursed for it: 'the serpent beguiled Eve and was cursed,' declared Justin.[6] Although Justin is ambiguous on this, it was probably then that Satan fell. He who was called the serpent 'fell with a great overthrow, because he deceived Eve'.[7]

According to Justin, when the Devil came to Jesus, he attempted to bring about his downfall by asking Jesus to worship him. But 'Jesus destroyed and overthrew the devil [...] who is an apostate from the will of God.'[8] Thus, the power of Satan and his fallen angels and demons was only temporary. At the end of the world, both men and angels who had misused their free will would 'justly suffer in eternal fire the punishment of whatever sins they have committed'.[9] Christ foretold, Justin tells us, that he who is called 'the serpent, and Satan, and the devil' would be 'sent into the fire with his host, and the men who follow him, and would be punished for an endless duration'.[10]

Following Justin, his disciple Tatian (*c*.120–80) in his *Address to the Greeks* identified the Edenic serpent with the Devil. Before the creation of men, God had created the angels, among whom the 'first born' and chief was the Devil. More subtle than the rest of the demons, he it was who, misusing his free will, tempted men to accept him as their god. As a result, he was excluded from the presence of God. Men, originally made in the image of God, became mortal, but the first-born angel through his transgression and his ignorance became a demon.[11]

Unlike Justin, though, Tatian explicitly rejected the myth of the watchers. '[T]he demons who rule over men', he declared, 'are not the souls of men,' that is, the spirits of the giants.[12] As a result, it is difficult to give an account of the origin of the demons apart from their chief. Consequently, Tatian's account of the fall of the angels after the fall of man reads a little lamely: 'and they who imitated him [the first-born angel], that is his illusions, are become a host of demons, and through their freedom of choice have been given up to their own infatuation.'[13] The Devil fell as a result of his ignorance of the true nature of God. The fallen angels tried to be divine: 'For, being turned by their own folly to vaingloriousness, and shaking off the reins [of authority], they have been forward to become robbers of Deity.'[14]

In line with his Gnostic tendency to view matter as evil, Tatian saw the fallen angels as having received their structure from matter. But none of them was made of flesh: 'their structure is spiritual, like that of fire or air.'[15] Living in the air, they perverted men's minds and disabled them from reaching the path that leads to heaven. They were the gods whom the Greeks and Romans worshipped. Zeus and the Devil were one and the same. God would allow them to sport themselves until the end of the world, at which time they would be punished for as long as they lived.

Although we can reasonably construe Justin as referring to the Devil's involvement in the fall of man, he did not *explicitly* link the Devil with the serpent and the Edenic fall. We do find, however, the first unambiguous account of the involvement of an angel in the fall of man in the second book of Theophilus of Antioch to Autolycus, known as the 'Apology to Autolycus' (late second century). It was Eve, Theophilus tells us, who was 'deceived by the serpent, and become the author of sin, the wicked demon, who is also called Satan, who then spoke to her through the serpent, and who works even to this day in those men that are possessed by him [...] And he is called "demon" and "dragon" on account of his revolting from God.'[16] The implication is that Satan's fall followed the fall of man. As for the fallen angels, Theophilus gave no account of them.

Neither Justin, Tatian nor Theophilus gave any reason why the Devil should have wished to tempt man. Irenaeus was perhaps the first to do so in his 'Against Heresies' (182–8). He blamed it on the Devil's jealousy of man. The Devil, we read, envious of God's workmanship (man), 'took in hand to render this [workmanship] at enmity with God'.[17] As a result, God banished the Devil from his presence.

If, for Irenaeus, the cause of the Devil's envy was man himself, for Tertullian (170–220), the first Latin theologian, it was envy, impatience, grief and maliciousness at God's having given man dominion over creation.[18] For Irenaeus, the Devil fell after the fall of man. Tertullian, though, believed that he fell before the fall of man, at the time when he formed the inclination to tempt man. Before he became the Devil, Tertullian declared, he had been created as an archangel, the greatest of the angels, 'the wisest of creatures' and 'good after the fashion of His good works'.[19] On the day that he was created, he was placed in a mountain paradise, where God had also placed the 'angels in a shape which resembled the figure of animals'.[20] Tertullian was in fact giving an angelic reading of the story in the book of Ezekiel (28.11–16) of the fall of the King of Tyre, before which he was 'the signet of perfection, full of wisdom and perfect in beauty', residing in the garden of Eden on the holy mountain of God until 'iniquity was found in you', and 'I cast you as a profane thing from the mountain of God.' Providing as it does a Biblical foundation for the goodness of the Devil at his birth, Ezekiel is a key text for the story of Satan as an originally good angel gone astray.

Thus, because the Devil was created with free will, the choice to be corrupt was his. Theologically, the key to the Devil's having been created with free will, and evil being a consequence of his misuse of it, is that it leads away from any assumption that evil was 'by nature' built into the creation of the world and thus attributable to divine intentions. Rather, as a consequence of the misbehaviour of a being created good but with the capacity to do evil, the existence of evil was accidental, and not necessary. So, as a result of his inclination to sin and his tempting of man, the Devil was punished, 'cast headlong from on high',[21] 'cast down like lightning'.[22] When the rest of the angels fell because of their lusting after women, he became the chief of fallen angels and the demons that resulted from the mating of the angels with the daughters of men.

From that moment on, Tertullian believed, they had all worked for the ruin of mankind. Demons and angels 'breathe into the soul and rouse up its corruptions with furious passions and vile excesses, or with cruel lusts accompanied by various errors'.[23] Their subtle and tenuous bodies allowed them access everywhere: 'Every spirit is possessed of wings. This is a common property of both angels and demons. So they are everywhere in a single moment; the whole world is as one place to them; all that is done over the whole extent of it, it is as easy for them to know as to report.'[24] Every individual had his own demon within to tempt him. The Devil's power had been diminished by the suffering and death of Christ, with the result that demons could now be repelled through faith in Christ. Eventually, the power of the Devil, his demons and angels would end at the Last Judgement.

Tertullian made one decisive contribution to Christian demonology. Justin, as we have seen, demonised the enemy outside – Judaism and the Greco-Roman religions. But Tertullian demonised those within Christianity whom he deemed to be heretics. The Devil was the source of both idolatry and heresy.[25] Tertullian had thus provided the demonological grounds for the late medieval and early modern persecution of witches construed as heretics in league with Satan.

## Pride Cometh before a Fall

The most important text for the story of the fall of Satan during the early Christian period was the *Life of Adam and Eve.* It was written sometime between the third and fifth centuries and probably Christian in origin; versions in Greek (originally), Latin, Armenian, Georgian, Slavonic and Coptic attest to its broad geographical spread.[26] It reached forward into the medieval period in numerous European translations, through to the Renaissance, and influenced the account of the fall of the Devil in the Qur'an.[27]

The Latin *Life of Adam and Eve* begins with Adam and Eve having been cast out of the Garden of Eden, mourning the loss of Paradise. After seven days, becoming hungry, they looked for food but found none. Adam then suggested to Eve that, if they were to repent deeply, God would pity them and provide sufficient for them to live by. Adam then determined to fast for 40 days and to spend the time standing in the waters of the river Jordan. He told Eve to go to the river Tigris, take a stone and stand on it in the water up to her neck without speaking for 37 days.

After 18 days had passed, Satan became angry and, transforming himself into an angel of light, went to Eve and found her weeping. He was about to tempt her for the second time; as if grieving with her, he began himself to weep. He told her to cease weeping, for God had forgiven her and had sent him to lead her to the place where the food she had had in Paradise had been prepared. She came out of the water, and the Devil led her to Adam. Adam knew instantly that she had again been seduced by the Devil and asked her how she had again allowed herself to be so led astray. Eve's sorrowing and lamenting was doubled.

Both Eve and Adam asked the Devil why, since they had not harmed him, he should pursue them so vehemently. The Devil told Adam that he was responsible for his expulsion from heaven, and to Adam's query,

The devil replied, 'Adam, what are you telling me? It is because of you that I have been thrown out of there. When you were created, I was cast out from the presence of God and was sent out from the fellowship of the angels. When God blew into you the *breath of life* and your countenance and likeness were made *in the image of God*, Michael brought you and made [us] worship you in the sight of God.' [...] And Michael went out and called all the angels, saying, "Worship the image of the Lord God, as the Lord God has instructed." And Michael himself worshiped first, and called me and said, "Worship the image of God, Yahweh." And I answered, "I do not worship Adam." And when Michael kept forcing me to worship, I said to him, "Why do you compel me? I will not worship one inferior and subsequent to me. I am prior to him in creation; before he was made, I was already made. He ought to worship me."

'When they heard this, other angels who were under me refused to worship him. And Michael asserted, "Worship the image of God. But if now you will not worship, the Lord God will be wrathful with you." And I said, "If he be wrathful with me, I will set my throne above the stars of heaven and will be like the Most High."

'And the Lord God was angry with me and sent me with all my angels out from our glory; and because of you, we were expelled into this world from our dwellings and have been cast onto the earth.'[28]

Envious of the happiness of Adam and Eve in the Garden of Eden, Satan attacked Eve. Before he did so – as we read in the Greek version of *Life of Adam and Eve*, also known as *The Apocalypse of Moses* – Satan tempted the serpent. The story is told by Eve to her children and grandchildren. According to her, God allotted different parts of Paradise for her and Adam to guard, she the south and the west, he the north and the east. The male animals were in Adam's part of Paradise, the females in hers. The Devil went into Adam's section, where he told the serpent that he had something to tell him:

> [T]he devil said to him, 'I hear that you are wiser than all the beasts; so I came to observe you. I found you greater than all the beasts, and they associate with you; but yet you are prostrate to the very least. Why do you eat of the weeds of Adam and not of the fruit of Paradise? Rise and come and let us make him to be cast out of Paradise through his wife, just as we were cast out through him.'[29]

The serpent became the mouthpiece of the Devil; Eve and Adam ate of the forbidden fruit and were thrown out of Paradise. The serpent was deprived of his hands and feet, his ears and wings.

The *Life of Adam and Eve* was demonologically significant for four reasons. First, while envy of man's place in Paradise after his fall motivated the Devil in his temptation of Eve, it was his pride in his position in the created order of things that brought about his fall. Self-love above obedience to God became here the primordial sin and the root of all others. Pride had demonologically become the dominant cause of the fall of Satan, and theologically of the fall of man.

Second, the *Life of Adam and Eve* had not only provided an account of the fall of Satan, in this case before Adam had entered the Garden of Eden but also filled in the gap in demonological theory that had been created by the decline in the myth of the watchers at the time of Noah as the origin of the fallen angels. The fall of the Devil *and* that of his angels now occur at the same time.

Third, the fall of the Devil and at least some of the angels is the consequence of a deliberate and direct revolt against God. Only after they had been cast down as a consequence of their rebellion did Satan set about tempting Adam and

Eve into disobedience of God. This was to become the classical Christian account of the fall of the Devil and his angelic followers.

Fourth, and most significant, declaring his rebelliousness against God, the Devil claimed, 'I will set my throne above the stars of heaven and will be like the Most High.' In so saying, he was referencing what was to be the most important Biblical text for the fall of Satan, namely, Isaiah 14. Lucifer and the Devil were about to become one and the same.

## Lucifer Descending

In the *Life of Adam and Eve*, mankind was still involved in the fall of the angels. But it was an angelic reading of Isaiah 14 that made possible an account of the fall of Satan as having occurred, not as a consequence of the creation of man, and not with the involvement of man, but before the creation of the world. For this addition to classical Christian demonology, we need to turn to the Alexandrian theologian Origen (*c*.185–254).

Like Tertullian, Origen gave an angelic reading of the passage in Ezekiel (28.11–16) about the fall of the King of Tyre that saw Satan as having first been one of the heavenly beings. Origen's most significant innovation was his identification of Satan with the 'Day Star' of Isaiah 14, that is, 'Lucifer', the Latin translation of the Hebrew *hêlel* and the Greek ἑωσφόρος ('heosphoros'). Thus did 'Lucifer' become an alternative name for the Devil, a fallen being of light. In his *On First Principles* and having quoted Isaiah 14.12–22, Origen declared,

> It is most clearly proved by these words that he who formerly was Lucifer and 'who arose in the morning' has fallen from heaven. For if, as some suppose, he was a being of darkness, why is he said to have formerly been Lucifer

or light-bearer? [...] In this way, then, even Satan was once light, before he went astray and fell to this place.[30]

The passage from Isaiah also provided a reason for Satan's fall. It was his hubris or pride in wishing to make himself like God that brought him down.[31] It was the sin of pride that came to dominate explanations of the cause of the fall of the Devil, and it became fixed as the original sin: 'by his pride he had once commenced to sin,' Augustine was later to write in *The City of God*.[32]

Origen's argument was intended to counter those Gnostics who, committed to a radical dualism, saw the Devil as a being opposed to God and evil by nature. The fall of the Devil and his angels was rather, Origen believed, a consequence of beings created good with the capacity to do evil, rationally and freely choosing to turn away from God. Both angelic and human evils were the result of this misuse of free will.

Origen's understanding of the fall of the angels and of men is bound in with his accounts of the pre-existence of souls and of there being no essential difference between angels, demons and men. According to Origen, all souls – those of men, angels and demons – had come into being at or near the time of the original creation of the world. All were created equal, with freedom of will. This enabled Origen to give an account of apparently innocent suffering as the result of already-present sin: 'For if this [pre-existent sin] were not so, and souls had no pre-existence, why do we find some new-born babes to be blind, when they have committed no sin, while others are born with no defect at all?'[33]

The Devil determined to resist God and God drove him away. Others revolted along with him: 'Some sinned deeply and became daemons, others less and became angels; others still less and became archangels; and thus each in turn received the reward for his individual sin.'[34]

There were, however, other souls who had not sinned sufficiently to become demons, nor so lightly as to become angels. These were to become men, their souls bound in material bodies.

The world was then created as a vale of punishments, and a possible vale of 'soul-making', for the various fallen souls – hierarchies of angels and demons, the spirits of the heavenly bodies and the various races of men. Corporeality, though not evil in itself, whether angelic, demonic or human, was a consequence of the fall. The world was organised by God according to the merits of those beings who would inhabit it.[35]

Theoretically, with men occupying the moral space between angels and demons, demons ought to have been located beneath the earth at its centre, at the furthest remove from heaven. This would be to minimise their activities in the world. Hence, in order to allow their continual interaction with men, Origen, like other early Church Fathers, located them in the air with aerial bodies, where they could 'feed on burnt offerings and blood and the odour of the sacrifices'.[36]

Demons' proximity to men allowed also for their allocation to nations and to individuals. Every individual, like every nation, had his own angel and his own demon. So the battle between good and evil was conducted, not only at the cosmic, but also at the national and the individual levels. Although Christ defeated the Devil and his angels, they would have power until Christ came again. God allowed the Devil to continue to tempt us, but we remained free to resist, and were therefore personally responsible for our deeds and misdeeds: 'Each person's mind is responsible for the evil which exists in him, and this is what evil is. Evils are the actions which result from it.'[37]

This location of evil, neither in God, nor in a principle of evil, nor in matter itself, but in the free will of spiritual beings led Origen to his most radical conclusion – that no spiritual being, including the Devil and his angels, was ultimately irredeemable. It is unclear whether Origen believed that the Devil would eventually be saved. On the one hand, his doctrine of free will would necessitate that even the Devil, were he ultimately to choose the good, could thus attain salvation. On the other hand, Origen also seemed to believe that, by virtue of the Devil's continually choosing evil, he had become so habituated to it that, although he had the choice to do good, he would never have the desire to do so.[38] He had become 'natured' to evil and thus would, in fact, never choose the good and would never be saved.[39] There may, as a consequence, be a contradiction in Origen's theology between the divine will that all will be saved and the Devil's will not to be.

However that may be, neither Origen's doctrine of the pre-existence of souls, nor his account of the possible ultimate salvation of all beings (perhaps including Satan) were embraced by Christianity at large. Augustine was sympathetic, if a little condescending, to those 'tender hearted Christians' who declined to believe in the eternity of hell's torments. He went on to reject the 'even more indulgent' Origen for believing 'that even the devil himself and his angels, after suffering those more severe and prolonged pains which their sins deserved, should be delivered from their torments, and associated with the holy angels'.[40] The Catholic humanist Erasmus of Rotterdam (*c.*1466–1536), in keeping with his commitment to freedom of the will and the virtues of personal merit against Luther's (and Augustine's) emphasis on salvation by grace, declared that 'A single page of Origen teaches more Christian philosophy than in ten of Augustine.'[41] But the sixteenth-century reformers were generally opposed to Origen, not only for his emphasis on the freedom of the will, but also for his belief that the love of God required the possible salvation of all, in contrast to their belief that the justice of God demanded that the wicked be punished eternally.

Yet there was a significant reassertion of Origen's commitment to pre-existence and universal salvation in a work published anonymously in England in 1661, probably written by the Anglican George Rust, later bishop of Dromore. *A Letter of Resolution Concerning Origen and the Chief of his Opinions* supported not only the doctrine of the pre-existence of souls, but also the eventual restoration of all. Of the prospect of God's being reconciled to all his creatures, even those confined to the realm of darkness, he enquired, 'what difference is there in the distance between a *devil* made an *angel*, and an *angel* made a *devil*? I am sure the advantage is on the ascending part rather then on the descending, for the mercy and compassion of God to all his works of his hands may reasonably be supposed to help them up though undeserving.'[42]

In terms of the story of the Devil, Origen's legacy was twofold. He had given a new name to the Devil – Lucifer – through his identification of the Devil with the Day Star of Isaiah 14. And, perhaps more important, his locating of the revolt of Satan and his angels before the creation of the world as the result of the sin of pride became a commonplace. His belief, or at least the belief attributed to him, that Lucifer and his angels would eventually be saved was to gain little purchase in classical Western demonology. Lucifer and his angels had fallen, and they were not to rise again. In the words of Richard Montagu in the mid-seventeenth century:

Before the creating of man upon earth, millions of Angels, created in glory, and subsisting with God in place of blisse, abandoned that first and original state, which they did then enjoy, and might with their Maker have enjoyed for ever. This act of Apostasie, and aversion from God, instantly ensued their first creation, it was *irrecoverable*, and their sin *impardonable; God sware to them in his wrath, they should never more returne unto his rest.* For that one act of rebellion and disobedience, God threw them everlastingly out of heaven: They are and shall be ever Ταρταραθέντες [those cast into hell], as the Apostle phraseth it, cast into, and irremediably detained in chaines of outward darknesse, unto the judgement of that great day.[43]

## The Battleground of History

By the end of the second century, then, along with other stories of his beginnings, what was to become the dominant story of the origin of Satan and his angels had taken its final shape. Created before the world or mankind, the chief of the angels, with a number of others, rebelled against God through their own pride and were expelled from heaven. The existence of the Devil and his fallen angels before the creation of man could now lead to the diabolisation of the story of Adam and Eve. The Devil, having been identified with the serpent (or having literally entered into it) now became ultimately responsible for the fall of man, the expulsion of Adam and Eve from the garden, and the alienation of man from God through his disobedience.

The Christian tradition was committed to the doctrine of one God whose primary attribute was goodness. Thus, in its search for an explanation of evil, it had rejected the possibility that an opposing principle of evil had existed from eternity. Similarly, the goodness of God was endangered if it were the case that he himself had created a being who was, by nature, evil. The doctrine that Satan and his demons were originally angels with free will reinforced the goodness of God (on the grounds that it was better for God to have created beings with free will who were able to choose between good and evil than beings not able to so choose). The existence of evils in the world could then be claimed to be the misuse of free will by freely choosing beings (including both angels and men).[44]

The rejection of the possibility mooted by Origen that even Satan was in principle redeemable – that, as George Rust put it, if angels became demons why couldn't demons become angels – had important 'negative' consequences for Christianity. It would entail that, before the creation of the world, there was in existence a being of absolute evil who would never desire to choose the good: an Anti-God or at least an Antichrist implacably opposed to God. This meant that, as long as history endured, it had to be read primarily, not as the story of God working his purposes out as year succeeded year, but as the story of a world over which God had lost ultimate control, not only as the result of the fall of Satan and his angels, but also as the consequence of the serpentine Satan tempting man into rebellion against God. Demonic will and human will were running riot. Thus, within the Christian story, evil and history are, in this sense, coterminous – evil is present from the time of the creation of the world and absent only at its end. Therefore, in order to regain some control of history, God himself had to enter it in the person of Jesus Christ.

# CHAPTER THREE

# Hell's Angel

The Son of Man came not to be served but to serve, and to give his life a ransom for many.

Matthew 20.28

## Paying off the Devil

For the early Church Fathers, the life, death and resurrection of Christ was set within the context of the historical battle between God and the Devil that ranged from the fall of Satan, before the beginning of history, until its end. As Frances Young put it, 'With the powers of evil, God had to do battle or business, and the supreme moment of victory was the Cross of Christ [...]. "Christus Victor" conquered death by his resurrection, spiritual blindness by the light of his teaching and ignorance by his revelation.'[1] All of these aspects of Christ's victory were brought together in the conviction that the Devil and his angels had been defeated (see Plate 8). It was a conviction predominantly expressed in the so-called ransom theory of atonement.

For Irenaeus, as a consequence of man's capitulation to the temptations of the Devil, man had become the Devil's possession. He was in the Devil's power, and death was the major consequence of his fall. Had God left man in this situation, it would have been tantamount to the total defeat of God and the overcoming of his will by that of Satan. In becoming man in Jesus Christ, in recapitulating in Christ

49

the first man Adam, God took back the control of history. Thus, according to Irenaeus,

> [B]y means of the second man [Christ] did He bind the strong man, and spoiled his goods, and abolished death, vivifying that man who had been in a state of death. For a[s] the first Adam became a vessel in his [Satan's] possession, whom he did also hold under his power, that is, by bringing sin on him iniquitously, and under colour of immortality entailing death upon him. For, while promising that they should be as gods, which was in no way possible for him to be, he wrought death in them: wherefore he who had led man captive, was justly captured in his turn by God; but man, who had been led captive, was loosed from the bonds of condemnation.[2]

This ransom theory was to become the dominant orthodox view of the work of Christ for the first millennium. Two adaptions to Irenaeus' theory were made. The first of these was that God ultimately won the liberation of men from the Devil by trickery. The second was that, against Irenaeus' view that the Devil was wicked and illicitly took men hostage, the Devil had legitimate rights over men.

Although Irenaeus was not as clear as he might have been, the overall drift of his argument amounts to the fact that it was to the Devil that God gave himself in order to free men from Satan's captivity.[3] This becomes much clearer in Origen where he comments on the passage from Matthew 20.28 with which we began this chapter.

> But to whom did He give His soul as a ransom for many? Surely not to God. Could it be then to the evil one? For he [the Devil] had us in his power, until the ransom for us should be given to him, even the life [or soul] of Jesus, since he (the evil one) had been deceived, and led to suppose that he was capable of mastering that soul,

and he did not see that to hold Him involved a trial of strength [...] greater than he was equal to. Therefore also death, though he thought he had prevailed against Him, no longer lords it over Him, He [Christ] having become free among the dead, and stronger than the power of death, and so much stronger than death, that all who will amongst those who are mastered by death may also follow Him [i.e. out of Hades, out of death's domain], death no longer prevailing against them. For every one who is with Jesus is unassailable by death.[4]

The key idea in this passage is that the Devil has exacted from God the death of Christ as a payment for the release of mankind from the punishment of sin which is death. There is also a hint that the Devil had been tricked, for he had not seen that to hold Christ in the bonds of death involved a power greater than he had. Christ's overcoming of death in the resurrection meant that the Devil had been tricked out of the ransom that he believed God had paid in delivering Christ up to him to die.

This 'divine deceit' was elaborated much more in the ransom theory of the Greek theologian Gregory of Nyssa (*c.*330–*c.*395). According to Gregory, in order to secure man's ransom from the Devil, God disguised himself in human form. With his divinity hidden beneath his humanity, Christ appeared an easy prey. Yet, seeing the power of Jesus over demons, diseases and nature, the Devil came to believe that the ransom paid through the death of Christ was a good deal for him, since it would gain him more than he would lose by liberating all others from death. Thus,

[I]n order to secure that the ransom in our behalf might be easily accepted by him who requires it, the Deity was hidden under the veil of our nature, that so, as with ravenous fish, the hook of the Deity might be gulped down along with the bait of flesh, and thus, life being introduced into the house of death, and light shining in darkness, that which is diametrically opposed to light and life might vanish; for it is not in the nature of darkness to remain when light is present, or of death to exist when life is active.[5]

The trick that God played on the Devil was justified by the ploy the Devil used on man in the Garden of Eden: 'by the reasonable rule of justice [...] [h]e who first deceived man by the bait of sensual pleasure is himself deceived by the presentment of the human form.'[6]

But there was a further innovation in Gregory of Nyssa's account of the ransom theory that was to resonate, via Augustine, through the medieval period. This was the notion that the Devil in some way had *rights* over men as a result of their having surrendered to the Devil. In Gregory of Nyssa, it was embedded in his idea that God, by virtue of his nature, in his dealings with the Devil *had to act justly*. God could not act arbitrarily and tear mankind away from the Devil by an act of force. This was because man had voluntarily bartered away his own freedom. It would have been unjust to the owner of mankind, the Devil, to use violence against him who had *legally* purchased humanity. Therefore, the only just method was 'to make over to the master of the slave whatever ransom he may agree to accept for the person in his possession'.[7] In offering himself as a ransom, rather than rescuing mankind by force, God demonstrated his goodness, his justice and his wisdom.[8] In sum, God did not stand outside the historical process and bring history back under control by external fiat, but himself took part in the historical drama.

All of the early Church Fathers were in agreement that the life, death and resurrection of Christ had altered the course of history, but not all agreed that it amounted to a ransom paid to the Devil, nor that there was divine deceit in play. John Chrysostom (*c.*347–407) rejected the ideas of ransom and deception. Whatever rights the Devil may have had over men before the coming of Christ, in seizing Christ he forfeited his rights over them, and neither a ransom needed to be paid, nor a trick to be played.[9] In his account of the work of Christ, therefore, Chrysostom marginalised the Devil and put God at the centre. To this end, Chrysostom turned to the other most common image to explain the death of Christ – that of a 'sacrifice' whereby, through substituting himself for sinful man, Christ paid to God the debt that men owed to him for their sin.

Both of these ideas flowed through to Augustine (354–430), for whom Christ's death was both a ransom paid to the Devil and a sacrifice made to God, with the result that man was both reconciled to God and, as a result of this, also freed from the Devil. As with Gregory of Nyssa, Augustine held that the Devil had a right of possession over men. It was necessary, therefore, for God to overcome the Devil in accord with justice.[10] Like Gregory of Nyssa, Augustine also invoked the image of the divine deceit, but Augustine's analogy was to the cheese in the mousetrap rather than the bait on the hook by which the Devil was deceived. As the commander of death, the Devil was delighted at the death of Christ: 'what he delighted in, that's where the trap was set for him. The mousetrap for the devil was the cross of the Lord; the bait he would be caught by, the death of the Lord. And our Lord Jesus Christ rose again. Where now is the death that hung on the cross?'[11]

## The Demonic Paradox

On the cusp of the close of antiquity and the beginning of the medieval period, the works of Pope Gregory the Great (*c.*540–604) are representative of Christian demonology of the time. In his writings, all of these themes become woven together. Although Gregory nowhere presented his demonology systematically, we can construct it from his works, and especially from his *Morals on the Book of Job*.

According to Gregory, before the creation of the world, angels were created with free will. Satan was the first of these created and was 'more eminent than the other Angels'.[12] Satan fell as a result of his pride, as did every evil spirit 'after the example of its chief, even Satan'.[13] Those angels who remained firm continued in the contemplation of their creator and were no longer consumed by temptation. They were organised in a ninefold descending hierarchy: archangels, angels, thrones, dominations, virtues, princedoms, powers, cherubim and seraphim. Angels, both fallen and unfallen, could adopt aerial bodies and be visible to men as necessary. Satan, however, could disguise himself as an angel of light.[14]

In contrast to man, Satan was irredeemable. It was fitting that man should be recoverable, for he was brought down by another – namely, Satan. But Satan fell by his own wickedness, parting from his angelic state 'without being persuaded thereto'.[15] Envious of man, the Devil entered the serpent and was able to draw man away from God to the pleasures of the flesh. Since then, death and suffering have been the lot of humankind, and God the creator and Satan the destroyer have been locked in a fierce battle, the angelical spirits who are the soldiers of God in perpetual conflict with the evil powers of the air.

The Satanic pride was however overcome by divine humility, the apostate spirit by human flesh.[16] Because the Devil nonetheless had rights over man, God paid the Devil a ransom to free humanity. The ransom paid by Christ, the second Adam, reversed the fall of the first man. The Devil was also tricked into overstepping his authority. As Gregory of Nyssa had, Gregory the Great envisaged God as setting a baited fishhook to snare the Devil:

So the almighty Father caught Leviathan [Satan] on a fishhook, because he sent his only-begotten Son, made man, to experience death [...]. The serpent was thus caught on the hook of the Lord's incarnation, for, as he swallowed the bait of his body, he was pierced by the barb of his divinity. For in Jesus was human nature which drew the devourer to him; and in him was also his divine nature, which pierced the monster [...]. The serpent was truly caught on the hook, because he died from this act of biting.[17]

At the same time, Christ's sacrifice of himself on the cross satisfied the debt that man owed to God for his sins.[18] It was this sacrificial account of the work of Christ that was to segue into the satisfaction theory of the life and death of Christ, exemplified in *Cur Deus Homo* of Anselm of Canterbury (1033–1109). Anselm rejected the ransom theory, arguing that the sacrifice of Christ was the debt owed by man to God to satisfy the demands of divine justice.

For Gregory, the victory of Christ left Satan imprisoned in the bottomless pit, though he would be released after a thousand years for a final cosmic battle at the end of history.[19] Satan and his angels would then be finally defeated and 'consigned to the eternal fires of hell'.[20] However that may be, the continued existence of evil in the world required explanation. Thus, while Satan was 'historically' imprisoned in hell, he was 'allegorically' still active in the world.[21]

The Devil's activity in the world, after Christ's 'defeat' of him, led Gregory to construct what we can call the 'demonic paradox': Satan was implacably in conflict with God in history, both within the world and in the hearts of men, and yet he remained God's enforcer and ultimately executioner. Here, for the first time, the demonology of the book of Job – in which Satan acted against Job only with the permission of God – entered the mainstream of Christian theology in conflict with the historical dualism already present. The afflictions caused by the Devil were *his* responsibility, but they were also the consequence of God's overarching providence. The Devil could not even attack a herd of pigs without God's permission. 'When then can he venture of his own accord to injure men who are made after the likeness of God, of whom is it doubtless quite plain, that he cannot presume to touch the swine, without permission?'[22] It was a paradox that saved the omnipotence and justice of God, but perhaps at the cost of the divine goodness.

## The Harrowing of Hades

For Gregory the Great, like his predecessor Augustine, the eternal destiny of individuals was fixed at the point of death; there was no possibility of repentance after death for those consigned to hell.[23] Thus, in spite of Gregory's belief that the death and resurrection of Christ had conquered death, he was not sympathetic to the plight of those in hell, nor therefore to the doctrine of the harrowing of hell. This was the belief that, between his death and resurrection, Christ had descended into Hades (or hell), had there preached to those already dead, had led the righteous thence to Paradise or heaven, and in so doing had defeated death and the powers of hell which had kept the dead there imprisoned (see Plate 9).[24] The key New Testament text was 1 Peter 3.19, according to which Christ preached to the spirits in prison. Clement of Alexandria and Origen were the first to use this text to include within the reach of salvation not only Old Testament worthies but also noble pagans and sinners in general. Augustine's position on whom Christ delivered from 'hell' is opaque, though he probably included Adam and the Old Testament patriarchs and prophets. Gregory the Great accepted that Christ descended into hell to free those who had led lives of faith and good works in expectation of his coming. Both Augustine and Gregory the Great were reflecting the majority opinion that Christ had descended into hell to free *only* those who believed that Christ would come.[25]

The most elaborate version of the harrowing of hell is to be found in *The Gospel of Nicodemus* (in its earliest form after the year 555). Apart from the New Testament Gospels themselves, this was perhaps the most influential and authoritative of all early Christian writings.[26] The second part of *The Gospel of Nicodemus*, which deals with Christ's descent into hell, is extant in both Greek and two Latin versions, the latter of which were the parents of versions in every European language.[27]

According to the Greek version, prior to Christ's arrival, Satan had come to Hades (both a place and a person) to ensure that Hades was ready to secure Christ.[28] Hades was worried that Jesus, having already taken Lazarus away from him, would remove the rest of the dead as well. Thus Hades asked Satan not to allow Christ to come: 'if thou bring him hither, not one of all the dead will be left in me.'[29] But, while they were speaking, a great voice was heard saying, 'Lift up, O Princes, your gates, and be ye lift [sic] up, ye everlasting doors, and the King of glory shall come in.' After Satan went out to try to stop Christ from entering, Hades ordered his devils to lock the gates and doors. Again the voice was heard, 'Lift up the gates.' As if he didn't know who it was, and following the script of Psalm 24, Hades asked, 'Who is this King of glory?' to which the angels with Jesus cried out, 'The Lord strong and mighty, the Lord mighty in battle.' Immediately the gates were broken, and 'all the dead that were bound were loosed from their chains.'[30]

Hades now seriously asked, 'Art thou then that Jesus of whom the chief ruler Satan said unto us, that by thy cross and death thou shouldest inherit the whole world?' Then Jesus took hold of 'the chief ruler Satan' by the head and delivered him to the angels, saying, 'bind down with irons his hands and his feet and his neck and his mouth.' And then he delivered him unto Hades, saying: 'Take him and keep him safely until my second coming.'[31] Hades then turned furiously on Satan, blaming him for having had Jesus crucified with the result that he and Satan should have lost the dead: 'Turn thee and see that not one dead man is left in me, but all whatsoever thou didst gain by the tree of knowledge thou hast lost by the tree of the cross.'[32] Hades told Satan, the 'head-devil', that he would practise evils upon him. While they were speaking, Jesus led Adam by the hand, followed by the rest of the dead, into Paradise.

The Hades of *The Gospel of Nicodemus* is more or less equivalent to the Hebrew dark underworld Sheol, where the dead resided. It was not traditionally a place of torments, but it was becoming so in *The Gospel of Nicodemus* as Hades took on a moral ambience as a place where sinners, along with the righteous, were located. Sinners were imprisoned there, 'bound in the chains of their sins that cannot be broken', sighing in their torments.[33] Wicked ministers were in charge of the dead. For the first time in Christian demonology, demons were described as both the keepers and (at least in the case of sinners) the tormenters of the dead. Just as significantly, Satan now had a role in the punishment of the wicked. If he was not yet himself actively engaged in the tormenting of the wicked, he was in charge of the torturers.

In the so-called Latin A version of *The Gospel of Nicodemus*, Satan remained in Hades for eternity, but in the Latin B version, there is a significant shift. There, Satan was not kept in Hades for eternity, but was cast into the fires of hell:

And behold, the Lord Jesus Christ coming in the glory of the light, in meekness, great and yet humble, bearing a chain in his hands bound therewith the neck of Satan, and also, binding his hands behind his back, cast him backward into Tartarus, and set his holy foot upon his throat and said: Throughout all ages hast thou done much evil and hast never been quiet at any time. To-day I deliver thee unto eternal fire.[34]

For *The Gospel of Nicodemus*, then, Hades – the place to which all the dead were assigned from the time of Adam onwards – was emptied between Christ's death and his resurrection. The Greek text was ambiguous on whether Christ led *all* of the dead or only Adam together with the patriarchs, prophets and the righteous generally out of Hades. Latin version A is similarly ambiguous,[35] but Latin version B clearly restricts the harrowing of Hades to the patriarchs, prophets, martyrs and the righteous. It allocates the remainder – sinners, demons, Satan and Hades himself – to hell. And we can assume that the demons who tormented sinners in Hades now become their tormenters in hell.

Thus, Christ's work not only liberated the righteous from Hades and opened up the possibility of a heavenly salvation for the righteous to come, it also inaugurated the fiery abyss for sinners already in Hades and for the wicked yet to come. The condition of the saved after Christ would be significantly better than before his death and resurrection, the condition of the damned infinitely worse. And, for the first time in Christian demonology, we have demons in hell both tormented *and* tormenting the damned. Satan has at last, in principle at least, assumed the role of the overseer of the punishments of the damned in hell.

This binary between heaven and hell in Christian thought would be mitigated in Christian theology by the development of a ternary system through the invention of an intermediate state (and later a place) between the two. After the year 1200, 'purgatory' comes into existence as a place in which those who are not sufficiently good to merit heaven nor sufficiently wicked to deserve hell can be purged or purified of their sins immediately after death (with a chance of going to heaven) before Christ comes in final judgement, at which time purgatory ends.[36] But if demons now had a role in the tormenting of the damned in hell, did they have a similar part in purifying those in purgatory?

This is a question that can only be asked after 1200, when purgatory becomes a third place, located beneath heaven, but distinguishable from hell. By around the year 1250 this question was asked by the Franciscan Bonaventure in his commentary on the *Sentences* of Peter Lombard. 'Is purgatorial punishment inflicted by the office of demons?' he asked. 'The punishment of Purgatory is not inflicted by the ministry of demons or by the ministry of good angels,' he replied, 'but it is probable that souls are taken to Heaven by good angels, and to Hell by bad ones.'[37] At around the same time, Albertus Magnus agreed that, while demons may take souls to purgatory, they do not purge them there.[38]

Essentially the same answer was given in the *Summa Theologica* of Thomas Aquinas. He accepted the possibility that demons took souls to purgatory, and even that they stood by enjoying and rejoicing in their sufferings. But he rejected the idea that they had any part in their punishments:

As after the Judgment day the Divine justice will kindle the fire with which the damned will be punished for ever, even so now the elect are cleansed after this life by the Divine justice alone, and neither by the ministry of the demons whom they have vanquished, nor by the ministry of the angels who would not inflict such tortures on their fellow-citizens.[39]

The more that purgatory became separated from hell, the less likely became the involvement of demons in the purification of souls located there. Thus, Dante's purgatory was closer to heaven than hell, and it was demon free, with angels assisting in the purging of sins. But the more *infernalised* purgatory was thought to be, the more active became the role of demonic punishers. Thus, for example, in the *Golden Legend* (*c*.1260) of the Dominican Jacobus de Voragine, hell and purgatory are virtually indistinguishable. So it is not surprising that demons were involved in a hierarchy of torments: 'It is done by the evil angels and not by the good. For the good angels torment not the good souls, but the good angels torment the evil angels, and the evil angels torment the evil Christian souls.'[40] It is perhaps some small comfort that the good angels often visited those in torment to comfort them and to warn them to suffer patiently pains that went beyond anything they could have experienced in this world.

## In Hell, and in the Air

Although the time when Satan was imprisoned was imagined at various points in his life, the idea that he was so incarcerated along with his demons was a tradition that went back via the book of Revelation in the New Testament to *The First Book of Enoch*. However imprisoned the Devil and his minions were in hell, they yet remained present in the air, in time and in history. It was a problem over which many puzzled intellectually, not least the bishop of Paris Peter Lombard (*c*.1100–60).

The four books of Lombard's *Sentences* brought together Christian theology as it was in the middle of the twelfth century, both its unity and diversity, into a systematic whole. For the remainder of the medieval period it became a standard textbook of theology. We find Lombard's demonology in the second book of the *Sentences*, distinction six. There, Lombard presented a number of views with which we are already familiar. Of the many angels that fell, declared Lombard, one had been more excellent than the others, namely Lucifer. He, like the many others, fell as a result of pride, 'and the dwelling of this gloomy air caught them falling'.[41]

Thus, the Devil and his fallen angels lived in the air beneath heaven. In order that they should not excessively harass men, they were located above the earth, 'in this gloomy air of ours, which was deputed for them as a prison even unto the time of Judgment'.[42] For this reason, Lucifer was called 'the Prince of the air'. On the Last Day, they would all be cast down into the pit of hell (*baratrum inferi*), according to the verse, 'Go you accursed into the eternal fire, which has been prepared for the Devil and his angels' (Matthew 25.41). Like the angels, the demons were organised hierarchically, at least until the Day of Judgement. They also had different offices. Some presided over one province, others over one man, others over specific vices – 'the spirit of lust', 'the spirit of pride', 'Mammon' over riches – 'because from that vice, by which he is named he can tempt men most of all'.[43]

Lombard now moved to a series of issues that were much less clearly determined. It is commonly asked, he wrote, whether all the demons are in this gloomy air, or whether some are in hell. His answer was decidedly ambiguous. Devils come from and go to hell on a daily basis.[44] That there are always some there to detain and torture souls, though perhaps at alternate times, is likely true.[45] This was hardly a persuasive compromise. Still, what he was certain of was that the souls of the wicked descend there and are there punished, along with those whom Christ left behind when he led the just out of hell.

Lombard was, however, much less certain about the location of Lucifer. He recognised that there were certain authors of the opinion that Lucifer had been bound there since he was conquered by Christ and did not have access to man to tempt him. Lombard cited the book of Revelation (20.7) that Satan would be loosed from prison after a thousand years. Still, 'whether he was plunged into Hell, or not', declared Lombard, it was believable that he would have a greater capacity to approach men in the time of the

Antichrist when he would be released, than he currently had.[46] Even now, he believed, the saints were able to disempower demons.

In spite of his deference to Lombard, the Franciscan Bonaventure (1221–74) in his commentary on the *Sentences* of Lombard was quite clear on the location of the Devil. He simply ignored the issue of his being bound in hell and located him in the air, along with his fallen angels. Bonaventure's rhetorical fire was directed against the argument that the demons were confined to hell subsequent to their fall and were there permanently confined. Against this, Bonaventure argued that, since the Devil was known as 'the Prince of power of this air' in Paul's letter to the Ephesians (2.2), and since where there was power there was substance, the Devil was located in the air where he tempts us. Moreover, since there is no redemption in hell, were the fallen angels to be located there, they would be unable to ascend therefrom to tempt us. Consequently, Bonaventure declared, 'the place of the demons after [their] lapse up until the Day of Judgment is not the subterranean place, which we call "Hell", but the gloomy air, in which, generally, the multitude of the demons inhabit.'[47] He claimed not to know whether some at least had been cast down into hell, but he did believe that some did descend to hell to torture souls according to various 'offices of malediction'.[48] As to their purpose in the air, it was in accord with the divine purposes to test men. The gloomy air corresponded to their sin, its subtlety to their mobility, for demons 'frequently fly around us just as flies [do]'.[49]

The *Summa Theologica* (1265–74) of the Dominican Thomas Aquinas, arguably the greatest of all systematic Christian theologies, was also unable to resolve the paradox of Satan's being bound in hell and his still being active among men. At least, this is the conclusion we can draw from Aquinas's not having taken up the issue. Nevertheless, although it would be incorrect to see

Aquinas's demonology as anything like a central feature of his thought, the authority of Aquinas in Catholic theology was to ensure that his demonology provided a framework for Catholic demonology from that time onwards.

According to Aquinas, angels were not naturally evil. Rather, they were intellectual beings with free will able to sin by virtue of the fact that they could choose not to align themselves with the divine will. As incorporeal beings, angels could not be tempted to sins that arose from the body. The Devil was the highest of the angels. The desire for excellence was highest in the chief of the angels, and this was the motive for the Devil's pride. Pride and envy were the core demonic sins, not only in the Devil but in also those lower angels.[50]

The Devil did not sin at the instant of creation; this would have been tantamount to his not having had the opportunity to have exercised his free will and to his having been created evil (which would deny God's goodness).[51] Thus, there was a moment (we might say a nanosecond) between the creation of the Devil, his realising that he was not like God, and his desiring to be so. Although more angels stood firm than fell, the Devil was the cause of the fall of the others, not as a consequence of his compelling them, but as the result of his exhorting them to do likewise. Those angels who fell were not only from the highest (or the lowest) order. Rather, free will being established among all angels, some fell from each order. According to Aquinas (and many others), Origen had erred in believing that the freedom of the will entailed that Satan and the fallen angels were capable of eventually choosing the good, and thus of being saved. It was an opinion that Aquinas rejected by arguing that, as the angels were confirmed in goodness from that time on, so those angels who fell were fixed in their obstinacy.[52]

As with the angels, so also with men: the Devil and his demons could not force men to sin but were only able to *persuade* them to do so. The assaults upon men were the consequence of the malice of the demons 'who through envy endeavor to hinder man's progress; and through pride usurp a semblance of Divine power, by deputing certain ministers to assail man, as the angels of God in their various offices minister to man's salvation'.[53] In line with Gregory the Great, Aquinas saw God as responsible for demonic assaults upon men. So Aquinas too was unable to escape from the paradox of Satan as divine opponent and divine enforcer.

Still, the contradiction was ameliorated to some extent by Thomas Aquinas's distinction between revelation and reason. Not all sins are committed at the instigation of the Devil. Had Satan and his demons not fallen, men would still have been capable of sin and would have sinned. Hence within Thomist demonology the explanation of evil did not *rationally* depend on the existence of Satan. Rather, the misuse of free will by angels and men was sufficient to explain it. And thus, as Jeffrey Russell puts it, 'Christian Scripture and tradition require belief in the Devil, but natural reason and logic do not.'[54] Nevertheless, when a man commits sin, whether instigated to do so by the Devil or not, he 'becomes a child of the devil thereby, in so far as he imitates him who was the first to sin'.[55] Thus, as Christ is the head of the Church, so 'the devil is the head of all the wicked, inasmuch as they imitate Him.'[56]

According to Aquinas, the Devil and his angels were cast down from heaven. Although by virtue of their sin they deserved to be in hell, they dwelt predominantly in the gloomy air, where they could tempt men. Good angels assisted men to follow the good and avoid evil. Good was also realised through men's overcoming the assaults of the demons. However, just as some of the angels were with the holy souls in heaven, some of the demons were 'even now in hell, to torment those whom they have led astray'.[57]

For Aquinas at any rate, the uncertainty about the freedom of Satan and his demons, and their location, would be solved on the Day of Judgement. Then, Satan and his followers would be permanently located in the fires of hell: 'But after the judgment day all the wicked, both men and angels, will be in hell, and the good in heaven.'[58] Yet, if their location was clear, the ambivalence of the roles of Satan and his angels would continue after the Day of Judgement into eternity. For they would be both themselves punished and themselves punishing the damned: 'the demons execute the Divine justice on the wicked. Nor does this in any way diminish the punishment of the demons, since even in torturing others they are themselves tortured, because then the fellowship of the unhappy will not lessen but will increase unhappiness.'[59] The paradox of Satan and his angels as both God's agents and God's enemies was one that remained for eternity.

Aquinas was similarly unable effectively to resolve the paradox of Christ's having overcome Satan in his crucifixion and resurrection, and yet sin and evil were still present in the world. As a result of the temptation in the Garden of Eden, and man's fall, God left man in the power of the Devil. However, the death of Christ released man from the power of the Devil. This was because, in conspiring to bring about Christ's death, he exceeded the limit of power assigned him by God. Aquinas went on to quote Augustine to the effect that 'the devil was vanquished by Christ's justice: because, while discovering in Him nothing deserving of death, nevertheless he slew Him. And it is certainly just that the debtors whom he held captive should be set at liberty since they believed in Him whom the devil slew.'[60]

Crucially, this liberty was not the consequence of a ransom paid to the Devil. Aquinas, following Anselm of Canterbury, rejected the notion that the Devil had rights and that therefore God needed to act in accord with justice. Thus, the debt was owed not to the Devil but to God. In effect, the image of 'sacrifice' rather than 'ransom' was driving Aquinas's account of Christ's work. He was primarily indebted to Anselm's *Cur Deus Homo* for a theory of atonement according to which Christ offered satisfaction to God for man's sins. 'Through Christ's Passion', declared Aquinas, 'we have been delivered from the debt of punishment [...] inasmuch as Christ's Passion was sufficient and superabundant satisfaction for the sins of the whole human race.'[61] For Aquinas, as we have noted, the Devil remained active – with God's permission – after the death and resurrection of Christ, tempting and assaulting man. However, Christ's passion did provide a remedy whereby man 'can safeguard himself against the enemy's assaults, so as not to be dragged down into the destruction of everlasting death'.[62] In spite of appearances to the contrary, then, Christ's victory was not entirely Pyrrhic.

Still, the failure of the ransom theory did entail that the Devil was not bound in hell. And, in so far as the emphasis moved from Christ's victory over the Devil and his being bound in hell to Christ's paying satisfaction to God, it left the Devil just as active in history after the passion of Christ as he had been before it. Indeed, even more so, for reasons we shall see later. As Pope John XXII put it in a sermon in 1332, 'Indeed, the damned, that is, demons, could not tempt us if they were secluded in hell. That is why one must not say they reside in hell, but in fact in the entire zone of dark air, whence the path is open to them to tempt us.'[63] John XXII's sermon reflected a new interest in the Devil and his demons that arose in Western theology from the middle of the thirteenth until the end of the seventeenth century. In order to understand why this was the case, we need to come to terms with the history of the relationship between Satan and magic.

# CHAPTER FOUR

# The Devil Rides Out

Be sober, be vigilant; because your adversary the devil, as a roaring lion, walketh about, seeking whom he may devour.

1 Peter 5.8 (KJV)

## A Pope Bewitched

The demise of the ransom theory had one important unforeseen consequence. Satan and his fallen angels, no longer imprisoned in hell, were once again free to roam the world, doing as they wished. John XXII, pope from 1316 to 1334, was surrounded on all sides by demons, both human and suprahuman. Or at least, so he believed. On 22 August 1320, Cardinal Guilhem de Peyre Godin sent a letter in the name of the Pope to the inquisitors for Carcasonne and Toulouse, Jean de Beaune and Bernard Gui. It was a request that they take action against those who practised demonic magic, and in particular against those who invoked demons or made pacts with them. 'Our very Holy Father and master, Lord John XXII', wrote the cardinal,

> fervently wishes to banish from the center of God's house casters of evil spells who kill the flock of the Lord; he orders and confers the task to you to make inquiries and to proceed, while conserving the modes of procedure which the canons have set down for you [...] in matters concerning

heresy, upon encountering those who sacrifice to demons or who worship them or pay homage to them. [You must also proceed] against those who make explicit pacts with those demons, or who create or have created any image or anything else to connect themselves to the demon or to perpetuate any evil by invoking demons, against those who, by abusing the sacrament of baptism, baptize or have baptized an image made of wax or other materials, or who, through other means and with the invocation of demons, create or have created those images in some way, against those who, with full knowledge, reiterate baptism, the order or the confirmation, against those who use the sacrament of the Eucharist or the consecrated host and other sacraments of the Church or some part of these sacraments in form or in matter to abuse them for their sorcery or evil spells.[1]

The importance of the letter was twofold. In the first place – in contrast to an ancient and long-standing tradition that viewed heresy as a matter of false opinion – this letter reflected Pope John XXII's revolutionary doctrine that heresy was as much a matter of acts and deeds as of wrong belief.[2] It was a doctrine that was to underpin not only the fourteenth-century condemnation of magicians, but also the witchcraft persecutions that were to begin in the century following.

In the second place, the letter iterated the belief that the practices of demonic magic, far from being on the margins of the Church were at 'the center of God's house'. John XXII believed that he, himself, had been the intended victim of malevolent magic. In 1317, the bishop of Cahors, Hugues Géraud, was accused of attempting to kill the Pope by poison and by wax image magic, the ashes of spiders and toads, the gall of a pig and so on.[3] It was a crime to which he confessed, before being tortured, whipped and burned at the stake.

## Cathars, Moderate and Extreme

More generally, the belief that the Devil and his minions were particularly active was the result of a surge of interest in the Devil and demonology from the middle of the thirteenth century. This was the consequence of four intellectual moments during that period: first, the rise of the Cathars; second, the rise of academic angelology and its demonological counterpoint; and third, the arrival in the West of Arab learning and the occult sciences. Finally, as we shall see in a later chapter, it was the result of an apocalyptic thematic in the theology of Joachim of Fiore.

It was the Cathars who put dualism back on the theological agenda as their response to the perennial Christian contradiction between an all-good and all-powerful God and the existence of evil in the world, though it was a dualism that went well beyond the historical dualism that I have identified as awkwardly embedded within the Christian tradition. Now the Cathars took Satan with absolute seriousness. The core of their theology was that the world, and all that was in it, had been created not by God but by the Devil. The moderate wing within Catharism was divided from its more extreme believers over the issue of the origin of Satan: the former maintaining, more in keeping with orthodox Christian theology, that Satan was God's subordinate, the latter that Satan was (or was the son of or the commander-in-chief of) a principle of evil independent of God.

The Cathars were all agreed that the earth and the firmament above it was a battleground between God and Satan, but they disagreed on how this had come about. The position of the moderates was best reflected in a twelfth-century work entitled *The Secret Supper* or *The Book of St John*. The text elaborates, in the form of a dialogue, on the conversation held between Jesus and John at the Last Supper. John asked Jesus about Satan before his fall. Jesus responded by telling him that Satan had been originally God's second-in-command, presiding over the heavens and right down to hell. Passing through all the regions between the heavens and hell, Satan progressively seduced many of the angels by offering to reduce their obligations to God. For this, he was cast out from his place before God's throne and from his heavenly office to the firmament below the heavens, taking a third of the angels with him. But Satan and his fallen angels could find no peace there, and he beseeched God to forgive him. God was moved with pity and gave him peace to do what he wished until the seventh age of the world.

Satan then created the world and all living things within it, including man. He ordered an angel from the second heaven to enter the body of the man that he had made. From the body of the man, he took a part, made another body in the form of a woman and 'bade an angel of the first heaven to enter into it'.[4] The angels grieved deeply that they now had mortal forms imposed upon them. Satan ordered them to have sex but they did not know how. Thus Satan created a paradise, and placed the man and the woman there, along with a serpent made from his spit. The Devil then entered into the serpent, aroused Eve's desire and had sex with her with the tail of the serpent. The same sexual desire was aroused in Adam and both 'angels' – he and Eve – 'were affected by a lust for debauchery, together begetting children of the devil and of the serpent, until the consummation of the world'.[5] As a result of their fall, the spirits of heaven were trapped in bodies of clay and delivered up to death.

The reign of Satan, supported by Moses and Enoch, was to last for seven ages. Satan convinced men that he was the one true God. For this reason, God decided to send his son so that people might 'recognize the devil and his wickedness'.[6] To this end, he first sent an angel, called Mary, the mother of Jesus. When Christ descended, he entered and came forth through her ear. In response, Satan sent his angel, John the Baptist. The Day of Judgement would come when 'the number of the just shall equal the number of those crowned [angels] who fell.'[7] The just would receive everlasting life. A 'hell of fire' would burn over all the earth, even up to the air of the firmament. Then Satan and all his host, along with sinners, would be bound and cast into the fire.

In contrast to the moderate dualists who saw the creation of the world to be the work of the Devil, subordinated to God, the extreme dualists attributed it to the work of an independent, eternal principle of evil. For the author of *The Book of the Two Principles*, this was the inevitable consequence of the truth of the doctrine of God's goodness, foreknowledge and the existence of evil. Foreknowing that some of the angels that he intended to create would fall into evil, God recognised that he would therefore be ultimately responsible for the choice they made and therefore for the existence of evil. As a result, his goodness could not be maintained. 'For this reason,' the author concluded, 'we are required to acknowledge two principles. One is good. The other is evil, the source and cause of the imperfection of the angels and also of all evil.'[8]

Consequently, the goodness of God was affirmed, but at the cost of his all-powerfulness. The view of the moderate Cathars that the world was the result of the creative act of the Devil, a subordinate being created by God, was also rejected. For, according to *The Book of the Two Principles*, this too implicated God in the origin of evil. Rather, this world was the result of the direct action of an evil God, coeternal with the good God. 'I believe', declared the author, 'that there is an evil god who created heaven and earth, the great whales, and every living and moving creature, and every winged fowl according to its kind, and made man and woman; who formed man of the slime of the earth, and breathed into him the breath of life.'[9]

Surprisingly, however, this belief did not entail the denial of the good God as creator, but rather the existence of dual creations, and hence of two creators. The key Biblical text was Ecclesiasticus 42.24: 'All things are double, one against another' (KJV). Thus, each God created his own angels and his own universe, such that there was both a good universe, the 'land of the living' (Psalms 27.13), and a bad universe, each with its own heavens and earth, and each the mirror image of the other. Or rather, perhaps, our world was the 'evil twin' of the good universe. Thus, John of Lugio thought, wrote Rainier Sacconi, 'that the good God has another world wherein are people and animals and everything else comparable to the visible and corruptible creatures here'.[10] The people who inhabited this heavenly universe were not merely spiritual beings but had bodies too.[11]

In short, Satan had changed sides. No longer a subordinate of the good God, he had now become the evil God's commander-in-chief. At the beginning, the two creations had been separate. But the Devil sneaked into the 'land of the living' and led astray the people there, the souls of whom descended into hell – that is, into our world. The Devil, puffed up by his success, then took his demons into the good universe, where they engaged in battle with Michael and his angels before being defeated and driven back to the evil realm. Still, the Devil and his demons were able to carry away into their kingdom a third of the creatures created by God. Their existence (or rather our existence, for all those on our earth are such fallen creatures) was not the consequence of their misuse of free will (which the Cathars denied) so much as of their having been made prisoners of war. Thus, while the bodies and spirits of those who fell remained in the 'land of the living', their souls were imprisoned in the earthly realm in the bodies of men and women, birds and warm-blooded animals, there to be continually reincarnated until such time as they would be brought back to the heavenly universe.[12]

The series of lives led on this earth, the Cathar equivalent of hell, enabled souls to do a kind of purgatorial penance until their eventual reunion with their bodies in the 'land of the living'. This was the Cathar reading of the doctrine of the final resurrection of the dead. Under this scenario, there would be no final judgement. Rather, the resurrection of the dead was a continual process. The evil universe would end only when all souls held captive there had been delivered from their earthly prison. Release was dependent, however, on having become one of the Cathar 'perfecti' after a long period of training in Cathar theology and ritual. The perfect would be freed from the cycle of reincarnation upon their deaths. They would then be reunited with the bodies which the good God had originally given them in the 'land of the living'.

That such 'salvation' was eventually possible for *all* was the result of the work of Christ. The doctrine of the incarnation among the Cathars is particularly complicated, Christ having *both* really *and* only apparently been made flesh. Sense can be made of this apparent contradiction in their theology through the notion of the two creations. John of Lugio believed that even in the good universe, evil was present. According to Sacconi, John of Lugio said that 'marriages and fornications and adulteries take place there, from which children are born.'[13] Thus, the incarnation of Christ and the atonement occurred in the 'land of the living'. Christ really assumed flesh from the blessed virgin and really suffered, was crucified, died and was buried, then rose again on the third day, and ascended to his heavenly father. But the passion, death and resurrection of Christ took place 'in another, higher world, not in this one', that is, in the universe of the good God.[14]

Christ nonetheless also descended into this evil realm, the Cathar equivalent of hell, to help those who had been imprisoned here by Satan. Christ did so only apparently and not really, since he could not take a human body created by the evil God. Of course, he did not have to, for the literal atonement had occurred in the good universe.

Granting that, Christ's descent to the earthly universe (identical with hell) was the equivalent of the harrowing of hell in orthodox theology. The doors to the prisons of those souls held on earth were opened, and the possibility of salvation made available to those who had previously descended from the empire of good to that of evil, at least to those who were the 'perfect ones' among the Cathars.

## Angels and Demons

The increasing interest in the Devil and demons was also part of a more general burgeoning of interest in spiritual beings. The development of demonology from the middle of the twelfth century was the flip side of the creation of angelology. Until this time, Gregory the Great's teaching on the nine orders of angels, primarily in his *Morals on the Book of Job*, remained the dominant interpretation of the angelic hierarchy. But the translation of the Greek works of Pseudo-Dionysius (recognised for the last century to be sixth-century writings) into Latin, first by Abbot Hilduin of Saint-Denis near Paris in around the year 838 and subsequently by John Scotus Erigena in the year 862, gave apparent authority to the study of the angelic hierarchies, not least because these works – especially *The Celestial Hierarchy* – were assumed to have been written by the Dionysius whom Paul had converted when he preached in front of the Areopagus in Athens (Acts 17.34). The works were subsequently shown to have been written in the sixth century, and the author is now generally referred to as Pseudo-Dionysius. Once Pseudo-Dionysius found his way into the *Sentences* of Peter Lombard, he became something of a cottage industry in academic theology in the Middle Ages and beyond.[15] For the same reason, from Peter Lombard onwards, the dark side of angelology – demonology – became embedded in theology.

In Aquinas's *Summa Theologica*, demons were discussed in two of the fourteen questions in 'The Treatise of the Angels', but the first demonology of significance in Western theology can be found, not in the *Summa Theologica*, but in the last section entitled 'On Demons' in Aquinas's work *De Malo (On Evil)*.[16] This was a much-extended discussion from that in the *Summa Theologica* and independent of the angelology to which it was appended in that work. There were a number of issues both in the *Summa Theologica* and in *De Malo* that were critical for the development of demonology.

The first of these concerned the corporeality of demons. The capacity of demons to assume bodies will play, as we will see later, a critical role in demonological debates about their capacity to have sex with men and women.[17] The second addressed the question of whether demons could perform miracles. The answer for Aquinas was no. Only God had the power to do miracles – that is to say, to cause events beyond the ordinary course of nature.[18]

Nevertheless, demons could produce *apparent* miracles: events that went beyond human power and understanding. They could *appear* to have performed the impossible through imaginary apparitions.[19] This was by virtue of their knowing the power of natural causes better than human beings do, the ability to put them together faster, and thus the capacity to produce greater effects than human powers or skills can.[20] For reasons that will become clearer later, we can say that the Devil was an expert in 'occult' causes and 'wonderful' (but not miraculous) effects.

Thus was the Devil a master of illusions. He could himself appear in a virtual embodied form, he could create the illusion of other virtual bodies to our external senses and he could even create illusions in our internal senses by entering our minds. In short, the Devil could make me aware of his presence, he could fool me by making me think somebody was present when they were elsewhere (to my external senses) and, by entering my mind, he could make it appear (to my internal senses) that *I* was something else (a werewolf or a cat, for example).

Since demons have no powers outside the ordinary course of nature, any more than we do, demonology was thus a part of the investigation of the natural world and a part of natural philosophy (or what we would call 'science'). Demonology was the 'science' of determining the powers of the Devil within the limits imposed by the ordinary course of nature. The tenacity of demonology was thus not the consequence of the Devil's ability to act supernaturally, but the result of his capacity *only to act 'naturally'*. The outcome of this was that the study of his nature and power was embedded within the study of nature more generally for the next four hundred years.

## The Demonisation of Magic

The Devil was not only a master of illusion, but also a master of magic (itself often concerning the production of illusions). Hence, the third reason for the surge of interest in matters diabolic from the twelfth century onwards was the rise of learned magic, both natural and demonic. Alongside the common traditions of magical healing and divining that the Middle Ages had inherited from classical antiquity, the influx of Arabic, Greek and Jewish texts and learning into the cathedral schools and universities of the West from the eleventh century led to the cultivation of natural magic, particularly in the areas of astrology, astral magic, image magic and alchemy.[21] In contrast to natural magic, which looked for the efficacy of its practices to occult or hidden powers within nature, there also developed 'necromancy' or demonic magic; or better, since it involved the invoking and commanding of both demons and angels, 'daemonic magic'.[22] The enemy was 'within'; necromancy, whether for malevolent or benevolent ends, was primarily practised within an educated and clerical elite, the underside of a culture attuned to the ritual display of priestly power (see Plate 13).[23] For this reason, unlike the 'ritual magic' for benevolent ends practised within the sacramental life of the Church, this was 'ritual magic' for malevolent purposes.

The magical and the diabolic had been intertwined in Christian thought since its beginnings. Thus, for example, according to the New Testament Acts of the Apostles 13, Paul and Barnabas found in Paphos on the island of Cyprus a man by the name of Bar Jesus who was a magician (a 'magos'), a false prophet and a Jew. The magician had tried to turn the proconsul Sergius Paulus away from Christianity. But Paul, 'filled with the Holy Spirit, looked intently at him and said, "you son of the Devil, you enemy of all righteousness, full of all deceit and villainy, will you not stop making crooked the straight paths of the Lord?"' (Acts 13.9–10).

It was Simon Magus who was to become, within the Christian tradition, the magician in league with the Devil par excellence. He made his first appearance in Acts 8.9–24, where, impressed by the wonders performed by Peter and John, he offered them money for their power. The apostles rejected his offer, urging him to pray for forgiveness. Although there is no mention of demons in the story in Acts, this was nonetheless the starting point for the many narratives from the second and early third centuries onwards that created Simon Magus as a master of illusion, portrayed the battle between Peter and Simon as one between divine and demonic forces and constructed Simon as the exemplary demonic magician. This is nowhere better exemplified than in the story of the death of Simon as told in the apocryphal text the *Acts of the Apostles Peter and Paul*. It was a story that, incorporated into the *Golden Legend* of Jacobus de Voragine in the middle of the thirteenth century, was transmitted in both art and literature for the next three hundred years.[24]

1 The three archangels drive Lucifer from heaven into hell. *The Three Archangels* by Marco d'Oggiono (sixteenth century).

2 Adam and Eve are tempted by Satan in the form of a four-legged virgin-headed serpent. *The Fall of Man and the Lamentation* by Hugo van der Goes (1470–5).

3 The angel of the Lord, described as a 'satan' ('adversary'), is called out by God to stop Balaam from cursing the people of Israel. 'Balaam and the Angel' from *The Mirror of Human Salvation* (fifteenth century).

4 Job, covered in boils, is assailed by God's emissary the Satan. 'Job and the Devil' from *The Mirror of Human Salvation* (fifteenth century).

5 Christ is tempted by the Devil. 'The Temptation of Christ' from *The Mirror of Human Salvation* (fifteenth century).

6 Demons delighting in tempting Saint Anthony in the desert. *The Temptation of St Anthony of Egypt* by Hieronymus Bosch (1450–1615).

7 The Devil presents Saint Augustine with the *Book of Vices. St Augustine and the Devil* by Michael Pacher (*c.*1480).

8 The Angel, holding the keys of hell, enchains the Devil in the shape of a dragon who is then bound in the pit. 'The Angel Enchains the Devil' from a commentary on the book of Revelation by Beatus of Liebana (*c.*776).

9 Christ harrows hell between his death and resurrection, rescuing those held captive. 'Christ Harrows Hell' from a northern English manuscript (fifteenth century).

10 At the request of Saint Peter, the demons enabling Simon Magus to fly allow him to fall to his death. *The Fall of Simon Magus* by Lorenzo Lotto (fifteenth century).

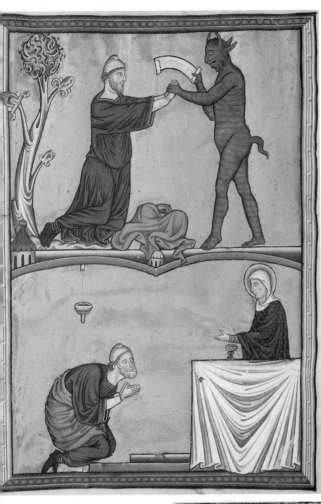

11 In the top panel, Theophilus makes the first written pact with the Devil. In the second panel, regretting his deal with the Devil, Theophilus begs the Virgin Mary to intercede with God on his behalf. 'Theophilus and the Devil' from the Ingeborg Psalter (twelfth century).

12 Faust makes a circle in the dust with a wand. Then he begins to call on Mephostophiles the spirit, and to charge him in the name of Beelzebub to appear there. 'Dr Faustus in a Magic Circle' from *The Historie of the Damnable Life and Deserved Death of Doctor John Faustus* (1648).

13 The Devil attempts to seize a magician who has formed a pact with him but is prevented by a monk. 'The Devil and the Magician' from *Chroniques de Saint-Denis* (thirteenth century).

14 The Devil appears as the sin of vanity. The lady looks in the mirror but all she sees is Vanity's backside. 'The Devil and the Coquette' from *Der Ritter von Turm* (1493).

15 A witch rides backwards on a goat. While referencing the canon
*Episcopi* in which women ride on beasts at night with the goddess Diana,
it invokes the tradition of witches flying to the Sabbath. *Witch Riding a
Goat* by Albrecht Dürer (*c*.1500–1).

According to the *Acts of the Apostles Peter and Paul*, Peter engaged in a magical contest with Simon Magus before the Emperor Nero in Rome. Nero had become persuaded that neither Peter, nor Paul, nor Simon Magus could be relied upon to tell the truth. Simon told Nero that, in order to demonstrate that Peter and Paul were liars, he would fly up to heaven on the following day. At Simon's request, Nero ordered a high tower to be built in the Campus Martius from which 'my angels may find me in the air; for they cannot come to me on earth among the sinners.'[25] Nero ordered Paul and Peter to be present, telling them that the truth would then be made clear.

On the following day, Simon, crowned with laurels, ascended the tower, spread his arms and began to fly. When Nero saw Simon flying, he said to Peter, 'This Simon is true; but thou and Paul are deceivers.'[26] Peter, looking steadfastly at the flying magician, replied, 'I adjure you, ye angels of Satan, who are carrying him into the air, to deceive the hearts of the unbelievers, by the God that created all things, and by Jesus Christ, whom on the third day He raised from the dead, no longer from this hour to keep him up, but to let him go.'[27] Immediately the demons let Simon go and he fell to his death at a place called Sacra Via (see Plate 10). In spite of this, Nero ordered Peter and Paul to be arrested, Paul to be beheaded and Peter to be crucified, at the latter's request upside down, 'for I am not worthy to be crucified like my Lord'.[28]

In the Greco-Roman world, magic was viewed as a practice that could be put to benevolent or malevolent ends. Only harmful sorcery was viewed as illegal. But for early Christianity, magic per se was reprehensible because demons were at the heart of it. Thus Christianity distinguished between the practice of Christianity (as the true religion) and the practices of all other religions (as demonic magic). It was an opposition made possible by the Christian identification of the gods and lesser spirits (*daemones*) of the Greco-Roman religions with demons (*demones*) – a view which, as we saw in an earlier chapter, goes back to *The First Book of Enoch.*

The definitive early Christian formulation of the demonic nature of magic is to be found in Augustine. Thus, for example, in *On Christian Doctrine* (396–427), all magical arts and superstitious practices were classified as demonic.[29] Similarly in *The City of God*, Augustine found that the demonic was present in all superstitious and magical transactions. So the distinguishing feature of magical practices, whether benevolent or malevolent, was the involvement of demons. The miracles of the Bible, declared Augustine, were intended to recommend the worship of the one true God, and to prohibit the worship of false gods. They were performed by simple faith and godly confidence and 'not by the incantations and charms composed under the influence of a criminal tampering with the unseen world, of an art which they call either magic, or by the more abominable title necromancy, or the more honorable designation theurgy'.[30] Within the broad category of the magical arts, Augustine included demonic pacts, haruspicy (divination through entrails), augury (divination through the flight of birds), medical magic, superstitious omens and signs and astrology and horoscopes.[31]

For the most important comprehensive account of magic and divination in the early medieval period we must look to the *Etymologies* of Isidore, bishop of Seville, a work left incomplete by his death in the year 636. After the Bible, it was arguably the most influential book in the Latin West for over a millennium.[32] Section nine of book eight, entitled *De Magis* (*On Magi*), offers what has been called 'the first definitive western Christian taxonomy of unauthorized practitioners'.[33]

Isidore, like Augustine before him, was committed to the view that magic was demonic. He bookended his taxonomy of practitioners with this in mind. Thus, after a brief account of the history of the magic arts, which he traced like many others to Zoroastrian Persia, he prefaced his account with these words: 'Consequently, this foolery of the magic arts held sway over the entire world for many centuries through the instruction of the evil angels.'[34] And in what appears to be at least a preliminary conclusion to his discussion, he wrote, 'In all these the craft of demons has issued from a certain pestilential alliance of humans and evil angels. Hence all these things are to be avoided by a Christian and entirely repudiated and condemned.'[35]

Still, if the overarching theme of *De Magis* is the diabolic nature of magical practices, the overall pattern of Isidore's taxonomy suggests a more nuanced account. First, there is in *De Magis* a reasonably clear distinction between magic and divination. Second, as we move through the spectrum from magic to divination, the means of the practices are progressively less overtly demonic, and the ends of the practices progressively less wicked. Third, therefore, as we move through this spectrum, there is a progression from magical and divinatory practices that overtly involve demons to divinatory practices that are completely 'natural' (in our sense of the word).

So, regardless of the *theoretical* demonisation of all magical and divinatory practices within *De Magis*, there was nonetheless a recognition in this work that, in fact, distinctions could really be made between those practices that were intentionally demonic and malevolent on the one hand, and those that were intentionally natural and benevolent on the other. Thus we find embedded within the West's first taxonomy of magic a new distinction in Western thought – between demonic magic and natural magic. From the twelfth century onwards, this distinction underpinned a new conflict in the history of the Western interpretation of magic that would remain unresolved for the next six hundred years, until rendered irrelevant by the collapse of both magic and demonology. This is the conflict between those proponents of natural magic who attempted to distinguish it from magic explicitly invoking the Devil and his demons and strove to find a place for natural magic within the mainstream of Christian theology, those who tried to find a place within the Christian context for a non-demonic form of conjuring spirits, and those who believed that the Devil was involved in *all* magical practices, whether benevolent or malevolent, angelic, demonic or natural.

## Magic Defined, Damned and Defended

The result of this conflict was that magic was often defined, occasionally defended, but more often condemned. Thus, for example, the Augustinian monk Hugh of St Victor (*c*.1096–1141) constructed in his *Didascalicon* a taxonomy that distinguished between 11 different types of magic – nine different forms of divination, the illusions of conjurors and the enchantments of sorcerers.[36] There is no suggestion in the *Didascalicon* that all these forms of magic were demonic; only the last two are so described. Conjurors were those who 'with their demonic art make sport of human senses through imaginative illusions about one thing's being turned into another'. Sorcerers, he went on to say, 'are those who, with demonic incantations or amulets or any other execrable types of remedies, by the cooperation of devils and by evil instinct, perform wicked things'.[37] So Hugh was aware that there were many forms of divinatory magic that were 'natural', yet he had no doubt that even these forms of divinatory magic had no place within legitimate knowledge. At best they were evil; at worst they led to engagement with the demonic.[38]

Still, if Hugh defined different forms of magic only in order to damn them, Michael Scot (d. *c*.1236) did so in order to defend some permissible kinds. A legendary account has him as a diviner who foresaw that he would die as the result of a stone falling upon his head. In an attempt to prove his own prophecy wrong, he took to wearing an iron skullcap to forestall his death. He was nonetheless fatally wounded when he removed his helmet one day in church. It was a story that reflected his brief notice as a magician in Dante's *Inferno*: 'That other who is so spare in the flanks was Michael Scot, who truly knew the game of magic frauds,'[39] and as a consequence he was doomed to spend eternity with his head facing backwards, along with other diviners of antiquity and the Middle Ages.[40] It seems more than likely that Dante drew on Scot's own reading of the psychological meaning of 'spare ribs' in his *Liber Physiognomiae* to indicate that Scot was someone who was basically bad but still knew what the good was.[41]

Dante's judgement derived from Scot's attempt to differentiate permissible and impermissible magic. Thus, he was particularly concerned to distinguish astrology (*astronomia*) from prohibited forms of magic and divination, although he did identify a superstitious form of astrology (*superstitiosa astronomia*), under which he listed divination from the letters in a person's name and the days of the moon, geomancy and sorcery. Although he repeated the definition of Hugh of St Victor that the magic art was not acceptable in philosophy, that it destroyed religion and corrupted morals, he nonetheless listed 28 varieties of divination, all of which he believed to be true, although they were forbidden as infamous and evil – for example, augury by song of birds, interpretation of dreams, observance of days or divination by the blood of corpses.[42] To doctors of medicine, he gave the following advice: 'In cases of grief, melancholy, deceit, or other difficulty, where medicine fails, the physician should advise the patient to go to diviners and enchantresses, although this may seem wrong [*inhonestum et nephas*], or contrary to the Christian faith, but true nevertheless.'[43]

Like Scot, William of Auvergne, bishop of Paris from 1228 until his death in 1249, attempted to find space for some forms of magic while appearing to condemn all. In orthodoxy, to know any of the magical texts was to be suspected of dabbling in the worst of them, so it is a matter for little surprise that William of Auvergne excused his knowledge of them as the errors of a misspent youth.[44]

Such a disavowal, though it had the rhetorical form of a condemnation, was nonetheless in effect actually clearing intellectual space for a defence of 'natural magic' that, William declared, was the eleventh part of natural philosophy or natural science (*scientia naturalis*). And natural magic – unlike the openly demonic forms of magic including image magic, and those forms of astrology that denied human free will – operated with 'natural powers' (*virtutes naturales*) in accord with the order of nature. Although the boundaries of the natural were much disputed, it was an order that implied theories of cosmic and human analogy, astral influences, universal signs and correspondences, and sympathies and antipathies between plants, stones and animals. Magical practice within this domain consisted of 'strictly natural operations, in which human industry has the role of a steward, merely assisting the occult natural powers, which it helps combine, harmonize and interweave'.[45] The world of natural magic was, in short, the world of marvels, beyond the ordinary course of nature, but nonetheless located within it.[46]

This concern to distinguish between natural and demonic magic was driven by the worry that those texts that contained legitimate knowledge might be damned along with those that were illicitly demonic. It was this that led the *Speculum Astronomiae* (*c.*1260s), traditionally attributed to Aquinas's contemporary Albertus Magnus, to draw up an annotated bibliography of astrological and magical texts, to discriminate between useful astrological texts and harmful necromantic ones.[47]

Like William of Auvergne, the author of the *Speculum Astronomiae* claimed that, having long ago examined many of the illicit works and having shrunk 'with horror from them', his memory of them was less than perfect.[48] We should read this only as a rhetorical device to distance himself from any accusations that he was still a peruser of such works; for the detailed account that he gives of them belies his claim. Although the distinction is an opaque one, he divided the necromantic works into the categories of the abominable, which involved the invocation of demons, and the detestable, which was 'effected by means of inscribing characters which are to be exorcized by certain names'.[49] These too ought to be left alone, 'for it is suspected that something lies under the names of the unknown language, that might be against the honour of the Catholic faith'.[50] Even so, he concluded in the final chapter of the *Speculum Astronomiae* that these books, rather than being destroyed, should be put aside, for the time was at hand when, although care needed to be taken, 'it will be useful on occasion to have inspected them.'[51]

Like the *Speculum Astronomiae*, the English Franciscan Roger Bacon (*c*.1215–*c*.1292) was also concerned that good and useful magic would be thrown out along with its demonic versions. Unlike William of Auvergne, Bacon did not attempt to defend magic by discriminating between its legitimate and illegitimate forms. 'Magic' and 'magician' for Bacon were always terms of disrepute, and always set against 'philosophy' and 'philosophers' (or 'science' and 'scientists'). But this was not a genuine condemnation of magic. Rather, his disparagement of magic and magicians was strategically intended to distance his own interest in issues magical from condemnation, the better to incorporate magical practices intended for good within the category of science.[52]

For Bacon, the opposition between magic and science was located in evil or good intentions. Those magical practices intending good were included within an enlarged domain of science.[53] This enabled Bacon to include not only certain kinds of astrology and alchemy within science, but also and more controversially the magic of the power of words (*virtus verborum*), spoken and written.[54] Thus, at the end of his section on the study of languages, Bacon told a story that exemplified the importance of intentionality. He informs us that a man he knew, when still a boy, came across a man in the fields having an attack of epilepsy. The boy wrote some verses, hung them around the neck of the epileptic, and immediately he was cured. The disease did not return until much later when his wife wished to confuse his mind because of the love she had for a certain cleric. She had him remove his clothes in order to bathe, so that he might take off the amulet around his neck to protect it from the water. At once his disease seized him again. His wife, frightened by the miracle, again tied the amulet on him and he was cured once more. It was not a piece of magic that Bacon could view as demonic. 'Who will venture to put an evil interpretation on this and ascribe it to demons,' Bacon enquired, 'even as some inexperienced and foolish people have ascribed many things to demons, which frequently have happened by the grace of God or by the operation of nature and the power of the excellent arts?'[55]

One of the inexperienced and foolish people that Bacon was referring to was St Augustine. That such magic could not but be demonic was, for Augustine, a consequence of his theory of the relationship between words and things. Augustine believed that, at least since the fall of man, the relationship between words and things was an arbitrary or conventional one. Thus, words had no natural power to produce magical effects; in so far as they did, it was the consequence of a language shared by magicians and demons, with demons bringing about the effects in the world upon receiving the verbal signs from the magicians.[56] Since all magic operated by means of signs, all magic was consequently demonic. To the extent that an Augustinian 'model of language as conventional and consensual was accepted (as it generally was in the thirteenth century), it was impossible to defend the power of words as a natural phenomenon'.[57]

By contrast, for Roger Bacon, words uttered 'with profound thought and great desire and firm intention and strong confidence' at the right astrological times had a *natural*, albeit occult, power to bring about effects in the world.[58] Thus, declared Bacon, together with the power of the sky, 'an astrologer can form words at times which are chosen to have an ineffable power [...]. By this power dangerous animals are put to flight, some kinds of wild animals are summoned to your hand, snakes are called forth from caves and fish from the depths of the water.'[59]

It was a power with which the Devil was familiar, always ready to use it for evil ends. The Devil, in this register, was the supreme natural magician. All the more need to cultivate the magic of words now, declared Bacon in apocalyptic mood, in order to combat the Antichrist as the end of time approached: 'I write these things, not only for the consideration of the wise, but because of the dangers which are now arising and will arise for Christians and the Church of God, from infidels, and most especially from the Antichrist, because he himself will use the power of wisdom [*potestas sapientiae*], and will turn all things to evil.'[60]

# Conjuring Demons
## and Conversing with Angels

From the twelfth to the fourteenth centuries, with natural magic distinguished from demonic magic (or philosophy from magic), the domain of natural magic had broadened. It had become less demonised, more 'normalised' and more mainstream. As a consequence, the fear of the Devil's involvement in *all* forms of magic was to that extent lessened (at least for some). Still, if demonic involvement in natural magic had become more of an intellectual stretch, the fear of Satan and his minions was no doubt increased by the circulation from the twelfth century onwards of magic texts explicitly intended to invoke demons for (albeit generally petty) malevolent ends.[61] The demonic magicians or necromancers 'saw themselves as invoking the sacred powers of heaven [angels, Christ, the Virgin Mary, the rulers of the demons or God] by which they could constrain the equally numinous but malign and treacherous powers of hell'.[62] It was fear of just this kind of magic that had motivated the letter that Cardinal Guilhem de Peyre Godin sent in the name of Pope John XXII to the inquisitors for Carcasonne and Toulouse, with which we began this chapter.

The so-called 'Munich Handbook of Necromancy', produced by a member of the lower or middling clergy in the fifteenth century, exemplifies the genre of miscellancies of demonic magic.[63] With few exceptions, the rituals in this book fall into three main categories – illusionist, psychological and divinatory. Among the first of these we can include rituals to conjure such illusions as a banquet, a castle, a means of transport such as a horse or a boat or a flying throne, to make the living appear dead and vice versa, and invisibility. Among the second, we find rituals – often using images – to induce madness, to arouse a woman's love or desire, to gain dignity and honour, to cause hatred among friends, to cultivate the powerful and to constrain another's will. The divinatory techniques (primarily 'scrying')[64] are intended to gain knowledge of things future, past, distant, stolen or hidden.[65]

Of the verbal formulas in the Munich Handbook, most are conjurations of demons, and there is a clear acknowledgement by the author that the commanding of evil spirits is at the core of his activities. The following erotic conjuration is representative:

> I conjure you demons inscribed in this circle, to whom is
> given the power of seducing and binding women in the

love of men, by the virtue and power of the divine majesty, and by the thrones and dominations and powers and principalities of Him who spoke and they were made, and by those [angels] who do not cease to cry out with one voice, saying 'Holy, holy, holy, Lord God of Sabaoth, heaven and earth are full of thy glory. Hosanna in the highest. Blessed is he who comes in the name of the Lord. Hosanna in the Highest,' and by these names which cause you fear and terror: Rator, Lampoy, Despan, Brulo, Dronoth, Maloqui, Satola, Gelbid, Mascifin, Nartim and Lodoni, and by this ring which is here, and by the innumerable powers that you and your superiors possess, that wherever you are, you should rise up from your places without delay and go to so-and-so, and immediately without deception lead her here, and take her back when I wish. And let no one be aware of this or take account of it.[66]

As this suggests, it was crucial to the necromancers' beliefs that they could, with God's permission and aid, compel, command and exploit the demons. To their opponents, however, it appeared that, far from controlling evil spirits, they were controlled by them. Thus, for example, one of the 1398 University of Paris articles against ritual magic condemned the belief that 'such arts truly force and compel demons and not vice versa, i.e., that the demons pretend they are forced [in order] to seduce men'.[67] But the necromancers themselves saw their powers as comparable to those with which priests exorcised demons, following the example set by Christ in casting out unclean spirits. From their perspective, whether conjuring or exorcising, they were in control of the diabolical.

Demonic magic undoubtedly led to a proliferation of named demons. In the Munich Handbook, we recognise Belial, Beelzebub, Lucifer and Sat(h)an, but most of the 189 demons named are unfamiliar and have a large variety of forms and functions. Thus, ritual number 34 gives a description of the rank, appearance and function of 11 named spirits. As well as a king, a prince and a seneschal, there are dukes, counts, presidents and marquises. They appear in various forms often belying their more terrifying natural appearance – a human with large teeth and three horns, a man with a leonine face with a viper in hand, a knight with lance, banner and sceptre or on a black horse, a boy with two heads and the wings of an angel riding on a dragon, a beautiful woman riding a camel, a man with a woman's face. Their roles are similarly various: to reveal the past, present, future and hidden matters, to locate hidden treasures, to give knowledge about occult matters, the trivium, astronomy and other liberal arts and languages, to procure the love of women, to secure favours or dignities, to provide excellent knights, to cross seas, rivers or regions quickly and to give power over serpents.[68]

The author of the Munich Handbook could not but have been aware that he was invoking fallen angels, but there are occasions in the manual in which the demons invoked are unfallen. They are called 'angels', 'most benign spirits' (*spiritus benignissimi*), 'most pleasant, happy, and joyful spirits' (*spiritus iocundissimi, ylares, et gaudentes*) or 'illustrious spirits' (*spiritus illustres*). One spirit is addressed as 'O most high and benign King Orient'.[69]

The 1398 University of Paris articles were clear that this distinction between angels and demons was not a legitimate one. All those invoked were, from its perspective, fallen angels, and neither unfallen angels nor sublunary *daimones* of ambivalent moral status. Thus, it rejected the belief of the magicians that 'some demons are good demons, others are omniscient, still others neither saved nor damned.'[70] But the necromancers themselves were not dualists. Although their intentions were evil at worst, spiteful at best, they nonetheless sought divine not Satanic approval. Their necromancy had an orthodox flavour. And since angels, demons, or any other spirits could only be invoked and controlled with the aid of heavenly powers, the distinction between them was irrelevant. So in practice, if not in theory, demonology, angelology and daemonology were all interwoven and indistinguishable. Hence, in the texts of ritual magic generally, the boundaries between demonic and angelic magic were permeable. Some practitioners of magic, though, did focus on rituals that called only on angelic powers for *benign* ends – to obtain visions, gain heavenly or worldly knowledge or to improve intellectual capacities.

The last of the University of Paris's 28 articles in 1398 condemned the belief that ritual magic 'can lead us to a vision of the Divine Essence or to the spirit of the Saints'.[71] In so doing, it may well have had in mind the work known as the *Liber Sacer sive Juratus* (*Sacred or Sworn Book*), pseudonymously written by a magician who called himself Honorius of Thebes, son of the mathematician Euclid, some time during the early part of the fourteenth century.[72] The uniqueness of this work was that it contained a magical rite to obtain the beatific vision, the end to which all Christians aspired – the vision of God as he is in himself in the fullness of his being. Thus, at the end of a highly defined, rigorous and complex ritual process of prayer, fasting, purging of sin, attending mass and receiving the host that lasted some 28 days, the magician was told to 'sleep and say no more, and you shall see the Celestial Palace, and the Majesty of God in his glory, and the Nine Orders of Angels, and the company of all Blessed Spirits.'[73] As ascetic and interior practices intended to evoke visions of the divine, angelic magic and Christian mysticism were coalescing.[74]

On the face of it, there seems little Satanic in this ritual, either in its procedures or its intended ends. Honorius went to some pains to offer an apology for his magical practices.[75] In addition, he declared, only virtuous Christians could engage in such activities. Those pagans who worked in the magical arts could not bind or constrain the spirits: 'The spirits feign themselves to be bound by the words of their law so that they may make them commit adultery and never turn to the true faith. Because their faith is naught, their works are naught.'[76] Similarly, since the coming of Christ, the Jews had lost their pre-eminence. They could no longer work any magic, 'because they are not alive in Christ'.[77] Only a Christian, he concluded, 'can come to the Divine Vision and succeed in all other works'.[78]

This was not an argument likely to persuade the mainstream, especially because it was preceded in the prologue to the book by the diabolisation of all those who demonised angelic magic. There it claimed that the campaign against magic by the Pope and his cardinals was led by Satan and his fallen angels and not by God. More than likely, it was Pope John XXII whom Honorius had in mind:[79]

When wicked spirits were gathered together, intending to send demons into the hearts of men, so that they should destroy all things profitable for mankind, and to corrupt the whole world even to the uttermost of their power, they sowed among men hypocrisy and envy, and rooted bishops and prelates in pride. Even the Pope and his Cardinals were affected [...]. Moved by covetousness and envy under the similitude of truth, these bishops and prelates through demonic instigation spread abroad false and unlikely stories.[80]

By contrast, the Benedictine monk John of Morigny's *Liber Visionum* (*Book of Visions*) (*c*.1304–18), not concerned with beatific visions and such like, had a much more mundane intent, though one which all students, teachers and modern academics alike would dream of, namely, a magical shortcut to formal learning. Through a nine-week regimen of prayers to God, the angels, the heavenly court and especially the Virgin Mary, together with fasting and purifications, knowledge of the seven liberal arts, philosophy, theology, along with such other information as the individual desired, could be attained: 'That which in other books is often in itself grasped with difficulty by native wit, tediously and at excessive length over a long period of time in enormous and fussy volumes of books, is taught in this book by means of a few easy prayers, conveyed through the revelations of angels.'[81] I wish!

In spite of official condemnation of all magical practices as demonic, by the beginning of the fourteenth century the distinctions between natural and ritual magic, and within this latter category between angelic and demonic magic, were clear in principle, even though they often overlapped in practice. Renaissance magic further attempted to incorporate natural magic into the broadening domain of natural philosophy. Angelic magic too attained a certain legitimation, facilitated by the Christianisation during the Renaissance of Jewish Kabbalah, Neoplatonism and the Hermetic literature. The aim of the Renaissance magi to create an overarching theory of magic that could embrace all of them further blurred the distinctions, not only between natural and ritual, but between demonic and angelic magic. Ironically, both natural and ritual magic may have been seen as having more to offer the experimentally minded natural philosopher than a medieval natural philosophy that was more a body of wisdom to be acquired than of knowledge to be discovered.[82]

CHAPTER FIVE

# Devilish Bodies

For we wrestle not against flesh and blood, but against
principalities, against powers, against the rulers of the
darkness of this world, against spiritual wickedness in
high places.

Ephesians 6.12 (KJV)

## The Demonisation of Popular Magic

In the year 1320, when Cardinal Guilhem de Peyre Godin,
at the behest of Pope John XXII, wrote to the inquisitors
for Carcasonne and Toulouse, Jean de Beaune and
Bernard Gui, it was the solo practitioners of ritual magic,
'necromancy' or demonic magic that he had in mind; or
better, for reasons demonstrated in the last chapter, since
it involved the invoking and commanding of *both* demons
*and* angels, 'daemonic magic'. The enemy, then, was very
much 'within', for necromancy resided within an educated,
clerical and sometimes courtly elite, the underside of a
culture attuned to the ritual display of priestly power.

A century later and Satan had broadened his focus
beyond a necromantic elite within the Church, and
towards the practitioners of the magic of the everyday – a
much larger market. As Pope Eugenius IV wrote in 1437
in *A Letter to All Inquisitors of Heretical Depravity*, 'The
news has reached us, not without great bitterness of spirit,
that the prince of darkness makes many who have been
bought by the blood of Christ partakers in his own fall and

damnation, bewitching them by his cunning arts in such a way that these detestable persuasions and illusions make them members of his sect.'[1]

Since at least the time of Augustine, all magic had been condemned as Satanic. The *daemones* of the pagan religions were of course *demones*. Hence all magic was really demonic, always implicitly if not usually explicitly so. That it was tacitly but not necessarily overtly demonic led in late antiquity to an emphasis on its Satanic origins rather than its human practitioners. Misfortune was the consequence, not of the power of sorcerers, but of demons. And sorcerers were as much victims as perpetrators. Thus, in late antique literature, as Peter Brown reminds us, 'the human agent is pushed into a corner by the demon-host.'[2] But the rise of learned demonic magic from the twelfth century onwards, intended to invoke demons through necromantic rituals, led to an increased concern with the practitioners of magic. The emphasis now was on the *explicit* conjuration of demons by the magician, and theoretically at least his control over them rather than theirs over him.

Unlike modern scholars, late medieval ecclesiastical authorities made little distinction between elite and popular forms of magic. Consequently, concerns over the Satanic involvement of the elite necromancer were easily transferable to the popular sorcerer, and the latter were as easily viewed as in league with the Devil as were the former.[3] Thus, for example, when the inquisitor Bernard Gui incorporated the concerns of the Pope into his inquisitorial manual, the *Practica Inquisitionis Heretice Pravitatis* (*The Conduct of the Inquisition of Heretical Depravity*) (1321–4), the magic that he expected inquisitors mostly to come across was popular rather than elite. He told the inquisitors to ask what suspected sorcerers knew about casting spells (or lifting them) on infants, about peace and concord between husbands and wives, and enabling the barren to conceive, about curing diseases, about thieves to be imprisoned, about substances they gave to be eaten – hair, claws and other things – the method for the discovery of thefts or the disclosure of secrets and the method of gathering herbs.[4] These were all aimed at the concerns and the practices of popular sorcerers and not to the elite. But he had no doubt that popular sorcerers, like the elite practitioners of demonic magic, turned 'their attention to spirits of evil and the teaching of demons'.[5]

The letter that Pope Eugenius IV wrote to his inquisitors in 1437 went a step further. He declared that sorcerers were members of a new Church, an upside-down version of the true one. They were no longer mere invokers of demons but devil worshippers and evildoers, heretical and criminal members of a secret ritual sect united in a Satanic conspiracy against the Christian faith:

> They sacrifice to demons, adore them, seek out and accept responses from them, do homage to them, and make with them a written agreement or another kind of pact through which, by a single word, touch, or sign, they may perform whatever evil deeds or sorcery they wish and be transported to or away from wherever they wish. They cure diseases, provoke bad weather, and make pacts concerning other evil deeds [...]. In their sorcery they are not afraid to use the materials of baptism, the eucharist, and other sacraments. They make images of wax or other materials which by their invocations they baptize or cause to be baptized. Sometimes they make a reversal of the Holy Cross, upon which our Savior hanged for us. Not honoring the mysteries, they sometimes inflict upon the representations and other signs of the cross various shameful things by execrable means.[6]

Thus, in the 1430s, there developed the notion that magicians were part of a secret heretical sect that rejected Christianity, gathered regularly in the presence of the Devil to worship him and performed evil deeds by magic. From this time onwards, in the history of Western thought, magic and witchcraft developed along separate intellectual paths. What we see in the early fifteenth century is the invention by the Church of the European witch as the evil servant of Satan. The key intellectual condition for the witch-hunts that were to come was then in place. While magicians were, theoretically at least, in control of demons, witches were controlled by them. As King James I of England was to note in his demonology in 1597, 'the Witches ar servantes onelie, and slaves to the Devil; but the Necromanciers are his maisters and commanders.'[7]

Magicians, however much they were in league with the Devil, were not perceived as a threat to society as a whole. The sect of Satan was a fantasy that expressed elite fears of ideological and social enemies within, of a hidden other working from inside society but outside the Church, to destroy it; it was an other that was addicted to abominable rites and practices.[8] As the story of this new Satanic sect spread throughout Europe, perhaps through the network of clergy who attended the Council of Basel (1431–40) and there heard of it,[9] the stage was set for the witch persecutions that were to last for the next three hundred years.

## Errors Not Cathartic but Satanic

The *Errores Gazariorum* (*Errors of the Cathars*) is one of the earliest accounts of a Satanic synagogue or sabbath as they were later more commonly known. It was anonymously written in the mid-1430s, probably in the region of Savoy. That the author had knowledge of particular witchcraft trials suggests that he may have been a clerical inquisitor. Although the title suggests that the work was about the Cathars, it was one of the foundational documents that established in the European mind the activities of the sect of Devil worshippers. In short, the heresy of the Cathars would metamorphose into that of witchcraft.

According to the *Errores Gazariorum*, when a person of either sex was first seduced by the Devil, they were given a container that was filled with an ointment to be used for the journey to their first synagogue. The ointment was used to anoint the staff (the witch's 'broomstick') by which the 'seduced man must go to the synagogue'.[10] When all those who had been thus seduced were assembled at the synagogue, the seduced person was presented to the Devil. The Devil appeared most often as a black cat, though sometimes as another animal, on occasion as an imperfect man. The Devil, rather like an inquisitor, then interrogated the applicant as to whether he wished to be a member of the sect and to remain so for the Devil's benefit. When the applicant had assented and made an oath of fidelity to the Devil, he then swore that he would be faithful to his new master, that he would assemble with other members as quickly as possible when any assembly was called and that he would not reveal the secrets of the society to any outsiders, not even on pain of death.

The candidate also swore to kill as many children under the age of three as was possible (sometimes even their own children and grandchildren), and to bring their bodies to the synagogue. By using *maleficia* (evil acts) and *sortilegia* (magic), he swore to impede sexual intercourse in every marriage wherever possible. He also agreed to avenge all injuries to the group, or any act that impeded or divided it. Finally, an explicit demonic pact was made. At least according to the confessions of some, the *Errores Gazariorum* tells us, when a new member entered the sect and made his declaration of loyalty, the Devil made a pact with him, written in blood (see Plate 18). This is discussed in more detail in the next chapter.

Having committed to the sect of Satan, the new member adored the presiding Devil and paid homage to him. As a sign of homage, he 'kisses the devil, whether the Devil appears as a human or some kind of animal, on the anus or the ass',[11] and bequeathed a part of his own body to the Devil upon his death (see Plate 17). In celebration of their new member, the sect ate a meal of murdered children together. After dinner had finished, the Devil ordered the lights to be extinguished and yelled, 'Mestlet, Mestlet'. At this command, the witches had sex together, a man with a woman or a man with a man, sometimes father with daughter, son with mother, or brother with sister, though apparently not with the Devil or other demons: 'the natural order is little observed.'[12] When these acts were completed, they prepared for the journey home.

At the time of initiation into the sect, the presiding Devil gave the initiate a jar of ointment for future use in travelling to the synagogue and taught him how to anoint the staff. This ointment was made from the fat of children who had been cooked. It was also combined with animals (toads, serpents, lizards and spiders) to produce an ointment lethal to the touch. In addition to ointments, lethal powders were made from the internal parts of children mixed with poisonous animals. When these were spread through the air on cloudy days, those who came into contact with them either died or suffered lingering illnesses. It was one explanation, the author declared, for high mortality rates in some regions, and constant bad weather in others.

That the actors in this sabbatical drama were considered to be heretical Cathars indicates that the sorts of activities which were essential to the witchcraft sect had been attributed to heretics in the past. In fact, the earliest report we have of Devil worshipping is from Paul, a Benedictine monk of Chartres. He wrote of a group of heretical clerics at Orléans in the year 1022 who gathered on certain nights, carrying candles and chanting the names of demons,

[U]ntil suddenly they saw descend among them a demon in the likeness of some sort of little beast. As soon as the apparition was visible to everyone, all the lights were forthwith extinguished and each, with the least possible delay, seized the woman who first came to hand, to abuse her, without thought of sin. Whether it were mother, sister, or nun whom they embraced, they deemed it an act of sanctity and piety to lie with her. When a child was born of this most filthy union, on the eighth day thereafter, a great fire was lighted and the child was purified by fire in the manner of the old pagans, and so was cremated. Its ashes were collected and preserved with as great veneration as Christian reverence is wont to guard the body of Christ, being given to the sick as a viaticum at the moment of their departing this world.[13]

In the 1430s, such activities were in the process of being transferred from heretics to practitioners of popular magic, and eventually from groups of men and women primarily to women.

## The Devil, Sex and Sexuality

For the author of the *Errores Gazariorum*, witchcraft was not sexed. Men and women seem equally to have been involved. The same can be said of the description of the sabbath by the French secular judge Claude Tholosan, who had himself conducted more than a hundred witchcraft trials. In the course of a work entitled *Ut Magorum et Maleficiorum Errores ...* (*c*.1436) – the name drawn from its opening lines, 'So that the errors of magicians and those who commit maleficia' – Tholosan reported on the new heresy of cannabilistic worshippers of the Devil. No distinction between men and women was drawn, so we can assume that, for Tholosan, men and women were both involved (see Plate 16).

In essence, Tholosan presents us with variations on themes similar to those of the *Errores Gazariorum*. Having drunk from a vase in which the Devil had urinated, the sect members renounced the laws of God and their faith. They then turned their naked behinds to heaven to show their scorn for God, 'drawing a cross on the ground, spitting on it and treading it underfoot'.[14] The Devil in the form of a man and of different animals then received kisses on the mouth from the witches, who offered him one of their children, who was then sacrificed and exhumed after burial. The fat of the dead children was extracted and eaten. Powders 'mixed with the devil's piss' and other poisonous ingredients were prepared to kill their enemies.[15] With other concoctions, they prevented conception in women, made men insane and drove them wild with sexual passion. The Eucharistic host was also used in witchcraft.

Necromancy, as we have seen, was about the domination of demons through the exercise of a cultivated intelligence and force of will. So it was conceived of as a predominantly male activity. Witchcraft, on the other hand, was focused on subservience and submission to Satan. Since these were qualities perceived as typically female, the demonologists soon came to imagine that women would predominate in the new sect of Satan. Thus, much demonological ink would be spent on theorising why this should be so.

In contrast to the *Errores Gazariorum* and Tholosan, Johannes Nider, again during the 1430s, was the first person to argue that it was women who were predominantly involved in the sect of Satan.[16] Thus, for example, in his *Formicarius* (*Anthill*), written in 1437 and 1438, he drew on traditional sources, Christian and classical, to suggest that women's nature tended towards the excessive, including the excessively evil.[17] Similarly, in 1438 in his *Preceptorium Divine Legis* (*Preceptor of Divine Law*), he gave a number of reasons why women were more likely than men to be witches: first, because they were more credulous and therefore susceptible to demons; second, because they were more easily impressed than men by visions and delusions, third because they had 'slippery tongues' and could not help but tell other women about the evil arts; and, finally, because they were physically weak, they sought revenge by *maleficia* (see Plate 14).[18] In general terms, they were, as the New Testament put it, 'the weaker vessel' (1 Peter 3.7).

That women were more susceptible to Satan than men had been embedded in the story of the fall in the Garden of Eden since the time that the serpent had been identified with the Devil. Thus, for example, John Stearne explained witchcraft as a female phenomenon since women were more easily displeased and revengeful of men since Satan's 'prevailing with Eve'.[19] That there was in women a greater facility to fall, as Alexander Roberts put it in his *A Treatise of Witchcraft*, led to their being one hundred times more likely than men to be witches.[20]

The importance of Nider's view that witchcraft was gendered was that the perception was incorporated into what is arguably the most influential of the Catholic demonologies, namely, the 1486 *Malleus Maleficarum* written by the Dominican inquisitor Heinrich Kramer. As a consequence, that witches were women became a key component of the persona of the witch. Kramer went a step further than Nider. He located the propensity of women to be witches, not only in their lack of faith and their ambition, but above all in their being more carnal than men. 'Everything is governed by carnal lusting,' he declared,

> Which is insatiable in them [...] and for this reason they even cavort with demons [*cum demonibus*] to satisfy their lust. More evidence could be cited here, but for intelligent men it appears to be reasonably unsurprising that more women than men are found to be tainted with the Heresy of sorceresses. Hence, and consequently, it should be called the Heresy not of Sorcerors, but of Sorceresses, to name it after the predominant element.[21]

Hence the title of the work, *Malleus Maleficarum – The Hammer of Sorceresses*. No longer the involuntary victims of Satanic assaults, female witches were now willing participants in Satanic sex. Thus female sexuality and evil were intimately connected. And, in order to show the 'reality' of demonic sex, Kramer argued that women found it enjoyable, at least as much as with a 'normal' man: 'Regarding the question of whether the sexual pleasure is greater or lesser with incubus [male] demons in an assumed body than with men in a real body, if all things are equal, it seems that it must be said that [...] he clearly rouses no lesser feeling of lust.'[22] As Walter Stephens neatly puts it, 'the plausibility of demonic copulation, its *verisimilitude*, is a matter of *virisimilitude*.' Kramer's assumption that sexual pleasure could only come from being penetrated by a force unambiguously male, Stephens goes on to say, is unmistakably misogynist. However, it is not about hating women; it is about hunting women 'only to the extent that it focuses on exploiting their sexuality to discover something about demons. *Cherchez la femme* means *Cherchez le diable*.'[23]

The demonologists' interest in demonic copulation thus appears not to be (at least initially) the result of an inordinate interest in matters sexual, but about demonic reality. For example, the Dominican inquisitor Nicolas Jacquier (*c*.1440–72) in his *Flagellum Haereticorum Fascinariorum* (*Scourge of Heretical Enchanters*) argued that, since sexual intercourse could only take place when awake, confessions to demonic sex could not be explained away as dreams. Experience clearly teaches us, he declared,

> that sexual intercourse [*operationes Venereae*] and the transports of carnal delight cannot take place or be consummated by people who are asleep, even though such experiences might originate in sleep by means of illusions or filthy fantasies [...]. It is clear that such apparitions take

place in reality, and not to people who are dreaming, but to those who are wide awake.[24]

The reality of demonic sex could also be demonstrated by affirming that it was considerably more pleasurable than human intercourse. Thus, for example, in the dialogue *Strix, sive de Ludificatione Daemonum* (*The Witch, or on the Deception of Demons*), written by the Italian philosopher Gianfrancesco Pico Della Mirandola in 1523, the sceptic Apistius could not understand why sex with the Devil was so pleasurable. The judge, Dicasto, replied that witches claimed that there was no pleasure like it on earth, and for three reasons, he thought: first, because the demons put on a pleasing face; second, because their 'virile members' were uncommonly large. 'With their faces', he declared, 'they delight the eyes, and with their members they filled up the most secret parts of the witches.' In addition, he said, the demons pretended to be in love with them. Probably, he concluded, 'they can stimulate something very deep inside the witches, by means of which these women have greater pleasure than men.'[25]

On the other hand, the reality of demonic copulation – that it took place 'in reality' and not merely 'in the imagination' – could be 'empirically' verified as much by the qualitative difference between human and demonic sex as by its similarities, by its displeasure as much as an equivalence in or a surfeit of it. Thus, for example, the jurist Henri Boguet, in the section headed 'Whether Such Copulation Exists in the Imagination Only' in his *Discours des Sorciers* (*Discourse on Sorcerers*), first published in 1590, looked to the confessions of witches as empirical evidence of its reality:

> But the witches' confessions which I have had make me think that there is truth in this matter; for they have all admitted that they have coupled with the Devil, and that his semen was very cold; and this is confirmed by the reports of Paul Grilland and the Inquisitors of the Faith.

Jacquema Paget added that she had several times taken in her hand the member of the Demon which lay with her, and that it was as cold as ice and a good finger's length, but not so thick as that of a man. Thievenne Paget and Antoine Tornier also added that the members of their demons were as long and big as one of their fingers; and Thievenne Paget said, moreover, that when Satan coupled with her she had as much pain as a woman in travail. Françoise Secretain said that, whilst she was in the act, she felt something burning in her stomach; and nearly all witches affirm that this coupling is by no means pleasurable to them, both because of Satan's ugliness and deformity, and because of the physical pain which it causes them, as we have just said [...]. For all these reasons I am convinced that there is real and actual copulation between a witch and a demon.[26]

What of male witches? Figures on the gender balance in witchcraft persecutions are notoriously slippery. Still, what we can say is that, while women were undoubtedly in the majority overall (though in the minority in some regions at some times), significant numbers of men were tried for witchcraft over the period.[27] Although Kramer in the *Malleus Maleficarum* constructed witchcraft as a predominantly female crime, he did not have any apparent qualms in recognising the existence of male witches. Indeed, he went as far as to recognise three kinds of sorcery that were specific to men.[28]

It would have been hard for him not to do so. It was at the request of Kramer and his inquisitorial colleague Jacob Sprenger that Pope Innocent VIII (1484–92) issued the famous bull *Summis Desiderantes*, subsequently included in at least some editions of the *Malleus Maleficarum*. This bull made no distinction between male and female witches. 'It is not without great vexation', declared the Pope, 'that it has recently come to Our hearing that [...] very many persons of both sexes have forgotten their own salvation and deviated from the Catholic Faith.'[29]

Although there were exceptions, most demonologists accepted that demons refrained from sodomy (and 'perverted' sexual practices generally). It was an assumption that went back to Thomas of Cantimpré (d. *c.*1270–2), who devoted a chapter of his *The Universal Good Concerning Bees* to 'Devils Blush over the Sin against Nature'. William of Auvergne similarly declared that sins against nature were so heinous that demons did not practise sodomy among themselves, nor had ever done so.[30] Aquinas too denied that demons engaged in sexual acts against nature, which included any sexual practices not conducive to procreation.[31] Their disinclination so to do was a residue of the angelic nature in which they were originally created.

In the *Malleus Maleficarum*, Kramer took his lead from Aquinas. Although Kramer recognised the possibility of sex between men and female demons, it was a matter in which he was not particularly interested. Later demonologists were not so reticent. But with respect to the matter of sex between men and male demons, Kramer's attitude was clear. Immediately after he had recommended that the heresy be known as the 'heresy of sorceresses', he went on to say, 'Blessed be the Highest One, Who has, down to the present day, preserved the male kind from such disgraceful behaviour, and clearly made man privileged since He wished to be born and suffer on our behalf in the guise of a man.'[32] It has been suggested that Kramer is here denying that men were involved in witchcraft at all,[33] but his intended meaning becomes clear if we recognise that, when he referred to women cavorting with demons [*cum demonibus*] immediately above, he explicitly meant male demons. The rejection of homosexual demonic sex then becomes clear. It is having sex with male demons from which God has preserved men. This interpretation is reinforced by the fact that he was actually citing William of Auvergne, who had used virtually identical language to thank God that men had never been sodomised by fallen angels.[34] Thus, although Kramer could have 'feminised' male witches by allowing them to have sex with the Devil as women did – thus 'gendering' his male witches as females – he chose not to do so. His horror of sodomy was too great to allow this.

Only during the sixteenth century was there a gradual move away from the dominant view that the Devil and his demons did not engage in sexual acts 'against nature'. This last vestige of their original angelic nature was finally removed. In 1521, the Dominican inquisitor Silvestro Prierius – most remembered as the first formal Catholic respondent to Martin Luther's Ninety-Five Theses – published his *De Strigimagarum, Demonumque Mirandis* (*On the Wonders of Witch-Magicians and Demons*). According to him, demons were more than willing to commit acts against nature if it resulted in the sinning of witches. He referred to the confessions of female witches who admitted to having sex with demons with bifurcated penises (*membro genitali bifurcato*) such that they were penetrated both anally and vaginally simultaneously.[35] But it was Pico Della Mirandola in *Strix*, only a few years after Prierius, who made the transition from demonic heterosexual activity that was 'against nature' to homosexual demonic activity. It was the one key issue on which he disagreed with the *Malleus Maleficarum*.[36] With the Devil no longer restrained by 'nature', the emphasis on unorthodox sexual practices between witches and demons increased over the next century. Thus Henri Boguet wrote: 'Satan couples with witches sometimes in the form of a black man, sometimes in that of some animal as a dog or a cat or a ram.'[37]

The pleasure to be gained by a woman from sex with the Devil was, according to the *Malleus Maleficarum*, at least equivalent to that with a man, but the Devil and his angels gained no such pleasure. Demons made themselves into succubi and incubi, Kramer wrote, 'not for the sake of pleasure, since a spirit does not have flesh and bones, but […] that through the fault of debauchery they may harm the nature of both aspects of man (the body and the soul), so that in this way humans will become more inclined to all faults'.[38] In the absence of flesh and bones, no pleasure was to be had from sex. This was a theory endorsed by Pierre de Lancre in the middle of his description of the sabbath, arguably the most sensational of seventeenth-century accounts of the ceremony. His 1612 work *Tableau de l'Inconstance des Mauvais Anges et Demons* (*Portrait of the Inconstancy of Evil Angels and Demons*) drew on his experience of witch-hunting south of Bordeaux in 1609. 'Now this lecherous operation', he wrote, 'is not performed and practiced by them for the pleasure that they take from it; because they are simply spirits, they cannot take any joy or pleasure from real things.'[39] The Devil wants only to insult God, to offend nature and to destroy and dishonour humankind.[40]

Now de Lancre really was quite obsessed with Satanic sex. He had no qualms in declaring that the Devil engaged in practices against nature, even if he qualified this by claiming that Satan got no more 'pleasure' from these than from any 'natural' practice. This was the result of his appearing at the sabbath as a billy-goat. According to de Lancre, the Devil sat on a golden throne. He danced with the most beautiful girls and women, sometimes leading the dance, sometimes putting himself into the hands of those whom he favoured the most. The Devil passed in ugliness 'the most horrible billy-goat that nature ever created'.[41] De Lancre was amazed that the Devil could find a woman depraved enough to wish to kiss him on any part of his body.[42] In an attempt to instil into the girls and women whom he interrogated some sense of the horror of their actions, he often asked them what pleasure they got from going to the sabbath,

Given that to get there they were carried violently through the air at great peril; that there they were forced to renounce and abjure their Savior, the Holy Virgin, their mothers, fathers, the generosity of heaven and earth, in order to adore a demon in the form of a hideous billy-goat, and to kiss him and caress the dirtiest parts of his body, to endure sexual contact with him that is as painful as childbirth. Moreover, they had to watch, kiss, and suckle, scratch and eat toads, and dance back to back in such a perverted way that even the most shameless of them should cast down their eyes in shame. At the feasts they had to eat the flesh of people who were hanged, dead bodies, the hearts of unbaptized children; they had to watch the debasement of the most precious sacraments of the church and other desecrations so abominable that just to hear them makes one's hair stand on end, giving one goosebumps and making one shiver all over. Nevertheless, they freely admitted that they went there and watched all these desecrations with obvious pleasure.[43]

The Satanic dance was a seductive one, with sex during or after. The Devil took the most beautiful woman 'for his carnal pleasures', but most often he honoured the queen of the sabbath, as well as the woman he favoured most, by having her sit next to him. According to the 16-year-old Jeannette d'Abadie, de Lancre tells us, the Devil would command the men and women present to form couples and have incestuous sex: a daughter with her father, a son with his mother, a brother with her sister. She herself had lost her virginity at the sabbath when she was 13. She said that she herself had never felt any semen, except when he deflowered her, on which occasion it felt cold, while that of other men was normal. She further said that when the Devil knew them carnally, they experienced a sharp pain. She saw women return to the sabbath, all bloody and complaining of pain. This was because the Devil's organ was covered with scales that tightened up as the Devil entered and pinched as he withdrew. De Lancre was able to extract various descriptions from his suspects of the Devil's penis: it was as long as an alder bush, though twisted and wound up like a snake; it was half as long as an alder bush, of modest size, red, dark, twisted, very stiff and pointy at the tip; whether appearing as a man or a goat, the Devil's penis was like a mule's, long and as big as an arm; it was one half iron, and the other half flesh, all along its length; or it was made out of horn which was why women screamed so. De Lancre had read Boguet's *The Examen of Witches*. 'This is completely opposite to what Boguet says,' he concluded, 'namely that the women from his country never saw his [the Devil's] organ to be longer than a finger and just as wide. Thus all the female witches of the Labourd are better served by Satan than are those of the Franche-Comté.'[44] Johannés d'Aguerre, de Lancre tells us, said that the Devil, appearing as a billy-goat, had his penis attached to his backside and that he would have sex with the women by moving and pushing it against their bellies. Marie de Marigrane, 15 years old, living in Biarritz, said that she had frequently seen the Devil have sex with a great many women. She said that, typically, he had sex with the pretty ones from the front and with the ugly ones from behind.

While de Lancre denied that demons gained any pleasure from sex as the consequence of their being spirits, for him they were not merely that. Like other demonologists, he was aware that demonic sexuality was the consequence of demons not being pure spirits but also having some form of embodiment at some times. This is all possible, declared de Lancre, because 'the demons make themselves a body of air with which, while this seems to be something marvelous and quasi impossible, they can practice the arts of Venus.'[45]

## Embodied Demons

The possibility of Satanic sex crucially depended upon the Devil's 'corporeality' (in some sense or other). This matter of the corporeality of demons was one that had already had a long history in the Christian tradition. At least until the time of Augustine, their embodiment was assumed. Thus, Christian readings of the 'coupling' of the fallen angels with the daughters of men implied embodied demons, and unproblematically so. For the early Christian period generally, if demons could be described in some way as immaterial, they were so only in complicated 'material' ways.

The issue was, then, not that the Devil was embodied, but that he could be so in such a multiplicity of ways. For the Neoplatonic philosopher Porphyry (c.232–303), demons had bodies made of *pneuma* (like thin air) that enabled them to become visible and to change shape.[46] Such demons rejoiced in sacrifices and were fattened up by the smoke from sacrificial blood and flesh. Like Porphyry, Origen believed that demons needed the smoke from sacrifices, and the foods that corresponded to their bodies, not only to be able to survive but, thus 'weighed down', to be able to remain close to the earth where the air was most dense, and they were nearer to people.[47]

Satan and his demons found a particular delight in appearing in embodied ways to St Anthony (c.251–356), traditionally viewed as the founder of Christian monasticism, in their attempts to draw him away from the ascetical life (see Plate 6). Thus demons appeared to him not only as a woman and a black boy but in numerous animal forms – lions, bears, leopards, bulls, serpents, asps, scorpions and wolves. 'The noises of all the apparitions together in the same place', we read, 'were terrible, and their outbursts of fury ferocious.'[48] Demons also appeared as giants, troops of soldiers, even as monks. Since the time of their fall, they

111

have been continually flying about the earth close to people. Because they have bodies different to ours, 'they can enter, even when the doors are shut, and take possession of all the air, they and their chief, the Devil.'[49] That they were predominantly 'air' meant they could be, literally, blown away. Thus, a very tall demon appeared to Anthony with a procession of spirits offering whatever he wanted. Anthony 'blew his breath at him, calling on the name of Christ', threatening to punch him as well.[50] Immediately, the demons departed. On another occasion, a demon posing as a monk looked like smoke as he went out of the door.[51]

Their subtle bodies gave them a remarkable speed that explained their apparent foreknowledge of events.[52] Apart from the capacity to be visible and invisible at whim, demons had the same powers as men, only highly enhanced – rather like Superman. Their bodies were so fine that they could 'literally' mess with our minds by entering physically into men's heads. They tempted humans not only from the outside but they could also do evil from within. In short, Satan could possess *our* bodies.[53]

Thus, from the beginnings of Christian monasticism, the battle with the Devil was a battle for men's thoughts, the 'internal' movements of their minds.[54] It was a matter of psychology, but mediated through a physical assault by the Devil on our minds. Thus, for Evagrius Ponticus (346–99), influenced by both Origen and Anthony, the Devil and his angels were the key opponents to spiritual progress. With bodies made of condensed, heavy and ice-cold air (here is the origin of the notion that sex with the Devil was an 'icy' experience), demons constantly used their superior knowledge and skills to delude their victims. They remained invisible until they took on shapes and they could enter men's bodies in the air inhaled through the nose on tiny wings in order to work on their brains.[55]

For Augustine too, demons had bodies of air, in contrast to their unfallen former angelic colleagues, who retained their ethereal bodies. As such, they could enjoy the sins of the body. The superhuman capacities of demons were the consequence, at least in part, of these aerial bodies. Through the powers of perception that belonged to the insubstantial body, Augustine wrote, demons readily surpassed the perception possessed by earthly bodies. Similarly, because of the superior speed and mobility of the aerial body, they exceeded the movements not only of men and beasts but also of birds. It was this that explained their apparent capacity to foretell the future. For, endowed with these two faculties of keenness of perception and speed of movement, 'they foretell and declare many things that they have recognised far in advance.'[56] As a result of these abilities, together with their long life-spans, demons not only foretell many things that will occur, but perform many marvellous acts.

Moreover, demons were able to persuade men who were avaricious and perverted in 'marvelous and unseen ways', entering into their bodies by means of the subtlety of their own bodies and influencing their thoughts.[57] The Devil crept through the entrances of the senses, adapting himself to colours, sticking to sounds, hiding in anger and lies, attaching to smells, infusing tastes and obscuring the understanding.[58]

This Augustinian account of embodied demons was to reach into the high Middle Ages by virtue of its endorsement by both Gregory the Great in his *Morals on the Book of Job* and Isidore of Seville in his *Etymologies*.[59] It was a view that lasted until the thirteenth century. The purpose of the discussion 'Of Demons' in *The Dialogue of Miracles* by the Cistercian monk Caesarius of Heisterbach (d. 1240) was to demonstrate by many exemplary tales that demons existed, that they were many in number and that they were malicious and hostile to men. They appeared in a vast array of forms, even in rather quirky human forms. Demons, declared Caesarius, 'have no hinder parts, and this is why a demon who appeared very frequently to a certain woman, when she asked him why he always walked backwards when he went away, replied: "We are allowed to take the human form, but nevertheless we have no backs."'[60]

Caesarius' clearest discussion of the nature of demonic bodies occurred in a chapter concerning how demons are in men. Here their 'natural' corporeality is implicitly asserted, in contrast to God's absence of it. According to Caesarius, it was impossible for the Devil to be within the human soul. To enter into the soul was only possible for God, 'because his substance is incorporeal by nature'.[61] The Devil could, however, be united to the soul 'by contact and pressure', and thence 'shoots in its wickedness like an arrow, by suggesting evil and fashioning the mind to vice'.[62] Thus, when the Devil is said to be in a man, it should not be understood as meaning that he is in the man's soul but in his body, 'because he is able to pass into its empty cavities such as the bowels'.[63]

Caesarius' view on the embodied nature of demons was already outmoded at the time of his writing in the mid-thirteenth century. The Augustinian view that demons (and angels) were embodied had been breaking apart for the previous century. It was an issue with which Peter Lombard was clearly already wrestling in the middle of the twelfth century in his *Sentences*, thus ensuring that the matter of demonic bodies would be a crucial part of theological discussion for the remainder of the medieval period. Lombard's strategy was to suggest that Augustine's position was much more ambiguous than it in fact was. On the one side, he wrote, were those who declared 'that all the Angels before [their] confirmation and/or lapse had bodies of air [*corpora aërea*] formed from a purer and superior part of the air [...] but to the evil angels [their] bodies were changed in [their] downfall, into the worse quality of the thicker [*spissoris*] air'.[64] On the other side were those who suggested that Augustine was merely

114

expressing the opinion of others concerning the embodied nature of angels and demons. These same writers, declared Lombard, 'taught unanimously [*concorditor*], that the Angels are incorporeal and do not have bodies united to themselves; but they assume bodies sometimes'.[65] That Lombard himself was more sympathetic to the latter position is implicit in his discussion that followed on how demons entered men, and in his conclusion that talk of demons entering men was more metaphorical than literal.[66]

Still, even if he was sympathetic to the non-corporeality of demons, Lombard ended by affirming that Augustine never solved the issue. By contrast, in his commentary on Lombard's *Sentences*, Bonaventure went a step further by declaring that Augustine doubted that the angels *were* naturally united to bodies. Having got around the issue of Augustine, Bonaventure made the following declaration: 'Angels, good and evil, do not have bodies, neither ones *naturally* united to themselves, nor ones bound [to them] inseparably.'[67] Nevertheless, he maintained, angels both good and evil could assume bodies primarily composed of air, 'an evil angel out of the inferior part, but a good [angel] out of the superior part'.[68]

Bonaventure's account was much complicated by his commitment to the Aristotelian notion that every living being was composed of both form and matter. Thus, although angels and demons lacked bodies, in order to exist they had to have matter. Only God existed as pure immateriality. On the face of it, this seemed to cut against his argument that spirits were incorporeal by nature. However, Bonaventure's solution was to argue that angels and demons (when disembodied) had 'spiritual matter'. Thus, matter was capable of being 'spiritual' when joined to spiritual forms, or 'corporeal' when joined to a corporeal form.[69]

This was an unnecessary difficulty that Thomas Aquinas would remove. He did so simply by making matter equivalent to corporeality. That is to say, for Aquinas –

rather like a modern physicist – to have matter was to be embodied, to be made of stuff, material, earth, air, atoms. As a result, Bonaventure's notion of 'spiritual matter' became a 'contradiction in terms'; 'spirit' and 'matter' were now by definition opposites. Thus, in answer to the question, 'Do demons have bodies joined to them by nature?'[70] Aquinas's answer was a resounding 'no'. It was a conclusion on which he disagreed with Augustine, although he was at pains to point out that Augustine did not think it mattered very much.

For Aquinas, then, both angels and demons were basically spiritual beings, which meant essentially 'incorporeal': 'to have a body united to it is not of the nature of an intellectual substance.'[71] Nevertheless, he argued, and here he and Bonaventure were in agreement, angels and demons could on occasion assume virtual bodies. It was clear from Scripture that they appeared not to the imagination but to the external vision of men, 'whereby the object seen exists outside the person beholding it, and can accordingly be seen by all'.[72] Thus, angels and demons could assume bodies of air appropriately condensed to form visible shapes.[73] In this way, Aquinas was able to reconcile the apparent conflict between reason and Scripture, where the former suggested incorporeality, the latter embodiment. Regardless of their difference over form and matter, for demonologists it was the agreement of Bonaventure and Aquinas on the capacity of demons to assume bodies that was crucial; it was this that made possible demonic sexuality.

According to Aquinas, then, the bodies assumed by spiritual beings were made of air, appropriately condensed, shaped and coloured by the divine power as the need arose. Such beings appeared in their virtual bodies to be living men, though they could not exercise those functions that are special to living subjects. Hence, they only appeared to perceive, talk and eat. Most crucially for later demonology, they could not procreate, though there was one activity in which they were almost genuinely human – sexual activity. By assuming the body of a woman they could take semen from a man and then, assuming the body of a man, deliver it to a woman.[74] This was essentially the same account as that given by Bonaventure.[75]

Both Aquinas and Bonaventure had the demon switching gender to steal and inject semen. This apparent demonic bisexuality was to trouble later demonologists. For example, the *Malleus Maleficarum*, generally concerned to keep demonic activities within the bounds of the 'natural', normalised it by the notion of a transfer of semen from one demon to another, thus in principle maintaining the heterosexuality of each demon. 'The succubus demon releases a seed from a criminal man; if the demon is assigned personally to this man and does not wish to make himself the incubus for the sorceress, he will hand the seed over to the demon assigned to the woman (sorceress), and the second one will make himself an incubus for the sorceress.'[76] Devils were very selective about whom they chose. The progeny that resulted was 'strong and large in body'.[77] As Aquinas knew, and we do too, there was Biblical precedent for this; the fallen angels who mated with the daughters of men in Genesis had, after all, produced giants.

Demonic sex was at the very centre of the Satanic heresy. Demonic corporeality, real or assumed, was central to demonic sex. Sex with the Devil was only taken off the demonological agenda a century after the *Malleus Maleficarum*, when Reginald Scot in 1584 and then more influentially Balthasar Bekker in the early 1690s denied any corporeality of the Devil, actual or virtual. The Devil, no longer capable of being incubus or succubus, was philosophically desexed from that time on. That was the key moment in the disappearance of the belief in the heresy of Satanism.

## CHAPTER SIX

# The Devil and the Witch

Thou shalt not suffer a witch to live.

Exodus 22.18 (KJV)

## Infanticide and Cannibalism

In the year 1612, the same year that Pierre de Lancre's *Portrait of the Inconstancy of Evil Angels and Demons* appeared, the assizes court at Lancaster in the north-west of England was transfixed by the story of a Satanic sabbath told by a 14-year-old girl by the name of Grace Sowerbutts. According to her, late in the previous year, she had accompanied her grandmother Jennet Bierley, her aunt Ellen Bierley and another woman Jane Southworth to a place called Red Bank on the northern side of the river Ribble near Samlesbury in Lancashire every Thursday and Sunday night for a fortnight. They had crossed the river magically from the Samlesbury side with the help of 'foure blacke things', that stood upright, yet did not have the faces of humans.[1] At Red Bank they found magical food which the other three women ate. Although Grace was encouraged to eat by her grandmother, the food looked too strange to her, and she did not have any. After they had eaten, the three women and Grace danced, each of them with one of the black things. After their dancing, she assumed that the three women had sex with three of the black things, for she herself too believed that 'the black thing that was with her, did abuse her bodie.'[2]

With magical transport, eating, dancing and sex with black things with (perhaps) the faces of animals, this meeting has all the features of a European witches' sabbath. In fact, it is the first description of an assembly of witches on English soil. But this was not all that Grace had to tell the court. She also said that she went one night with her grandmother and her aunt Ellen Bierley to the house of a Thomas Walshman in Samlesbury. All the household were asleep, and the doors were locked. Somehow, Jennet Bierley opened them, and the three of them entered the house. Jennet went alone into the room where Thomas Walshman and his wife were asleep. She brought out a small child that had been in bed with its parents and then sat Grace down by the fire with the child. Jennet Bierley then took a nail and thrust it into the child's navel. After that, she took a quill, placed it in the hole made by the nail, 'and did suck there a good space'.[3] She then placed the child back in bed again and the three of them returned to their own homes. Grace said that neither Thomas Walshman nor his wife were aware that the child had been taken. She added that, when Jennet pushed the nail into the child's navel, it did not cry out. The child had not thrived from that time on, she informed the court, and had subsequently died. Like the sabbath, up until this time, English witchcraft had had no tradition of infanticide or cannibalism. Grace had not been 'schooled' in this by any English investigating magistrate. So how did a 14-year-old girl know of such things?

The mystery became clear to the court when Grace admitted that a Master Christopher Southworth, 'to whom shee was taken to learne her prayers, did perswade, counsell, and advise her, to deale [...] against her said Grand–mother, Aunt, and *Southworths* wife'.[4] Christopher Southworth was in fact a Catholic priest who had been trained in Douai and Rome between 1579 and 1586 and was hiding out in his family's house, Samlesbury Hall. Grace Sowerbutts' mother, troubled by a set of behaviours that strongly suggested that Grace was possessed by the Devil, had taken Grace to him, probably in the hope of an exorcism. Christopher Southworth took the opportunity to use Grace to implicate Jane Southworth, his widowed aunt by law, and several of his family's tenants in witchcraft because they had converted to Protestantism and refused to return to the Catholic fold. He had seized the chance to do so by introducing Grace to some of the intricacies of elite European demonology that he had no doubt learned during his studies in Douai and Rome. So, to this little-known Catholic priest belongs the dubious privilege of being responsible for introducing the sabbath, infanticide and cannibalism to an English witchcraft trial for the first time.

Witches who killed children through sucking their blood were part of a European tradition that went back to the very beginnings of the witch-hunts in the early part of the fifteenth century. Thus, for example, in the 1420s, Bernardino of Siena preached a sermon in which he told of a number of women who, suspected of witchcraft, were taken into custody. 'And there was taken among others', he said,

> one who had told and confessed, without being put to torture, that she had killed thirty children or thereabouts, by sucking their blood; and she said that every time she let one of them go free she must sacrifice a limb to the devil, and she used to offer the limb of an animal; and she had continued for a long time acting in this manner. And furthermore she confessed, saying that she had killed her own little son, and had made a powder from him, which she gave people to eat in these practices of hers.[5]

Like blood-sucking, the eating of children by witches was also part of a European tradition from the beginning of the fifteenth century, though it had precursors in earlier stereotypes about medieval heretics.[6] Infant cannibalism exemplifies the metaphor of the witch as the anti-mother in a tradition of witches killing, burying, exhuming, cooking, and then eating children in their assemblies. Thus, for example, in the *Malleus Maleficarum*, Kramer elaborated on the story of demonic infanticide he had found in the *Formicarius* of Johannes Nider. According to Kramer, when asked about the method by which infants were captured, a certain captured sorceress replied,

> We prey on babies, especially those not yet baptized but also those baptized. [...] With our ceremonies we kill them in their cribs or while they lie beside their parents, and while they are thought to have been squashed or to have died of something else, we steal them secretly from the tomb and boil them in a cauldron until all the flesh is made almost drinkable, the bones having been pulled out. From the more solid matter we make a paste suitable for our desires and arts and movements by flight, and from the more runny liquid we fill a container [...] Whoever drinks from this container is immediately rendered knowledgeable when a few ceremonies are added, and becomes the master of our sect.[7]

## Travels Sabbatical

In the above passage, the murder of infants and travel to the sabbath are linked. It is the paste made from infants that enables witches magically to attend the gathering of witches. Later, the *Malleus Maleficarum* informed its readers that witches made a paste from the limbs of children and, following the Devil's instructions, smeared it on a seat or a piece of wood. Then they were immediately carried into the air by day or night, visibly and invisibly.[8] In other cases, it claimed, rather than using ointments, the witch was transported by means of demons in the form of animals, at other times merely by the Devil's invisible power.

Kramer, the author of the *Malleus Maleficarum*, was here linking the notion of infanticide with the idea already established by the *Errores Gazariorum* that the inducted witches were given an ointment with which to anoint their staffs in order to travel to the synagogue.[9] Johann Fründ in his *Bericht* in the 1430s made no mention of ointments, but he did have the 'evil spirit' (*der bös geist*) transporting the witches by night from one mountain top to another.[10] The *Malleus Maleficarum*, the *Errores Gazariorum* and Fründ's *Bericht* were in fact all drawing on an intellectual tradition of debate about 'night-flying women' that went back to the tenth-century canon *Episcopi*. The authority of this text, wrongly attributed to the Council of Ancyra held in 314, derived from its having been included in the mid-twelfth century in what was to become the most important collection of ecclesiastical law, namely Gratian's *Decretum*. There we read,

> It is also not to be omitted that some wicked women perverted by the devil, seduced by illusions and phantasms of demons, believe and profess themselves, in the hours of night, to ride upon certain beasts with Diana, the goddess of pagans, [or else with Herodias] and an innumerable multitude of women, and in the silence of the dead of night to traverse great spaces of earth, and to obey her commands as of their mistress, and to be summoned to her service on certain nights [...]. Wherefore the priests throughout their churches should preach with all insistence to the people that they may know this to be in every way false [...]. Whoever therefore believes that anything can be made, or that any creature can be changed to better or to worse or be transformed into another species or similitude, except by the Creator himself who made everything and through whom all things were made, is beyond doubt an infidel [and worse than a pagan].[11]

These 'night-flying women' were later to be identified with witches (see Plate 15). Thus, for example, Bernard Gui in his inquisitor's manual in the early 1320s associated witches with 'the fairy women, whom they call the "good folk" [*bonas res*], and who, they say, roam about at night'.[12] And the Spanish inquisitor Nicholas Eymeric in his *Directorium Inquisitorum* (*Directory for Inquisitors*) in 1376 declared that the women of the canon *Episcopi* 'offer sacrifices to the demons they invoke'.[13]

When Gui and Eymeric made this identification, the notion of the Satanic sabbath was yet to be invented. When it was, the passage from the canon *Episcopi* with its suggestion that 'night flying' was illusory was to be a core problem for those demonologists who wished to argue for the reality of magical travel to the sabbath. The 'theoretical' feasibility of the sabbath depended on the possibility of there being an 'intelligible' means by which many witches travelled long distances to it. Perhaps more importantly, Satanic sex was only 'really' possible when the witch was at the sabbath in person. Thus, as the inquisitor Nicholas Jacquier in his 1458 *Flagellum Haereticorum Fascinariorum* (*The Scourge of the Heretical Bewitchers*) clearly put it: 'Experience manifestly teaches that the operations of Venus and the passions of carnal pleasure are not able to be carried out or completed by those who are asleep, even if initiated in sleep by illusions or disgusting fantasies.'[14]

So the canon *Episcopi*'s notion that the 'night flying' was *illusory* and not real was a crucial problem that the demonologists had to overcome if the sabbath and sabbatical sex were to be possible. One way of doing so was to assert that the doings of the 'flying women' of the canon *Episcopi* were not relevant to those of more recent witches. Thus, for example, Bartolomeo Della Spina (*c.*1475–1546) in his *Quaestio de Strigibus* (*An Investigation of Witches*) suggested not only that the Council of Ancyra (whence he believed the canon *Episcopi* was derived) was not authoritative, but also that, even if it were, the witches of his time differed so much from those described in the canon *Episcopi* that its description of flying women was not relevant to contemporary circumstances.[15]

Della Spina was right: the folk belief in the flying women that the canon *Episcopi* declared an illusion did not have anything to do with sabbaths or the Devil, but this was a difficult argument to sustain. Moreover, the opinion of the canon *Episcopi* that night flying was nothing but dreams and illusions had been reinforced by a story from the *Vita Sancti Germani* (*Life of St Germain*). Written by Constantius of Lyon sometime before the year 494, the work was well known in the later medieval period as a consequence of its incorporation into the *Golden Legend* of Jacobus de Voragine (*c*.1228–98).

According to the *Golden Legend*, while visiting a house, St Germain was surprised to see the table being laid again. On asking why this was being done, he was told that the table was being prepared for certain good women who journeyed through the night. Germain stayed up to see who would arrive for the evening meal. He saw a troop of spirits enter in the form of men and women and enquired of his hosts if they knew these persons. They were identified as the neighbours (in Nider, the *female* neighbours) of the host. Germain forbade the spirits to leave and made inquiries in the homes of the neighbours, all of whom were found sleeping in their beds. He then called upon the spirits to tell the truth, and they declared that they were demons who in this way sought to deceive men.[16]

There was another possibility raised by the *Malleus Maleficarum* in response to the story from the *Life of St Germain*: 'it was clearly possible for the demons to set themselves alongside their husbands as they slept, as if the women were sleeping with their husbands, during the intervening period of time when the search for the wives was being conducted.'[17] In fact, the *Malleus Maleficarum* attempted to deal with a whole host of issues surrounding these sabbatical travels: the travel of witches to these sabbaths in their physical bodies; the apparent travel of witches in visions, dreams or imagination; the capacity of demons to impersonate at feasts the innocent who were lying by night asleep in their beds; and the capacity of demons to impersonate the witches at their feasts by replacing them in their beds at night.

Now the *Malleus Maleficarum*, in spite of the canon *Episcopi*, was strongly committed to the idea of witches' physical transport. How did it reconcile this with the claim of the canon *Episcopi* that the women who believed that they physically flew by night were deluded by the Devil? It did so, like Bartolomeo Della Spina did later, by distinguishing between the women described in the canon *Episcopi* and real witches who committed crimes and had made a bargain with the Devil, and by claiming that the delusions of the former did not also apply to the latter.[18] So, as the *Malleus Maleficarum* saw it, there was nothing in common between the two groups of women. Only thus was it able to sustain both the authority of canon law and its own commitment to the reality of sabbatical travelling.

Yet, the *Malleus Maleficarum* did want to keep both options open. It also argued that witches *truly* travelled to the sabbath *in their imaginations*. This enabled it to dispense with the problem discerned by St Germain, namely, the apparent presence of witches in their beds while putatively elsewhere. Additionally, in a piece of more than obscure casuistry, the *Malleus Maleficarum* claimed that the possibility that demons impersonated women at the sabbatical feasts, as St Germain had supposed, was mentioned only so that no one would believe in the *impossibility* of demons impersonating women in their beds.[19]

The need to demonstrate the 'reality' of the sabbath, and the 'reality' of the bodily transactions that there took place, drove many demonologists to argue for the 'real' transport of witches to the sabbath, even if they were willing to agree that witches travelled there also on occasions in the imagination only. Still, the weight of opinion was on the side of those who argued for real sabbatical travels. Thus, for example, the Jesuit Martín del Rio in his *Disquisitiones Magicae Libri Sex* (*Six Books on Investigations into Magic*) in 1599–1600 strongly supported *real* travelling to the sabbath. Having anointed themselves with a stick smeared with the ointment from the fat of dead children, 'they are usually carried away sitting on a staff, a pitch-fork, or a distaff; or they stand on one leg in a basket; or they sit on brooms, or a reed, or a bull, a pig, a male goat, or a dog.'[20]

Ointments were the link between infanticide, cannibalism and sabbatical travels. The connection of ointments to travelling to the sabbath, together with the canon *Episcopi*'s view that such travels were illusory, also opened up the potential for scepticism. Thus, for example, in his *The Discoverie of Witchcraft* in 1584, the English sceptic Reginald Scot completely rejected the possibility of physical travel to the sabbath. He did so by invoking the authority of the Neapolitan natural magician Johannes Baptista Neapolitanus, more commonly known to us as Giambattista Della Porta (1535–1615). He was a physician and sceptic to whom Scot, as a supporter of natural magic, would have been attracted. Scot was no doubt influenced to seek out Della Porta's *Magiae Naturalis* from his reading of Johann Weyer's 1563 *De Praestigiis Daemonum* (*On the Tricks of Demons*). For there, under the title of 'Ointments of the Lamiae and Certain Sleep-producing Plants which Greatly Disturb the Mind', Weyer had given an account of Della Porta's experiment.[21] Scot was no doubt delighted by Della Porta's test, and he translated it closely. After having detailed Della Porta's two recipes for transportation, the one based on the fat of young children, the other on the blood of a bat, he gave us Della Porta's account:

Now (saith he) when I considered throughlie hereof, remaining doubtfull of the matter, there fell into my hands a witch, who of hir owne accord did promise me to fetch an errand out of hand from farre countries, and willed all them, whome I had brought to witnesse the matter, to depart out of the chamber. And when she had undressed hir selfe, and froted [rubbed] hir bodie with certeine ointments (which action we beheld through a chinke or little hole of the doore) she fell downe thorough the force of those soporiferous or sleepie ointments into a most sound and heavie sleepe: so as we did breake open the doore, and did beate hir exceedinglie; but the force of hir sleepe was suche, as it tooke awaie from hir the sense of feeling: and we departed for a time. Now when hir strength and powers were wearie and decaied, shee awooke of hir owne accord, and began to speake manie vaine and doting words, affirming that she had passed over both seas and mountains; delivering to us manie untrue and false reports; we earnestlie denied them, she impudentlie affirmed them.[22]

Through Della Porta, Scot was able effectively to tie the use of ointments to illusory journeys of the imagination rather than the body. Della Porta was of help too in Scot's theory of the melancholic origins of sabbatical travelling, for Scot was able to suggest that, according to Della Porta, such imaginary journeys were false rather than true because they were the delusions of old mad women.[23] Thus, for Scot, Della Porta's account took care of both physical and imaginary sabbatical travels. It dovetailed nicely with Scot's own explanation of witches: that they were deluded and melancholic old women.

In his *An Examen of Witches*, Henry Boguet noted that he had read Johann Weyer. So he too knew Della Porta's account of his experiment with the ointments, and he saw the problem it posed for supporters of bodily sabbatical travels. Thus, to avoid the conclusions drawn by Della Porta, he drove a wedge between ointments and flying to the sabbath. Some travelled to the sabbath, he wrote, upon a white staff, others on a black ram, a black man, a goat, a horse, sometimes on a broom, generally leaving their house by the chimney. Some rub themselves with a certain ointment, he went on, while others use none. Some who are not even witches, after anointing themselves, do not fail to fly up the chimney and be carried away as if they were witches. Some even go to the sabbath without beast or staff to carry them. But it should be known, he concluded, 'that a beast or a staff is of no more use than the ointment, but that it is the Devil, who of his own power, is as a wind which bears them along'.[24] So concerned was he that sabbatical travel in the imagination was open to scepticism that he was willing to concede that it was impossible truly to travel to the sabbath *without* the body:

> For my part, I have never been able to believe that such a thing is in any way possible; for if it is true that when the soul is separated from the body, death must necessarily follow, how can it be possible for a witch, after having been in spirit to the Sabbat, to return to life by the help of the Devil? This cannot be except by a miracle, which belongs only to God and not to Satan, who only works by secondary and natural causes and therefore has no power to raise the dead to life.[25]

In ruling out 'true' imaginary travels by relegating them to the realm of the illusory, he left only one option – that of Satanic travels in the physical body; these would become increasingly unbelievable.

## The Satanic Pact

When Pope Eugenius IV wrote his *A Letter to All Inquisitors of Heretical Depravity* in 1417, he believed that, at the core of Satanic witchcraft, there was a pact made between the witch and the Devil. Witches, he declared, make with devils 'a written agreement or another kind of pact through which, by a single word, touch, or sign, they may perform whatever evil deeds or sorcery they wish'.[26] The *Errores Gazariorum* informed its readers that, when a new member joined the sect and had sworn his faith and had paid homage, 'the devil pricks his left hand with an instrument and draws blood from it, with which he writes a certain writing on a deed, which he then keeps.'[27] It was the pact, regardless of any criminal acts (*maleficia*) that may have resulted from it, that created the *heretical* moment (see Plate 18). As the English Protestant William Perkins was to put it two hundred years later, 'The Ground of all the practices of Witchcraft is a league or covenant made between the Witch and the Devill: wherein they doe mutually bind themselves to each other.'[28] As a result of this pact or its Protestant equivalent the covenant, Satan 'hath bound himselfe to them, for the effecting of rare and extraordinarie workes, which others, not ioyned with him in the like confederacie, are not able either by his helpe, or any power or pollicy of their owne to bring to passe'.[29] In short: no pact, no magic!

Thus, the pact between the Devil and the magician or the witch was perceived as a precondition of any and all magical powers. Following Augustine, superstitious practices in general, and witchcraft and sorcery in particular, were viewed as originating in a compact between men and demons. The pact could be either explicit or tacit. According to Aquinas, a pact was explicit when the sorcerer invoked demonic assistance, and tacit when, without acts of conjuration of demons, a person performed an act with the aim of effecting something which either did not naturally follow, or which was not expected as the result of the direct intervention of God.

This Thomist distinction was endorsed by the third of the 1398 University of Paris articles against ritual magic, which condemned entering into an implicit or explicit pact with demons, defining the former as 'every superstitious ritual, the effects of which cannot be reasonably traced to God or nature'.[30] It was a distinction that blurred the boundaries between popular superstitions on the one hand, and sorcery and witchcraft on the other, and it negated the difference between benevolent and malevolent magic. Thus, to be involved in any form of magic was to have made a pact with the Devil, even if unknowingly. But it was explicit rather than implicit pacts that were to attract the attention of the demonologists and, of these explicit pacts, the demonologists engaged most particularly with those made publicly at the sabbath more than those made privately between witch or magician and the Devil.

By the time of William Perkins, in the early seventeenth century, the simple pact between the witch and the Devil had been elaborated in accordance with the developing repertoire of witchcraft practices. In keeping with his Protestantism, Perkins's version of this was a verbal agreement between the Devil and man that reversed the divine covenant made between God and the Christian. According to Perkins, when a pact was made openly, the witch bound himself to the Devil by renouncing God and the Bible, the covenant made in baptism and his redemption by Christ; as a pledge and token of all of this he gave the Devil a written pact in his own hand or some part of his blood. The Devil, for his part, promised to be ready at the witch's command to appear in the form of any creature, to consult with him, to aid and help him in the procurement of pleasures, honour, wealth or preferment and to do whatever he was commanded.

In its most elaborate form, in the same year 1608, in Guazzo's *Compendium Maleficarum*, the pact comprised a complex ritual that inverted Catholic beliefs and practices. In this case, the witches denied the Christian faith and withdrew their allegiance from God. They repudiated the

Virgin Mary, heaping insults upon her. The Devil then placed his claw upon their brow, symbolically removing the holy chrism, thus destroying the sign of their baptism. He then bathed them in a new baptism and gave them a new name. He also made them deny their godmothers and godfathers, both of baptism and confirmation, and assigned them new ones. The witches then gave the Devil a piece of their clothing. Within a circle traced upon the ground, they swore allegiance to him and prayed that he would strike them out of the book of life and inscribe their names in the book of death. They then promised to sacrifice to him or to suffocate for him one child every fortnight or month, and vowed to give him a gift every year. He then placed his mark upon some part of their bodies. Having been marked, the witches vowed never to adore the Eucharist, to insult the Virgin Mary and images of the saints, to trample upon and destroy relics and images of the saints, holy water, blessed salt and bread, never to make confession to a priest and to maintain a silence concerning their bargain with the Devil. They also vowed to fly to the sabbath, take part in its activities and recruit all they could into the service of the Devil. The Devil promised to stand by them, to fulfil all their prayers in this life, and to bring them to happiness after death.[31]

In Western Europe, the origin of the notion of the Satanic pact went back to the translation from Greek into Latin in the ninth century by Paul, a deacon of Naples, of a text entitled 'A Miracle of the Virgin Mary Concerning Theophilus the Penitent'.[32] By the year 1500, it had been translated into virtually all European languages. According to the legend, Theophilus was a faithful priest in Asia Minor who was offered the bishopric upon the death of the previous incumbent. Theophilus was reluctant to accept the position and another was appointed. After the new bishop had been consecrated, certain clergy urged that Theophilus be removed from his position as steward.

As a result, he was demoted by the new bishop, and a new steward appointed.

The Devil then made Theophilus' heart 'to beat with perverse thoughts, instilling into him jealousy of the steward's power and the desire of honour'.[33] There was in the town a Jewish magician, 'a practicer of all sorts of diabolical arts'.[34] Theophilus went to him by night and sought his help. The magician told him to come back the next evening and he would take him to his master. The next evening, after Theophilus had promised not to make the sign of the cross at anything he heard or saw, the magician 'showed him suddenly a creature clad in white robes [...] and, seated in their midst, the prince. It was the devil and his minions.'[35] The Devil promised Theophilus that he would rule over all, even the bishop, if he would be the Devil's servant. Theophilus kissed the Devil's feet and begged to be his servant. The Devil told him to deny the son of Mary, and Mary herself, and all the things offensive to the Devil, and to put the agreement in writing. Satan entered into Theophilus and he said, 'I deny Christ and His mother.'[36] And he put his denial in writing.

The next day, Theophilus was recalled from retirement. The man who had replaced him was ingloriously removed, Theophilus was reappointed steward and given double the responsibilities he had had before. Everyone obeyed him in fear and trembling. But Theophilus soon regretted his arrogance, and he devoted himself to fasting, prayer and vigils. He then felt remorse for his deal with the Devil, repented of his sins and threw himself upon the mercy of the Virgin Mary. After 40 days of prayer and fasting, she appeared to him. He made a new confession of his faith, and Mary interceded as a mediator (*mediatrix*) between him and God.[37] Mary retrieved the written contract from Satan and Theophilus was forgiven by God (see Plate 11).

The legend of Theophilus is important for its part in the history of the cult of the Virgin Mary and for its role in the history of anti-Semitism. It is also a significant text within the history of demonology. On one intellectual trajectory, it feeds into the history of witchcraft, and the pact between the Devil and the witch; but on another trajectory it is part of the history of magic. The legend of Theophilus, combined with the figure of Simon Magus, becomes the legend of Dr Faust, the master magician and learned necromancer who had sold his soul to the Devil, the historical Dr Faustus (d. *c.*1539) having become even in his own lifetime inextricable from the mythology that surrounded him. The exemplary form of the legend can be dated to 1587, the year of the German *Historia von D. Johann Fausten*, published by Johann Spies. It was the English translation of this work published in 1592, *The Historie of the Damnable Life, and Deserved Death of Doctor Iohn Faustus*, that inspired Christopher Marlowe's *Doctor Faustus*,[38] whence, boomerang-like, it went back to Germany and the nineteenth-century *Faust* of Goethe.

According to the English Faust book, John Faust, in spite of his successful studies in divinity, progressively turned to the practice of necromancy, so much so 'that he could not abide to be called doctor of divinity but waxed a worldly man and named himself an astrologian, and a mathematician: and for a shadow, sometimes a physician, and did great cures, namely with herbs, roots, waters, drinks, receipts and clysters'.[39] His expertise in necromancy and conjuration was so advanced and his desire for knowledge so great that he determined to conjure the Devil. Going to a thick wood near Wittenberg, he made a circle in the dust with a wand, and within that more circles and characters. Then he began to call on Mephostophiles (sic) the spirit, and to charge him in the name of Beelzebub to appear there. At the appearance of the spirit, Faust commanded him to reappear at his house at midday the next day (see Plate 12).

At that meeting, the necromancer Faust, in apparent command of the spirit, told him that he wanted the spirit to serve and obey him in all things until his death, that the spirit should bring anything he desired, and that the spirit should always tell him the truth. Mephostophiles told Faust that such a promise was not his to give without the permission of his prince, Lucifer. Moreover, said the spirit, 'It is also certain, we have never as yet opened unto any man the truth of our dwelling, neither of our ruling, neither what our power is, neither have we given any man any gift or learned him any thing, except he promise to be ours.'[40] But Faust remained determined to obtain his requests of the Devil without the loss of his soul.

That same evening, Mephostophiles returned, having gained assent from Lucifer to whatever Faust wished, if Faust would promise to be his. Again, Faust laid out his demands, and in turn the spirit his: that in return Faust should give Lucifer his body and soul; that he should do so in writing in his own blood; that he would be an enemy to all Christians and deny his Christian belief; and that he never let anyone change his opinion on these matters. The spirit further promised that his wishes would be fulfilled for a certain number of years, at the end of which he would be fetched away. Faust agreed. The next morning, Faust wrote out the contract with his own blood in a saucer set on warm ashes:

I Johannes Faustus, Doctor, do openly acknowledge with mine own hand, to the greater force and strengthening of this letter, that sithence [sic] I began to study and speculate the course and order of the elements, I have not found through the gift that is given to me from above, any such learning and wisdom that can bring me to my desires [...] now have I Doctor John Faustus, unto the hellish prince of Orient and his messenger Mephostophiles, given both body and soul, upon such condition that they shall learn me and fulfil my desire in all things, as they have promised and vowed unto me, with due obedience unto me, according unto the articles mentioned between us.

Further, I covenant and grant with them by these presents, that at the end of 24 years next ensuing the date of this present letter, they being expired, and I in the mean time, during the said years, be served of them at my will, they accomplishing my desires to the full in all points as we are agreed, that then I give them full power to do with me at their pleasure, to rule, to send, fetch or carry me or mine, be it either body, soul, flesh, blood or goods, into their habitation, be it wheresoever: and hereupon, I defy God and His Christ, all the host of heaven, and all living creatures that bear the shape of God, yea all that lives; and again I say it, and it shall be so. And to the more strengthening of this writing, I have written it with mine own hand and blood, being in perfect memory, […] John Faustus, approved in the elements and the spiritual doctor.[41]

Like Theophilus, Faust was to live to regret his agreement. Unlike Theophilus, he had no Virgin Mary to come to his aid to save him from eternal damnation in hell, and no escape from his side of the bargain. At the end of the 24 years, after his last oration to his students on his last evening bemoaning his fate, he stayed alone. The next morning, his students, coming into the hall in which they had left him, 'found no Faustus, but all the hall lay besprinkled with blood, his brains cleaving to the wall; for the devil had beaten him from one wall against another, in one corner lay his eyes, in another his teeth, a pitiful and fearful sight to behold'.[42] His body they found in the yard, lying in the horse dung, 'most monstrously torn and fearful to behold'.[43]

## The Devil's Mark

In Protestant theology, and Calvinist thought in particular, the relationship established between God and man was a covenantal one in which the terms were established by

God alone. So it is perhaps a matter of little surprise that in Calvinist demonology, the emphasis was on the covenant made between the Devil and the witch. As the Genevan Calvinist Lambert Daneau put it in 1574, sorcerers work and infect things by their poison through Satan. 'There is no sorcerer,' he continued, 'but he maketh a league & covenant with the Divel, and voweth himselfe unto him.'[44] The covenant with the Devil was sealed by his marking the witch either with his teeth or his claws. It was a mark, declared Daneau, that the witch 'always beareth about him, some under the eye liddes, others betwene their buttocks, some in the roofe of their mouthe, and in other places where it may be hid & concealed from us'.[45]

Daneau's commitment to the idea that the pact with the Devil was sealed with the Devil's mark played little role in the writings of the early demonologists. The *Malleus Maleficarum*, for example, makes no reference to it. It was on other occasions referred to, if only to be refuted.[46] Catholic demonologists only came to it late in the sixteenth century. Nicholas Remy, for example, in his *Daemonolatria* (*Demonolatry*) in 1595 had no doubts that the Devil marked those whom he had newly claimed as a sign of his ownership of them. He reminded his readers that these marks could be found by their being insensitive to pain and not bleeding when pricked, however deeply. It was explained for him by the fact that areas exposed to extreme cold lose their sensitivity and, when touched by the talons of the Devil's icy cold body, they remained permanently affected. Henri Boguet similarly noted that 'the place where they bear these marks is so insensitive that they do not shrink even if they are probed to the bone in that place.'[47]

Still, Boguet did not want to make the discovery of marks necessary to a conviction. They are very difficult to find, he said, because they are very inconspicuous. The Devil often effaces them as soon as the witch is arrested. Moreover, some witches are never marked; the Devil only branded those whose loyalty was in most doubt. Thus for Boguet the absence of a mark should not be a conclusive piece of evidence suggesting innocence. '[T]hey are wrong,' he concluded, 'who are so scrupulous as to be unwilling to condemn a witch to death unless a mark can be found, as is the practice of a certain Republic [Geneva] which I shall not name.'[48]

The Scottish Reformer John Knox, exiled from his native Scotland from 1553 to 1555, had learned not only his theology but also his demonology from Calvinist Geneva. So it is not surprising that the Devil's mark, as evidence of the demonic pact, often accompanied by the 'pricking' of the witch in search of a mark insensible to pain and which did not bleed, was a common feature of witchcraft trials in Reformation Scotland from the late sixteenth to the early eighteenth century.[49] The Calvinist connection between covenant and mark is nowhere better demonstrated than during the last major Scottish witch-hunt, in a 1697 sermon to the trial judges by the minister of Kilallan, James Hutchinson. Based on the text from the book of Exodus 22.18, 'Thou shalt not suffer a witch to live,' it proposed a covenantal theology that provided legitimation for the trying of children as witches. Thus, according to Hutchinson, the term 'witch' is constituted by the 'real compact between Satan and that person either personally drawn up and made or mediately by parents [...] having power of the person, [Satan] adding thereunto his mark'.[50] Just as the children of professing parents when baptised were in covenant with God, so were the children of those parents who had made a covenant with Satan in covenant with the Devil. Those children that 'have received his mark and have been trained up by these parents in the way of witchcraft and have practised them may justly be looked upon as witches, formally constituted as being under a real covenant with Satan'.[51]

In spite of its prevalence in Scotland, Daneau's endorsement of the Devil's mark as evidence of the Devil having sealed the bargain was not a sign of witchcraft that became widespread in England. In England, where evil acts (*maleficia*) were more the focus of persecution than heresy, the notion of the demonic pact was less marked and consequently the belief in the demonic mark as key evidence of it was marginalised. Rather, the mark subtly changed in England as a result of that distinctive feature of English witchcraft – the keeping of familiar spirits.

The keeping and nurturing of familiars in animal or human form became in England one of the decisive features of witchcraft.[52] Witches paid a price for their familiars. They had to be fed bread, milk, animals – even the witch's own blood. Thus the European Devil's mark was supplemented in England by the witch's mark – a supernumerary nipple or teat by which the English witch fed her familiars. Where European witches were demonic lovers, English witches were demonic mothers. Or perhaps rather, in the English context the sexual, the maternal and the demonic were complexly interwoven.[53] Thus, the European search for the sign of the demonic pact was transformed in England into the search for the place from which the familiar was nurtured by the witch's blood, and the meaning of the marks became fluid and ambiguous.

Quite detailed accounts of familiars were present in English texts from as early as 1566. Thus, in that year, in the trial of Mother Agnes Waterhouse, the marks of the accused were examined at the request of the queen's attorney:

Agnes Waterhouse when dyd thye Cat suck of thy bloud never saide she, no saide hee, let me se, and then the jayler lifted up her kercher on her heade and there was diverse spottes in her face & one on her nose, then sayde the quenes attorney, in good faith Agnes when dydde he sucke of thy bloud laste, by my faith my lorde sayde she, not this fortnyght.[54]

No one at this time had put together the European Devil's mark – a sign of the Satanic pact, insensitive to pain and incapable of bleeding – with the English witch's marks caused by her feeding of familiars.

The two ideas continued to run parallel for another hundred years. Thus, for example, in the 1697 edition of Michael Dalton's *The Countrey Justice*, judges were encouraged to look for both nipples and marks, the former evidence of witches having familiar spirits, the latter of their having made a bargain with the Devil.[55] Still, as early as 1612, in *The Witches of Northamptonshire*, the two marks had become one in an expansion of a passage from the 1597 *Daemonologie* of King James. In his demonology, James had remarked that there were two ways to assist in the trial of witches: one was 'their fleeting [floating] on the water'; the other 'the finding of their mark, and the trying the insensibleness thereof'.[56] This was quite in keeping with the European tradition of the witch's mark, as we might expect from a Scottish king. But in *The Witches of Northamptonshire*, we read that there were two signs or tokens by which to detect and find witches: again 'their fleeting on the water', but this time also 'the marke *where the Spirits sucke*, and by the trying of the insensibleness thereof'.[57] This was a peculiarly English hybrid of the Devil's mark – both maternal and erotic. It was undoubtedly the consequence of the introduction of the European Devil's mark into England by a Scottish king, who as both James VI of Scotland and James I of England was something of a hybrid himself.

It was Reginald Scot in his *The Discoverie of Witchcraft* who in 1584 had told of the European Devil's mark to an English reading public, and he therefore holds the somewhat dubious honour of having been the first to do so. Still, true to his sceptical bent, Scot was having none of the mark, nor of the Satanic pact. The impossibility of it went to the core of Scot's argument, namely, that the pact of the sort described by the demonologists assumed something that was impossible, that is, the corporeality of the Devil:

> That the joining of hands with the divell, the kissing of his bare buttocks, and his scratching and biting of them, are absurd lies; everie one having the gift of reason may plainlie perceive: in so much as it is manifest unto us by the word of God, that a spirit hath no flesh, bones, nor sinewes, whereof hands, buttocks, claws, teeth, and lips doo consist.[58]

For Scot, no teeth or claws meant no mark; and no mark meant no covenant between the Devil and the witch. Scot's critique was an early sign that the edifice built by the demonologists was beginning to creak.

# CHAPTER SEVEN

# A Very Possessing Devil

And Jesus asked him, saying, What is thy name? And he
said Legion: because many devils were entered into him
[…]. Then went the devils out of the man, and entered into
the swine: and the herd ran violently down a steep place
into the lake, and were choked.

Luke 8.30–3 (KJV)

## The Possessed Body

To the Puritan family and household of Alexander Nyndge
in Herringswell in Suffolk, it appeared that he might have
been mad. On 20 January 1573, we are informed, Alexander
Nyndge demonstrated a whole range of behaviours
sufficient to lead them to this suspicion. His chest and body
swelled, his eyes bulged, he shook, he refused to eat, he
banged his head and other parts of his body against the
ground and the bedstead, he gnashed his teeth and foamed
at the mouth, a lump ran up and down his body between
the skin and the flesh, he was horribly disfigured and he
showed enormous strength.[1]

Alexander's brother Edward, master of arts from Oxford
University, read the symptoms quite differently. He saw
them as the result, not of madness, but of Alexander's being
possessed by a demon. It was a diagnosis which Alexander
himself accepted: 'Alexander Nyndge having his speech
then at liberty said unto the same Edward, "Brother, he is
marvellously afraid of you, therefore I pray you, stand by

141

me."'[2] Alexander now spoke from the place which Edward had constructed for him and in the role which Edward had determined for him, as a person possessed by the Devil. He physically showed the demon within: 'And within a little time after, the body of the said Alexander, being as wondrously transformed as it was before, much like the picture of the Devil in a play, with a horrible roaring voice, sounding Hell-hound, was most horribly tormented.'[3]

The period from 1550 to 1700 was the golden age of the demoniac. As Erik Midelfort remarks, 'Observers at the time were so impressed with this spread of possession that no previous age, with the exception of Christ's own age, seemed to have presented so many frightful examples of the Devil's rage.'[4] It is no coincidence that the age of the demoniac was also that of the witch. For the latter was, more often than not, taken to be the cause of the former. From Alexander Nyndge in Suffolk in 1573 to the possessions in Salem in 1692, the Devil was especially active in entering human bodies. Cases of demonic possession were common enough, as Daniel Walker notes, 'for ordinary people to understand them and believe in them'. On the other hand, as he points out and contemporary writings confirm, they were 'rare enough to be an exciting novelty and thus attract large audiences',[5] not least because the demoniac had the particularly numinous quality of being both terrifying and fascinating.

That the Devil could possess human bodies was the result of the conviction that the Devil too was embodied or at least, as we have seen, 'virtually' embodied. As a result, the body possessed was a site of conflict between good and evil. And demoniacs, in their battle with the Devil within, became exemplars of piety, even sanctity.

Though metaphor and reality often overlap in the description of the entrance and exit of the demon, the demonological tradition and the possession texts themselves have an overall commitment to a demonic quasi-corporeality. The jurist Henri Boguet in his *Discours des*

*Sorciers* was convinced that witches usually used food, most often apples, to introduce the Devil into a person:

> And in this connection, I cannot pass over what happened at Annecy in Savoy in the year 1585. On the edge of the Hasli Bridge there was seen for two hours an apple from which came so great and confused a noise that people were afraid to pass by there […]. Everybody ran to see this thing, though no one dared to go near to it; […] at last one man more bold than the rest took a long stick and knocked the apple into the Thiou […] and after that nothing more was heard. It cannot be doubted that this apple was full of devils, and that a witch had been foiled in an attempt to give it to someone.[6]

In this he found a precedent in Satan's use of an apple to tempt Eve in the Garden of Eden. He went on to retell the familiar story from St Gregory of the nun who, in eating a lettuce, swallowed the Devil hidden within it because she had failed to make the sign of the cross.

The Devil was seen to enter through bodily openings: nostrils, ears, wounds, the anus, and so on. But most commonly, he entered through the mouth, often mingling with the air that was breathed.[7] Having gained entrance, the Devil was not restricted to any one part of the possessed body, but could move around it. Thus, the demonologist Francesco Maria Guazzo developed a complex symptomology of possession, according to which the location of the Devil could be determined in the light of the symptoms presented by the possessed:

> If the demon is in his head, he [the demoniac] feels the keenest pains in his head […]. If he is in his eyes, he [the Devil] twists them about. If in the back, he bruises his limbs before and behind […]. If he is in the nobler parts of the body, as about the heart or lungs, he causes panting,

palpitation and syncope. If he is more towards the stomach, he provokes hiccoughs and vomiting so that sometimes they cannot take food, or if they do they cannot retain it.[8]

The demons would depart in similar ways – through the ears, the nostrils, the vagina, the anus, most often through the mouth – as the sixteenth-century Italian exorcist Zaccaria Visconti put it, 'like a fiery flame or a very cold wind or some creature'.[9]

Multiple demonic personalities could co-exist in the body of the demoniac. Possession by legions of demons had Biblical authority, not only in the Gerasene demoniac whom Jesus exorcised (Mark 5.1–20), but also in Mary Magdalene, who was possessed by seven devils (Luke 8.2). As a consequence, possession by many, both named and anonymous, was more the rule than the exception. The French demoniac Nicole Obry was at one time possessed by around 30, of whom the chief was the Beelzebub of Biblical renown.[10] Beelzebub was also active across the Channel in England, where the demons Brother Glassap and Brother Radulphus, who had taken up residence in the so-called boy of Burton, Thomas Darling, reported to him.[11] Rachel Pinder broke all records. She was said to have five thousand legions of demons within.[12] A sceptic such as the Anglican Samuel Harsnett could come up with good reasons for the presence of so many, not least that the expulsion of a large number prolonged the exorcism and heightened the reputation of the exorcist.[13]

## Possession, Medicine and Sceptics

The possessed body was not only a site of conflict between good and evil. In the seventeenth century, it was also a battleground between believers and sceptics. Anglican sceptics, such as John Deacon and John Walker, anxious to discredit Catholic exorcisms and to discourage Puritan exorcists alike, argued that when the Scriptures spoke of possession by demons they did so only metaphorically. To interpret possession literally, they maintained, 'would pester the Church with many absurd and inconvenient opinions'.[14] Similarly, Thomas Hobbes claimed that the Biblical accounts of Satan entering bodies were to be interpreted metaphorically. He went on to suggest that, since spirits are corporeal, and since two corporeal entities cannot occupy the same space at the same time, corporeal possession is therefore impossible.[15]

That there was conceptual space for sceptics was because the Devil's possession of a body was often indistinguishable from 'natural' diseases. Often reluctant to accept that their loved ones were possessed by the Devil, relatives generally consulted the medical experts. But many physicians, when unable to find a 'natural' reason for the symptoms of those afflicted, were not averse to suspecting that the Devil was active. Not necessarily – indeed, not often – opposed to demonic diagnoses, the physicians' judgements were often important in determining that the cause of the afflictions was beyond the medical.

Still, not all physicians would countenance a diagnosis of demonic possession. Edward Jorden, for example, explained the symptoms of possession in terms of the disease of hysteria or 'the suffocation of the mother'. Jorden was motivated by the possession of Mary Glover, and by the trial of the witch Elizabeth Jackson in December 1602 for having bewitched her. On that occasion, doctors Hering and Spencer testified to the preternatural origins of her illness, doctors Jorden and Argent to its medical origins. Judge Anderson, completely unconvinced by Jorden's 'naturalistic' explanations of Mary's symptoms, found Jackson guilty.[16]

According to Jorden, hysteria was 'an affect of the Mother or womb wherein the principal parts of the body by consent do suffer diversly according to the diversity of causes and diseases wherewith the matrix is affected'.[17] Jorden was following the tradition of including under 'hysteria' a whole range of symptoms, all believed to arise from gynaecological irregularities, which were often included as signs of possession. His book on hysteria was intended to demonstrate that 'divers strange actions and passions of the body of man, which in the common opinion, are imputed to the Devil, have their true natural causes, and do accompany this disease.'[18] While he did not go so far as to deny the possibility of demonic possession, he did plead for caution in the diagnosis, 'both because the impostures be many, and the affects of natural diseases be strange to such as have not looked thoroughly into them'.[19] Of the seemingly possessed cured by the prayer and fasting of others, Jorden had a ready psychological explanation in the confident expectation of the patient to find relief through those means.

Jorden's account was predicated on the assumption that 'naturalistic' and 'preternaturalistic' accounts of disease were incompatible. This was not readily acceptable to those who believed that Satan could be equally involved in both natural disease and supernatural possessions. As Stephen Bradwell wrote, 'Whereas he [Jorden] supposes by placing natural effects to call in natural causes, and by admitting natural causes to exclude supernatural out of doors, he is much deceived. For supernatural efficients can do all [that] the natural may and much more.'[20] Still, Jorden's account of possession as an illness did allow for the possibility that the symptoms of demonic possession did not have to be taken only as either genuine evidence of the diabolic or as the result of intentional fraud by the apparently possessed. Disease was, for Jorden, a genuine alternative to fraud or the activities of the Devil and his minions.

Thus, in the summer and autumn of 1605, the demoniac Anne Gunter was interviewed by King James I. Anne had become a matter of considerable public concern, sufficient to arouse the King's interest. Soon after the first of their meetings, Anne had been handed over to the sceptical Richard Bancroft, then archbishop of Canterbury, and thence to Samuel Harsnett, who had been earlier engaged in investigations of cases of alleged possession. As in the case of Mary Glover, Edward Jorden also became involved. At her final meeting with James on 10 October, Gunter confessed that her vomiting of needles and pins had been a fraud, but that she had long been afflicted with hysteria.[21]

Under formal examination, other demoniacs also put forward hysteria as an explanation of their behaviour in mitigation of their apparent fraud. Between the spring of 1585 and the summer of 1586, six demoniacs were exorcised by 12 Catholic priests, mostly in Denham, Buckinghamshire. Fifteen years later, Bancroft and Harsnett decided to investigate. Three of the demoniacs, Anne Smith, Sara Williams and Richard Mainy claimed to have been suffering from hysteria at the time of their supposed possessions.[22] To Harsnett, that they were really suffering from hysteria made the opportunism of the exorcising priests even greater:

> let them turn over but one new leaf in Sprenger, Nider, Mengus, or Thyraeus, and see how to discover a devil in the Epilepsy, Mother, Cramp, Convulsion, Sciatica, or Gout, and then learn a spell, an amulet, a periapt of a priest, and they shall get more fame and money in one week than they do now by all their painful travail in a year.[23]

Apart from hysteria, epilepsy was also often looked to as a possible natural explanation of demonic symptoms. When Thomas Darling's illness began, many believed that he was suffering from epilepsy or the falling sickness 'by reason that it was not a continual distemperature, but came by fits, with sudden staring, striving and struggling very fiercely, and falling down with sore vomits'.[24] Certainly, epilepsy and possession had comparable symptoms – falling down suddenly on the ground, grinding the teeth, foaming at the mouth, self-violence, deprivation of the senses, and swelling of the body.[25]

The diagnosis of a natural disease did not necessarily mean the denial of demonic involvement. The line between 'natural' disease and demonic causation was not that finely drawn. So, for some, natural diseases in general were demonically caused.[26] Others saw those suffering from natural diseases as good candidates for infection by the Devil. The Dutch physician Levinus Lemnius believed that it was frivolous to refer the causes of illness to evil spirits. But he did accept that the Devil could make naturally caused ailments worse.[27] The author of *Religio Medici*, Thomas Browne, testified in a 1664 witchcraft trial in England that the fits of some females 'were natural and nothing else but what they call the mother, but only heightened to a great excess by the subtlety of the Devil, cooperating with the malice of these which we term witches'.[28] In late seventeenth-century New England, Cotton Mather believed 'that the evil angels do often take advantage from natural distempers in the children of men to annoy them with such further mischiefs as we call preternatural'.[29]

Demonic possession was often also linked with melancholy, itself an illness which covered a vast array of symptoms. The Presbyterian divine Richard Baxter believed that Satan used melancholy to move men to despair and suicide.[30] For Robert Burton, religious melancholy was itself caused by the Devil, and demonic possession was included in his categories of diseases of the mind. 'The last kind of madness or melancholy', he wrote, 'is that demoniacal (if I may so call it) obsession or possession of devils which *Platerus* and others would have to bee praeternatural: stupendous things are said of them, their actions, gestures, contortions, fasting, prophecying, speaking languages they were never taught &c.'[31]

There were occasions when those suffering from what Burton would diagnose as religious melancholy (and we would diagnose as clinical depression) were believed to be possessed by the Devil. Suicidal impulses were seen as evidence of demonic activity. In August 1590, for example, John Dee diagnosed Ann Frank, a suicidal nurse in his household, as possessed by an evil spirit.[32] His attempts at exorcising the spirit were unavailing; she died in late September, having cut her throat. Suicidal impulses were common among those who, not merely melancholic, also showed the symptoms of possession.

For those of a more 'secular' frame of mind, the notion that an illness could be both 'natural' and caused by Satan was unacceptable, and the symptoms of demonic possession were totally subsumed into those of melancholy or other physical or mental diseases. Konrad Gesner in his *The Treasure of Euonymus* in 1559 prescribed a powder as a cure for demoniacs: 'Many also that be Limphatici, that is, mad or melancholic, whom they believed commonly to be resorted to by devils, we have cured them with the same.'[33] In 1601, the Anglicans John Deacon and John Walker included melancholy along with hysteria and epilepsy in the causes of the symptoms of demonic possession.[34] Their colleague Samuel Harsnett concurred: 'The Philosophers' old aphorism is, *cerebrum Melancholicum est sedes daemonum*, a melancholic brain is the chair of estate for the devil.'[35]

For his part, Samuel Harsnett saw manifestations of possession as reflecting any number of illnesses. If any have an idle or sullen girl, he wrote,

and she have a little help of the *Mother*, *Epilepsy*, or *Cramp* to teach her to roll her eyes, wry her mouth, gnash her teeth, startle with her body, hold her arms and hands stiff, make comic faces, girme, mow, and mop like an ape, tumble like a hedgehog, and can mutter out two or three words of gibberish, such as *obus*, *bobus*, and then with-all old Mother *Nobs* has called her by chance idle young housewife, or bid the devil scratch her, then no doubt but Mother *Nobs* is the Witch, the young girl is owl-blasted and possessed.[36]

While not denying the reality of the demonic realm, Deacon and Walker, like Harsnett, tried to drive an Anglican wedge of secularism between papists and Puritans. Reports of rare and strange feats arose not from diabolic, they declared, but from medical causes, 'from disordered *melancholy*, from *Mania*, from the *Epilepsy*, from *Lunacy*, from *Convulsions*, from the *mother*, from the *menstrual obstructions*, and sundry other *outrageous infirmities*.[37]

The medicalisation of demonic possession was a first sign of a significant shift in early modern demonology. On the one hand, it signalled the increasing dominance of a new understanding of demonic possession, one that did not entail a choice between only two possibilities – the Devil or deceit on the demoniac's part. The diseased and therefore deluded demoniac now became an option. In effect, those engaged in medicalising the Devil within were wrestling with a new understanding of what was to count as being in the domain of nature, and struggling with the possibility that the demonic should no longer be included within the 'natural'. They were edging towards the belief that the medical and diabolical explanations could no longer both be held. A choice – for the medical *or* for the diabolical, but not for both – now had to be made.

## Forensic Demonology

Still, even granting the capacity to distinguish the medical clearly from the demonic, fraudulent demoniacs were an ever-present option. In the face of diagnostic doubts and the possibility of fakes and charlatans, clear criteria of Satanic possession became crucial. The signs of possession on and in the bodies of the possessed provided the evidence that Satan had taken up residence within. Thus, itemisation of the criteria of possession, and the giving of evidence for the demoniacs having fulfilled the criteria, were common features of texts committed to establishing the authenticity of any particular possession.

These showed, at least, that the Devil was consistent. The manifestations of demonic possession differed little across the range of ages and across gender. Thus, male demoniacs showed the same behaviour as female, and older demoniacs had the same repertoire as younger ones. Although demoniacal behaviour was nuanced in terms of the denominational allegiances of the possessed, the same general features of possession were evident among the tormented in English Protestant and Catholic cases and, one might add, in the European Catholic and Protestant contexts more generally. Moreover, over the period from 1500 to 1700, there were no discernible shifts in the nature of possessions. What is clear is that children and adolescents were more prone to possession than adults.

Possession provided an excuse for outrageous behaviour, and a complete mitigation of it. Far from being condemned, the demoniac received sympathy and concern. It was the Devil, after all, that was making them do it. The language of demoniacs was clearly often obscene – at least to seventeenth-century ears. On occasion, if only rarely, so was their behaviour. William Sommers, for example, breached the boundary between the human and the bestial by trying to mount a female dog.[38] The Devil also pushed the limits of blasphemy. The young English woman Joan Harvey sometimes spat at the name of Jesus and blasphemed God, saying 'God is a good man I can do as much as he; I care not for Jesus, &c.'[39]

Across the English Channel, in Loudun, the symptoms among a group of possessed nuns in the 1630s was typical, though (as was not uncommon among Catholic female demoniacs generally), much more sexually charged. They breached the boundaries of both nuns and women generally. According to one 1634 account, *La Veritable Histoire des Diables des Loudun* (*The True History of the Devils of Loudun*), the nuns of Loudun gave daily proof of their possession:

They struck their chests and backs with their heads, as if they had their neck broken, and with inconceivable rapidity; they twisted their arms at the joints of the shoulder, the elbow and the wrist two or three times around; lying on their stomachs they joined their palms of their hands to the soles of their feet; their faces became so frightful one could not bear to look at them; their eyes remained open without winking; their tongues issued suddenly from their mouths, horribly swollen, black, hard, and covered with pimples, and yet while in this state they spoke distinctly; they threw themselves back till their heads touched their feet, and walked in this position with wonderful rapidity, and for a long time. They uttered cries so horrible and so loud that nothing like it was ever heard before; they made use of expressions so indecent as to shame the most debauched of men, while their acts, both in exposing themselves and inviting lewd behaviour from those present would have astonished the inmates of the lowest brothels in the country; they uttered maledictions against the three Divine Persons of the Trinity, oaths and blasphemous expressions so execrable, so unheard of, that they could not have suggested themselves to the human mind. They used to watch without rest, and fast five or six days at a time, or be tortured twice a day as we have described during several hours, without their health suffering.[40]

Signs multiplied, and the Devil's repertoire increased. Francesco Guazzo listed 47 signs of possession to distinguish it from a further 20 signs indicative of bewitchment.[41] The Italian exorcist Zaccaria Visconti gave 21 'signs of someone possessed of an evil spirit'.[42] From the depositions provided at the trial of William Sommers, the author of *A Breife Narration* in 1598 produced a list of 23 criteria 'proving that William Sommers of Nottingham of the age of twenty years was possessed by Satan, and did not counterfeit as some pretend'.[43]

Perhaps not surprisingly, the evidences of possession among demoniacs in the New Testament provided many of these. John Darrell, for example, pointed to 'crying, gnashing the teeth, wallowing, foaming, extraordinary and supernatural strength, supernatural knowledge, with sundry others to the number of eighteen'.[44] In addition to those listed above, the Biblical texts also included violence to self and others, inability to hear and speak, entering into coma-like states and pining away, nakedness and dwelling among graves and in the wilderness. Of these, only the last two failed to occur among early modern demoniacs.

The Biblical signs of possession were not the only ones. Nor were they considered definitive. It was recognised that some of the Biblical signs of demonic activity could appear among those suffering from natural illnesses, and others were reasonably easy to counterfeit. The Devil was seen to have extended his repertoire since Biblical times, and out of the Devil's creativity a theological virtue was made. Thus, for example, the author of *A Breife Narration* in 1598 argued for the necessity of other, and less ambiguous signs of possession: 'But seeing men in this matter are grown more incredulous than heretofore, it has pleased God, besides the signs of possession mentioned in Scripture, to give other signs also, more from cavil to make his glorious works most apparent and certain.'[45]

For many, the 'supernatural' signs of possession – those which appeared to be beyond nature – were the defining signs. Supernatural knowledge or clairvoyance, knowledge of other languages, levitation, knockings, smells, evidence of living things beneath the skin of those possessed, the vomiting of strange objects, all were seen as incontrovertible proofs of possession since, on the face of it at least, they defied natural explanation.

In particular, the ability to speak without moving the mouth, lips or tongue, generally from the stomach (ventriloquy), reinforced the belief that the vocal source here was not the demoniac but the Devil. Not only the eyes of the witnesses but their ears also testified to the presence of the demonic, for demoniacs spoke in tones different to their normal voices. For their later 'secularised' theatrical descendants, the ventriloquists' 'dummies', the purpose was to persuade the onlookers that their moving lips expressed their own thoughts, and not that of another. Unlike their wooden counterparts, the demonical 'dummies' did not move their lips. Therefore, to the onlooker, the voice which spoke from within expressed the thoughts of another presence within the possessed – the Devil. The disjunction between voice and body, and the consequent conviction that here was a voice (or voices) from the realms of hell, were no doubt reinforced when a voice with a low, deep, thick, male timbre emanated from a female body or from that of a young boy. Joyce Dovey, for example, spoke 'in a bigger and grosser tone than her ordinary speech, and when she speaks, she looks fiercely with something arising big in her throat, and commonly with swearing'.[46] In 1533, Thomas Cranmer wrote of a maid from whose belly a voice was heard which, 'when it told anything of the joys of heaven, it spoke so sweetly and so heavenly, that every man was ravished with the hearing thereof; and contrary, when it told anything of hell, it spoke so horribly and terribly that it put the hearers in a great fear.'[47]

The passive body in general was a sign of the presence of the demonic. To be possessed by the Devil was to be closed to sensations, impervious to the world outside. Thus, William

Sommers would lie as cold as ice, as if dead, 'senseless and speechless, his eyes out of his head like walnuts, his face black in a strange manner, and all his members and the parts of his body instantly cold for the space of an hour'.[48] Almost a century later, in 1698, Christian Shaw was 'struck dumb, deaf and blind'. Like many other demoniacs, her tongue was immobilised, 'drawn to a prodigious length over her chin'.[49]

Demoniacs were also thought to be insensitive to pain and not to bleed while in their states of trance. It was certainly one way to test their authenticity. William Sommers, for example, had 'pins thrust deep into his hand and leg to test if he did counterfeit. But he was senseless, and no blood flowed.'[50] It was reported of Katherine Waldron, visited by King James around 1597, that 'she would endure exquisite torments, as to have pins thrust into her flesh, nay, under her nails.'[51] Mary Glover demonstrated her insensibility when she failed to react to hot pins being applied to her cheek and close to her eye, and being burned with lighted paper in five places.[52]

The demoniacs' closure of their bodies to the world outside them was often reinforced by a refusal or inability to eat – a kind of unholy anorexia. The tightly clenched jaw of the possessed was a visible sign of the malice of Satan. Elizabeth Throckmorton's eating disorder progressed to the point where her jaws were so tightly clenched that she could not take milk through a quill forced between her teeth.[53] Similarly, Mary Glover did not eat for 18 days, 'save by way of injection, or forcible powering down with a spoon, and that but a little at once, it was so much resisted in passing down for all that'.[54] The Lutheran demoniac Judith Klatten appeared not to have eaten for almost five years, though she herself was to claim that 'little tiny men and maids wearing beautiful ornaments [...] brought her food from whatever was being cooked at home or roasted elsewhere.'[55]

Satan took up his abode in the place from which he spoke. So it is unsurprising that he controlled what went into the stomach. Nor is it a surprise that a sign of the Devil's presence was the regurgitation of objects which he had presumably brought with him. It was undoubtedly one of the more exotic evidences of his having taken up residence within the demoniac. In 1616, John Cotta, for example, reported that the possessed had been seen 'to vomit crooked iron, coals, brimstone, nails, needles, pins, lumps of lead, wax, hair, strawe and the like'.[56] He saw it as one of the certain supernatural effects of possession. To the list William Drage added knives, scissors, whole eggs, dogs' tails, pieces of silk, live eels, large pieces of flesh, bones and stones, wood, hooks and pieces of saltpetre, both vomited and 'voided by stool'.[57] Anne Gunter's repertoire was limited to pins, but she could vomit them not only out of her mouth, but from her nose, out of her chest and in her urine.[58] The 11-year-old Christian Shaw merely vomited, but her list of objects was large – different coloured hair, curled, plaited and knotted, hot pieces of coal the size of walnuts, straw and pins, sticks and bones, hay mixed with dung as if from a dung hill, feathers, stones, lumps of candle grease and eggshells.[59]

## Beyond the Borders of the Human

As we have seen, the Devil himself was often perceived as a mixture of man and animal, and evil spirits frequently appeared in animal form. In spite of the Devil being within, external visions of the Devil were common among demoniacs, not only at the onset of possession, but throughout it. Demons often appeared in animal form as rats, cats and dogs; on occasion as birds, and even as bears. They manifested to some as black men, often as children, black, white or red. Thus, Margaret Byrom was 'grievously molested and sorely frightened with a terrible vision [...] like a foul black dwarf, with half a face, long shaggy hair, black broad hands and black cloven feet'.[60] On 31 August 1590, Elizabeth Throckmorton cried out grievously about a vision of Mother Samuel with a black child sitting upon her shoulder.[61]

The possessed often behaved like animals. In so doing, they incarnated the demonic realm. Because the demonic and the animal overlapped, in occupying the border ground between the human and the animal, the possessed threatened that essential distinction between the animal and the human established by God in the Garden of Eden. Certainly, the possessed appeared to onlookers to mimic the acts of animals. Their behaviour was described in those terms; they were said to have barked, purred and meowed, to have croaked like frogs, crowed like cocks, roared like bears and grunted like pigs. Like the mad, they lost their human identity. They ran around on all fours, walked like spiders, scratched and bit themselves, growled, groaned, howled and bit like mad dogs, hopped like frogs and bounced like goats.

The Devil within also distorted the facial features of the possessed beyond the apparently humanly possible. Their heads were said to rotate through 180 degrees, and to wag prodigiously. Their jaws became dislocated, and their faces turned black. Their eyes bulged as if on stalks, or were sunk deep into their sockets, and on occasion changed colour. Their mouths were pulled awry. Some drew their chins up to their foreheads, others had extended tongues like calves'. Their bodies were capable of extreme contortions and acrobatics. They bounced up and down like balls, flew over the tops of beds, rolled around the room like hoops, wriggled like fish on dry land and ran up the walls and across the ceiling upside down.

They were dangerous to be around; they were violent and unpredictable. It was a violence combined with extraordinary strength. As evidenced in the Scriptures, strength was one of the sure signs of possession. William Sommers in his fits seemed stronger than four or five men. Two or three strong men could hardly hold the four youngest among the Lancashire seven, nor the 12-year-old William Perry. A strong man could not pin down the nine-year-old Jane Throckmorton.

The theology of possession was also complicated and messy. All were agreed that only with divine permission was the Devil able to enter into anyone. This was a simple consequence of the doctrine of the sovereignty of God. The French demonologist Jean Bodin declared, 'It may also occur that Satan is sent by God, since it is certain that all punishment comes from Him.'[62] On the other hand, both the possessed themselves and those involved in their deliverance were apt to give the firm impression that, in their case at least, the Devil was firmly in control, or at best, that God and the Devil were involved in a battle which it was possible for either to win.

As we have seen, this was an irresolvable ambivalence at the heart of Christianity itself. Satan was both divine emissary and divine enemy. It was a paradox often present in the literature of witchcraft and possession. Thus, for example, Levinus Lemnius informed his readers that God winks at the hurts brought upon men by the Devil; indeed, he 'partly instigates the devils and their instruments to rage against many that have deserved to be so punished'.[63] Lemnius also reminded them that, since Satan's chief end is to abolish the glory of God, he assaults man, both within and without, 'and sometimes he troubles the body, sometimes the soul, and sometimes both, to work their destruction'.[64]

The matter was further complicated by the possibility of two modes of possession. In the one case, the demoniac was possessed as a result of the direct action of Satan; in the other, as a consequence of the presence of witchcraft. The difference had important moral consequences. In general, where the Devil had directly entered the body of the demoniac, it was as a consequence of the sin of the latter. The possessed were ultimately responsible for their plight. Thus, in the case of Alexander Nyndge, his possessed body was the sign of *his* sinfulness, and the Devil was God's emissary. So the story of Alexander functioned as a reminder to its readers of the need for rigorous moral examination of the self to avoid the punishment of God.[65] In the case of William Sommers, God used the body of the demoniac to demonstrate the sins of the whole community: 'When Sommers began his gestures, Master Darrell affirmed that they were the signs, whereby the Devil showed the sins that reigned in Nottingham, and did himself interpret some of them [...]. By this course the people were very much amazed, as thinking the Devil to preach so unto them, and so note the sins that reigned in that town.'[66]

By contrast, where the Devil had gained entrance as a consequence of witchcraft, the demoniac was more likely to be construed as the innocent victim of the machinations of a witch. It is hardly, then, a matter of surprise that those who were possessed and their families were inclined to point the finger of responsibility elsewhere. Accusations of witchcraft were more the norm than the exception. Since witches had the power to send the Devil into their enemies, it is no surprise that the demonically possessed saw the cause of their suffering, not in their own sin, but in the *maleficia* of witches. The golden age of possession was also that of witches. And witchcraft and demonic possession created a particularly vicious and unvirtuous circle.

For those accused of sending the Devil into the possessed, the results were serious, usually fatal. As a result of the accusations of the possessed nuns of Loudun, the local priest Urbain Grandier was burned at the stake in 1634.[67] Alice Samuel, her daughter Agnes and her husband John were all hanged in Huntingdon as a result of charges of bewitchment made by the Throckmorton children.

On the word of Thomas Darling, Alice Gooderidge was imprisoned and died in gaol. The English cunning man, Edmund Hartley, was hanged twice, the second time successfully. William Sommers' accusations saw 13 persons making court appearances. Elizabeth Jackson was indicted for witchcraft on the basis of Mary Glover's accusations. Margaret Muschamp's illness was blamed on a variety of people, but only Dorothy Swinow, who had had a history of bad relations with Margaret's mother, was eventually indicted. In 1616, nine women were hanged as a consequence of Henrie Smith's accusations that they had sent their familiar spirits to torment him.

## Exorcising the Devil

Whether as the emissary of God or the agent of a witch, the Devil was an uninvited guest. And, like univited guests generally, he was inclined to stay a long time, and be hard to get rid of. Thus, for example, the Ursuline nun of Loudun, Mother Jeanne des Anges, was possessed from 1632 until 1638, Marie des Vallees, the so-called Saint of Coutances, from 1609 to 1655. Judith Klatten, a Lutheran girl from the German village of Helpe, was possessed for almost five years.

Protestant England did not witness the routinisation and ritualisation of possession that occurred in Catholic France. Still, possessions for months or even years were common, although sometimes with periods of remission. The Throckmortons were possessed for three and a half years until April 1593, the Lancashire seven from February 1595 to March 1597, with 18 months' remission during that time. Margaret Muschamp's problems lasted from August 1645 until February 1648, James Barrow's for nearly two years.[68]

The Devil's extended stays were not for want of trying to be rid of him. Catholic demoniacs were subjected to long and complex rituals of exorcism. Up until the end of the sixteenth century, it was very much a matter of improvisation that, as result of the difficulty in distinguishing exorcism from invocation, had often led to suspicions that the exorcist was in league with the Devil. But the proliferation of possessions by the Devil created the demand for manuals of exorcism, both to legitimate the reality of demonic possession and the role of the exorcist, and to manage formally the techniques of deliverance from Satan. These manuals were in the genre of 'Teach Yourself Exorcism'. As the subtitle of the most authoritative of collections of exorcism rites, the *Thesaurus Exorcismorum* of 1608, put it: 'Treasury of most terrible, powerful and efficacious exorcisms and conjurations with the most proven method, by which evil spirits, demons and all evil spells are driven from obsessed human bodies as if expelled by whips and clubs'.[69]

Included within this collection was the 1578 *Flagellum Daemonum* (*Whip of Demons*), the most successful exorcism manual of its time, written by the Italian Franciscan Girolamo Menghi (1529–1609). This contained a complex series of seven exorcisms, comprising both verbal formulae and liturgical actions. The latter consisted of such rites as the continual use of the sign of the cross, the laying-on of hands, sprinkling of the demoniac with holy water, the showing of the crucifix, fumigations of the demoniac and the possessing Devil with sulphur, the burning of a painting of the possessing demon and the use of herbs to fumigate and cause vomiting – rue, dill, garlic, frankincense and hypericon. Along with these went the use of prayers, Bible reading (especially the first chapter of the Gospel of John), asking the names of the demon and his companions, interrogation of the demons and adjurations to them to depart. The exorcist needed to ensure that the demon was driven from every part of the possessed's body: 'Get away, then, in the name of the eternal God, from the head, from the hair, from the top of the head [...] from the knees, from the legs, from the intimate parts,' and so on.[70] Where the demoniac had not been liberated, and for some reason the exorcism had to be terminated, then all the demons had to be ordered into the lower parts of the body 'such as the dead toe nails'.[71]

In line with the Protestant avoidance of elaborate rituals and anything that hinted at 'priestly magic', Protestant dispossessions were much less ornate affairs. It was a matter primarily of prayer and fasting. There was, of course, New Testament precedence for prayer and fasting as a means of deliverance from possession. In the face of his disciples' inability to cast out an evil spirit from a possessed boy, Jesus had explained to them that 'This kind can come forth by nothing, but by prayer and fasting' (Mark 9.29). For Protestants, the Biblical assertion that *this kind* only comes out by prayer and fasting came to encompass *all kinds* of evil spirits. It was a regimen that fitted Protestant spirituality more generally as extended periods of prayer and fasting were central features of a developing Protestant spirituality throughout the period and were believed to be efficacious for all manner of special needs.

Prayer and fasting for deliverance from demons chimed with the theological acceptance that such deliverance was up to God. But there was also the not unreasonable conviction that extended periods of prayer could wear the Devil down until he finally submitted and departed. That prayer and fasting worked was, for those involved, a cogent proof that Protestantism could be genuinely competitive with Catholicism. Even among the sceptics, there was sufficient recognition of its effectiveness to call forth an explanation. Thus, for the physician Edward Jorden, prayer and fasting was a *natural* not a supernatural remedy. When prayer and fasting work, he declared, 'it is not for any supernatural virtue in them, either from God or from the Devil [...] but by reason of the confident persuasion which melancholic and passionate people may have in them.'[72] It was a view in keeping with the common medical belief of the time in the power of the imagination over the body.

The Devil himself clearly resented the primary mode of deliverance – prayer. When Dr Dorington began to pray for the Throckmorton girls, 'at one instant of time all the children fell into their fits [...] wonderfully tormented as though they would have been torn in pieces.'[73] When the bishop prayed with John Harrison, 'the boy was so outraged that he flew out of his bed, and so frightened the Bishop's men that one of them fell into a swoon.'[74] Others reacted vehemently to the words 'God', 'Christ' or 'Jesus'.

In Protestant exorcisms, prayer and fasting were interspersed with preaching and reading the Bible. As the prime cultic object in Protestantism, the Bible provoked rage in the demon within. The exorcist Jesse Bee saw the Devil's reaction to his reading of the Bible in the presence of Thomas Darling as a way of inspiring 'due and godly regard' for the Bible among the spectators.[75] Bee would call Satan to battle by reading the first chapter of the Gospel of John. During the reading, Darling would fall into torments, often at the fourth verse, but also at the ninth, the thirteenth, the fourteenth and the seventeenth. On other occasions, he was thrown into fits at the fifth verse of the first chapter of the book of Revelation, and the twelfth and twenty-fifth verses of the twelfth chapter of the Gospel of John.[76]

Still, in spite of worries about priestly magic, even within Protestant demonology the printed word nonetheless had a quasi-magical power. When Mary Hall went to read the Bible, the two spirits which possessed her would say, '"Mary, do not read;" or "Mary you will not read, for books are all against us;" Her Father would say, "She will read in spite of all the devils," and so she did always without interruption; for when she read she was not molested.'[77]

Diabolical violence was also often provoked by the presence of sacred objects and rituals. When dwelling within

Catholics, the Devil was especially sensitive, not only to the Eucharistic host, but also to relics, holy water, the sign of the cross and the Bible. These reactions to sacred objects and rituals verified the presence of the demonic. Ironically, in his response to the cultic objects and rituals of Catholicism, the Devil was seen as legitimating Catholic doctrine and practice against the spurious claims of Protestantism. Vice versa, although in accord with the more limited range of Protestant cultic paraphernalia and rituals the Devil's reaction to Protestant objects and rituals was more restricted. For *his* part, the Devil was clearly more inclined to ecumenism of a sort than either Catholics or Protestants – he loathed them all.

The Protestant exorcist John Darrell recognised the strategic value that exorcism held for his Puritan cause against the claims of Rome. The practice of prayer and fasting to expel demons, he believed, would more effectively enable Protestants to 'stop the mouth of the adversary, touching the priviledge of theirs of casting forth devils wherein, with their other lying miracles, they glory so much'.[78] God, through his delivering of the demoniacs, would appear to be favouring the Puritan cause.

As aware of the strategic value of dispossessions as Darrell, and as sceptical as Darrell was credulous, the Anglican Samuel Harsnett suspected a disastrous outcome were Protestant dispossessions to become widespread: Protestant would turn against Protestant, and not only against Catholic. Were Darrell and his like not dealt with, wrote Harsnett, 'we should have had many other pretended signs of possession: one Devil would have been mad at the name of the Presbyter, another at the sight of a minister that will not subscribe, another to have seen men sit or stand at the Communion.'[79]

In fact, Harsnett's fears were not realised among Protestant demoniacs. The Devil in them was more interested in individual souls than ecclesiastical bodies, his presence more the outcome of bewitchment by a witch than a symbol of conflict between or within Christian groups. But Harsnett's concerns *were* confirmed by Catholic demoniacs. Harsnett was familiar with the French demoniac Marthe Brossier, for Abraham Hartwell had published a translation of a French account of Brossier in 1599, dedicated to the then bishop of London and Harsnett's 'boss' Richard Bancroft.[80] Brossier's Devil had declared that all the Protestants belonged to him.[81] The Catholic demoniacs at Denham, Sara and Friswood Williams, reported that their exorcists believed that most Protestants were possessed.[82] The demoniac Anne Smith declared that the priests would ask the demons within why they did not trouble them before when they were Protestants, and 'the devil would answer that there was no reason for them so to do because the Protestants were theirs already.'[83] In general, perhaps not surprisingly, the devils of Denham demonstrated the demonic status of Protestantism and the divine character of Catholicism.[84]

Of course, Harsnett's concerns were only valid ones if he assumed that the Devil should be taken as speaking the truth. In general, his word was so taken. Indeed, there was Biblical authority for the Devil's knowing religious truth. The unclean spirit within the demoniac in the synagogue cried out to Jesus, 'I know who you are, the Holy One of God' (Mark 1.24). The Gerasene demoniac recognised Jesus as the son of God (Mark 5.7). Thus, there was an expectation among both Catholics and Protestants that the Devil within the possessed would speak the truth. In this way, paradoxically, the Devil was a defender of the faith. His ability to possess, and the faithful's ability to deliver those possessed by him, were a defence against scepticism and atheism. Who knows, asked John Darrell rhetorically, 'whether God has therefore sent evil Spirits into sundry English persons to vex them in their bodies that thereby he might confound the Atheists in England? [...] for some special thing no doubt there is moving the Lord more at this time than in former times to send devils into men, Yea, into divers.'[85]

The demonic attestation of religious truth – or any sort of truth, for that matter – was something of a two-edged sword. It contained within itself the possibility of its own denial; Biblical authority also pointed in another direction. In the Gospel of John (8.44), Christ had called the Devil a liar and the father of lies. Thus, as early as 1593, the Nonconformist divine George Gifford expressed his doubts that the Devil within the possessed could be *compelled* to speak the truth. 'But how can it be proved', he asked, 'that the Father of lies may be bound, and forced through charge and adjuration in the name and power of God to tell the truth?'[86] The physician John Cotta reminded his readers in 1616 that, 'since he is oft a false accuser, and the enemy of God and truth, he may not be credited in himself, no nor truth it selfe simply as in his mouth.'[87] This had legal implications. Richard Bernard warned jurors to beware the naming of the witch by the possessed, 'because this is only the Devil's testimony, who can lie, and that more often than speak truth.'[88]

Moreover, the Devil was so tricky that he could produce the illusion of demonic possession. Satan, in his subtlety, declared John Darrell, 'has done in the boy [William Summers] some sleight and trifling things, at divers times, of purpose to deceive the beholders, and to bear them in hand, that he did never greater things in him: thereby to induce them to think, that he was a counterfeit'.[89] So convinced was Darrell of the Devil's repossession of Sommers that he refused to accept the boy's capacity to mimic his former fits.[90] In Darrell's world, Satanic activity was impervious to refutation, even if the demoniac confessed himself to be a fraud.

Where the opposition of fraud and demonic possession is undermined, truth is forever indeterminate. In short, where nothing can occur that would count against the Devil's activity, nothing can be said to count for it. As Stephen Greenblatt remarks, 'If Satan can counterfeit counterfeiting, there can be no definitive confession, and the prospect opens to an infinite regress of disclosure and uncertainty.'[91]

Convinced of the fraudulence of both the possessed and their exorcists, Samuel Harsnett viewed possession and deliverance as a theatre of imposture. The connection between theatricality and possession was noted by Shakespeare, who borrowed from Samuel Harsnett's 1603 *A Declaration of Egregious Popish Impostures* in his depiction of Edgar's madness, his *hysterica passio*, in *King Lear*. The Devil loved an audience, and demoniacs became very much actors in a public drama.

There is little doubt that the roles of demoniac, exorcist and spectator were played out, improvised, developed, embellished and refined in a series of ongoing negotiations and interactions between all the participants within the format of a loosely constructed cultural script known to all the participants. However, for those convinced of its reality, it was far more than drama. The fictive and the real overlapped indistinguishably. It was a reality play, one which created its own reality for demoniacs, exorcists and spectators alike. For this reason, then as now, it is difficult to determine where the real and the unreal begin and end.

# CHAPTER EIGHT

# The Devil Defeated

Therefore rejoice, ye heavens, and ye that dwell in them. Woe to the inhabiters of the earth and the sea! for the devil is come down unto you, having great wrath, because he knoweth that he hath but a short time.

Revelation 12.12 (KJV)

## The Binding and Loosing of Satan

The period from 1550 to 1700 was, as we have seen, the age when the demoniac flourished. For those who lived during that time, that there were many possessed by the Devil, was not a matter of surprise. On the contrary, it was to be expected. The issue of demonic activity linked with that of the end of the world, and the conviction that, as history drew to a close and Christ's return in judgement became imminent, Satan would be all the more active.

The book of Revelation (12.12) had prophesied that Satan's rage would increase as his time grew shorter. Thus James I had ended his *Daemonologie* in 1597 by reminding his readers that the consummation of the world 'makes Satan to rage the more in his instruments, knowing his kingdom to be so near an end'.[1] Even as late as the 1730s, William Whiston, Isaac Newton's successor as Lucasian Professor of Mathematics at the University of Cambridge (though even then he was something of a scholarly anachronism), believed that the power of exorcism had been preserved for the time of the Antichrist. It was a

168

power that, with the expected end of the papacy, was about to be restored.[2]

Both exorcists and demoniacs were aware of the apocalyptic context in which they lived. They grounded their activities in a cosmological context. John Denison, for example, began his introduction to the possession of Thomas Darling in 1597 by placing it within the context of the end of history and the prophecy that the Devil's wrath would increase, knowing that he has but a short time. 'This prophecy is fulfilled,' he declared, 'not only in the outrageous fury that Satan uses in raising persecution against God's Saints by his mischievous instruments, and corrupting men's minds by his wicked suggestions, but also in tyrannising, according to his limited power over them, by torments [...]. And this last kind of tyranny is also apparent, amongst other instances, in the pitiful vexing of this poor child.'[3] Darling himself had visions of heaven, hell and the Day of Judgement.[4] A century later, in 1689, the exorcism of the 'Surey demoniack' Richard Dugdale by the Nonconformist minister John Carrington and his colleagues was saturated with end-time expectations. Asked by Carrington why he tormented Dugdale, the Devil replied, 'My time is short, and I must take all advantages of carrying on my work, for which purpose this is a fit occasion.'[5]

That genuine possessions were to be expected in the last days was an important part of John Darrell's argument against his demoniacs being treated as frauds or sufferers from natural diseases. God is as ready to chastise men in these as in former days, wrote Darrell, '[a]nd the Devil in regard to the shortness of his time more ready than ever to do his service and best indeavour'.[6] Moreover the sufferings of the possessed on this side of the grave were a latter-day sign of the final destiny of those to be tormented in hell.[7] Even the 'sceptics' read demoniacal frauds as part of the imminence of the end.[8]

The bodies of the possessed were themselves sites of eschatological conflict. The increasing wrath of Satan at the end of his time in the body of the possessed mirrored the increase in his activity in the historical realm. The process of history was replicated in the body of the possessed, and as his defeat in the body of the possessed grew near, so he raged all the more. Thus, for example, the seven demoniacs of Lancashire were increasingly tormented as the time approached for the departure of the Devil.[9] 'I imagined', said John Swan as the deliverance of Mary Glover approached its conclusion, 'that his malice was rather grown greater towards the end of his kingdom. And so it fell out.'[10]

Christian eschatology (the doctrine of the last things) moved within a space framed by the Bible, and it was constructed from a pot-pourri of Biblical texts. As we have seen in an earlier chapter, that the Devil had only a short time was read in conjunction with the end of history and the return of Christ in judgement of the living and the dead (see Plates 22 and 23).

That Satan would be bound for a millennium prior to his release and eventual confinement in hell for eternity was a certainty. When this would happen or whether it had already happened, or whether all of this ought to be taken *more* or *less* literally, was much less clear. The key issue was whether the binding of Satan (and therefore the beginning of Christ's rule) had already happened at some point in the past, or whether it was yet to occur. This depended, crucially, on how Christ's reign during the millennial period was to be construed. For those who believed that Christ's thousand-year kingdom was to be on earth, the beginning of the millennium and Satan's binding was in the future and yet to begin. But for those who accepted that Christ's millennial reign was to be a heavenly (or spiritual) one, it was possible to view the binding of Satan and the beginning of the millennial period as having already begun.

That Satan was already bound was a reading of Revelation 20.2–3 that fitted neatly with the view that, in his life, death and resurrection, Christ had disempowered the Devil and liberated his captives.

This was an interpretation of Revelation that was to resonate throughout the medieval period, primarily as a result of its endorsement by Augustine. Although Augustine had once believed that the first resurrection would be a bodily one, and that there would be a thousand-year sabbath of spiritual delights for the saints, his considered position in *The City of God* was that the first resurrection had already occurred; it was a spiritual one, and the millennium had already begun. Thus, according to Augustine, the binding of Satan had happened as the result of the victory of Christ and he had already been thrown into the bottomless pit. The Devil is 'prohibited and restrained from seducing those nations which belong to Christ, but which he formerly seduced or held in subjection'.[11] Nonetheless, he dwells in the depths of the 'blind hearts' of those who hate Christians[12] and remains able to take even more possession of the ungodly, for 'that man is more abundantly possessed by the devil who is not only alienated from God, but also gratuitously hates those who serve God.'[13] Thus the Church, even now, was the Kingdom of God, and God's saints reign with him. The 'millennium' stands not so much literally for a thousand years as figuratively for all the years of the time after Christ until the end of history, the number of which only God knows.

Although Augustine read the millennium 'spiritually' and not historically, he remained committed to a literal end of history. He was perfectly clear on the nature of the events to come: 'Elias the Tishbite shall come; the Jews shall believe; Antichrist shall persecute; Christ shall judge; the dead shall rise; the good and the wicked shall be separated; the world shall be burned and renewed. All these things, we believe, shall come to pass.'[14]

Thus, for Augustine, at the end of time, Satan would be loosed again. Like the beast of Revelation 13.5, the Devil would 'rage with the whole force of himself and his angels for three years and six months'.[15] This is the time of the Antichrist (of whom more later). During this time the number of the faithful would be finally determined: '[T]hose who have not been written in the book of life', he declared,

> shall in large numbers yield to the severe and unprecedented persecutions and stratagems of the devil now loosed, so we cannot but think that not only those whom that time shall find sound in the faith, but also some who till then shall be without, shall become firm in the faith they have hitherto rejected and mighty to conquer the devil even though unbound.[16]

After Christ comes in judgement, the Devil and his angels, together with the wicked in their resurrected bodies, would be consigned to the punishments of everlasting fires in indestructible bodies.

## The Antichrist

Christian eschatology was rendered more complicated by the doctrine of the Antichrist (both a tyrannical ruler and a pseudo-Christ who would precede the coming of Christ at the end of the world) and the complex of ideas surrounding him: his relationship to Satan, his identification with the beast of Revelation 13 whose number is 666, with the seventh head of the dragon (the Devil) in Revelation 12, with the 'false prophet' of Revelation 16 and with an array of historical figures or historical groups – past, present or future (who may be the Antichrist, or at least one of the 'Antichrists' who prefigure him). And the loosing of Satan was intimately and intricately connected with the coming of the Antichrist. As Augustine had put it, 'then shall Satan be loosed, and by means of that Antichrist shall work with all power in a lying though a wonderful manner.'[17]

Although the Antichrist was identified in the Christian tradition with many of the figures in Revelation, he was not explicitly mentioned in that book. Rather, the key texts occurred in the first epistle of John: 'children, it is the last hour! As you have heard that antichrist is coming, so now many antichrists have come. From this we know that it is the last hour' (1 John 2.18). A little further on we are asked, 'Who is the liar but the one who denies that Jesus is the Christ? This is the antichrist, the one who denies the Father and the Son' (1 John 2.22).

These passages were augmented by those verses in the second letter of Paul to the Thessalonians (2.3–11) on the man of sin and the son of perdition who is identified with the Antichrist in the later tradition. The Christian interpretation of these verses, which sees them as referring to the Antichrist, gives us an account of the Antichrist as follows. Antichrist, the man of sin and the son of perdition, will appear before Christ's second coming. Nations and peoples will break away from Roman (imperial and ecclesiastical) power before the Antichrist leads a great apostasy. He will then raise himself up against God and his Church. He will rebuild the temple in Jerusalem destroyed by the Romans, claim to be God, and he will demand to be worshipped. The power of Antichrist (represented in his forerunners) is already at work, though the Roman Empire (or Church, or a kingdom in continuity with Rome) now restrains Antichrist. After the end of the Empire and at the end of the world, he will be revealed. Satan will give the Antichrist the power to work false signs and wonders in order to deceive the faithful. God will also allow the Antichrist to test Christians and to condemn those pseudo-Christians who prefer evil above truth. At the end of the world, he will be finally defeated and killed by Christ or by the archangel Michael.[18]

Even so, the Biblical allusions to the Antichrist were sufficiently opaque, and the interpretations of the Antichrist sufficiently varied, to create more apocalyptic fire than light. The Anglican bishop of Salisbury John Jewel (1522–71), in his commentary on the second letter of Paul to the Thessalonians – himself convinced like most of his Protestant contemporaries that the papacy was the Antichrist – lamented the confusions that had arisen since the time of the Emperor Nero:

> Some say he should be a jew of the tribe of Dan; some, that he should be bred up in Bethsaida and Corazin; some, that he should rise up in Syria; some that he should overthrow Rome; some, that he should build up the city of Hierusalem; some, that Nero was antichrist; some, that he should be born of a friar and a nun; some, that he should continue but three years and a half; some, that he should turn trees upside down, with the tops in the ground, and should force the roots to grow upward, and then should flee up into heaven, and fall down and break his neck. These tales have been craftily devised to beguile our eyes, that, whilst we think upon these guesses, and so occupy ourselves in beholding a shadow or probable conjecture of antichrist, he which is antichrist indeed may unaware deceive us.[19]

Read literally, the belief that Satan was bound during Christ's lifetime might have led to expectations that Christ would return around the end of the first millennium (and thus the loosing and eventual defeat of Satan) somewhere between the year 979 (a millennium from the then earliest presumed date of Christ's birth) and the year 1033 (a millennium from the then presumed date of his death). In spite of Augustine's non-literal reading of the thousand-year binding of Satan, there were among the ecclesiastical elite some at least from the middle of the tenth century

16 Witches gather at the Sabbath to worship the Devil depicted as a goat. The witch is about to kiss the goat's backside. 'The Witches' Sabbath at Vaudois' from *The Book of Occult Sciences* (fifteenth century).

17 The ritual kiss of the Devil's backside. 'The Infamous Kiss' from Francesco Guazzo's *Compendium Maleficarum* (1626).

18 The Devil explains his terms to the novice witches in the *Compendium Maleficarum*. 'The Devil Demands a Pact' from Francesco Guazzo's *Compendium Maleficarum* (1626).

19 The Antichrist with Christ-like features preaches. But it is Satan, whispering in his ear, who tells him what to say. *Preaching of the Antichrist* by Luca Signorelli (1499–1504).

20 The Antichrist supported by demons at the top is attacked by an angel. In the centre left, the Antichrist beguiles his listeners while the Devil whispers in his ear. 'The Reign of Antichrist' from the *Liber Chronicarum* (1493).

21 The Antichrist with three heads that represent the Pope (wearing the triple tiara), the Turk wearing the turban, and the Jew. 'The Three-headed Antichrist' (seventeenth century).

22 The angel and the demon weigh the good and the evil in the balance. 'The Last Judgement' by the Master of Soriguela (late thirteenth century).

23 One of the damned riding on a demon on the way to hell. *The Damned Taken to Hell* by Luca Signorelli (1499–1502).

24 The damned are tormented by demons in the mansions of hell. 'Vision of Hell' from Vincent of Beauvais's *Miroir Historial* (fifteenth century).

25 Satan, tortured by demons in the fires of hell, presides over the punishments of the damned. 'Satan Confined to Hell' from *Les Très Riches Heures du Duc de Berry* (fifteenth century).

26  William Hogarth's 1762 portrayal of witches and demons as the stuff of superstition. *Credulity, Superstition and Fanaticism* by William Hogarth (1762).

onwards who, while taking their basic apocalyptic soundings from Augustine, saw the millennium, and more particularly the coming of the Antichrist, as happening in the more or less immediate future.

One such was Thietland, abbot of the monastery of Einsiedeln in Switzerland in the middle of the tenth century. Although he was significantly influenced by Augustine's account of the end of times in *The City of God*, unlike Augustine he took literally the expectation that Satan would be loosed at the end of the millennium, which he dated at one thousand years after the passion of Christ, that is, in 1033. Thietland, perhaps writing in a context in which many of his contemporaries were expecting the arising of the Antichrist at any moment, should probably be read as intending to allay their fears by putting off the end for some seventy to eighty years in the future.

Thietland's views on Satan and the Antichrist occur in his commentary on the second letter of Paul to the Thessalonians, particularly those verses that had been interpreted as referring to the Antichrist (2.3–11).[20] Rejecting any supernatural origin for the Antichrist, Thietland declared that he would be 'a man born from man'.[21] Nevertheless, he is the inverse of Christ; for, as the fullness of divinity dwelt in Christ, so also 'the fullness of deception and malice will dwell in him,'[22] and he would exalt himself even over the son of God. The 'man of sin', he went on to say, stood not only for the Antichrist, but for the 'entire mass of evil people belonging to his body'.[23]

The key moment in Thietland's commentary lay in his discussion of the second letter of Paul to the Thessalonians (2.8): 'Then that lawless one will be revealed.' Thietland read the 'lawless one' as referring to Satan. According to Thietland, the angel who descended from heaven to bind Satan was Jesus Christ. This binding of Satan for a millennium occurred at the time of Christ's passion.[24] Satan would then be released for a period of three and a half years. He would enter into the Antichrist. Like a magician, he would be able to perform many things 'miraculously, though deceptively'.[25]

The Antichrist would then be able to lead Gog and Magog astray. And for Thietland, Gog represented the evil persons of his own time who signalled the imminent arrival of the Antichrist, and Magog the Devil.[26] Thietland, perhaps more concerned to provide a commentary on the signs of his times than to elaborate on the eventual defeat of Satan and the Antichrist, tells us no more about the end of history.

## Adso and the Antichrist

It is, however, to a contemporary of Thietland that we owe the first 'Life of Antichrist'. It was composed by Adso, the abbot of Montier-en-Der, around the middle of the tenth century.[27] Written at the request of Gerberga, wife of the French king Louis IV d'Outremer, Adso's *Epistola Adsonis ad Gerbergam Reginam de Ortu et Tempore Antichristi* (*Letter of Adso to Queen Gerberga on the Origin and Time of the Antichrist*) provided the first narrative account of the Antichrist and, in turning the traditional genre of the 'Lives of the Saints' upside down, it marked a key moment in the history of the legend of the Antichrist.[28] It would remain a key text for subsequent accounts of the Antichrist. Adso was describing a figure whom he believed would eventually come, although he himself was not expecting his arrival imminently. But he was writing in a context in which the coming of the Antichrist was anticipated by his contemporaries to be sooner rather than later.

According to Adso, the Antichrist is so called because he will be contrary to Christ in all things, and all his actions will be in opposition to Christ. As Christ came as a humble man, so the Antichrist will come as a proud man. As Christ came to raise the lowly, the Antichrist will cast out the lonely, exalt the wicked and magnify sinners. He will drive out Christianity, revive the worship of demons in the world, seek his own glory and call himself Almighty God. Adso followed the tradition of there having been many forerunners to the Antichrist of the last days, namely, the Roman emperors Nero and Domitian, and the Seleucid Emperor Antiochus Epiphanes. Even in Adso's own time, he declared, there were many Antichrists, 'for anyone, layman, cleric, or monk, who lives contrary to justice and attacks the rule of his way of life and blasphemes what is good [...] is an Antichrist, the minister of Satan.'[29]

Following the tradition that saw the Antichrist as a Jew who would pretend to take the place of Christ, Adso believed that he would be a Jew from the tribe of Dan. He rejected the tradition that, in keeping with the Antichrist being the Christ turned upside down, saw him as the product of the Devil and a virgin (or a whore). Like most commentators, he also rejected the tradition that the Antichrist, in imitation of Christ as God incarnate, was the Devil himself in human form. Still, he did undoubtedly edge towards the idea of the Antichrist as an incarnation of the Devil. Although Adso followed the dominant belief that the Antichrist would be born of human parents, the Devil would enter his mother's womb at the very moment of his conception:

> Just as the Holy Spirit came into the mother of our Lord Jesus Christ [...] so too the devil will descend into the Antichrist's mother, will completely fill her, completely encompass her, completely master her, completely possess her within and without, so that with the devil's cooperation she will conceive through a man and what will be born from her will be totally wicked, totally evil, totally lost.[30]

Thus, the Antichrist was, if only metaphorically, the son of Satan: 'not through nature but through imitation because he will fulfil the devil's will in everything. The fullness of diabolical power and of the whole character of evil will dwell in him in bodily fashion'[31] (see Plate 19).

While Christ was born in Bethlehem, the Devil knew the ideal place for the Antichrist to be born – Babylon, the seat of the pagan Persian Empire. And as Christ was brought up in Nazareth, so the Antichrist would be brought up in those towns condemned by Christ: 'Woe to you, Bethsaida, woe to you, Corozain' (Matthew 11.21).[32] He would have magicians, enchanters, diviners and wizards 'who at the devil's bidding will rear him and instruct him in every evil, error, and wicked art'.[33] Evil spirits would be his constant companions and friends.

Eventually, the Antichrist would come to Jerusalem, like a Messiah, and with various tortures (like Nero) would slay all the Christians who remained true to their faith, 'whether through sword, or fiery furnace, or serpents, or beasts, or through some other form of torture'.[34] All those who believed in the Antichrist would have his mark on their forehead. He would raise up the temple that Solomon had built that the Romans had destroyed. Then (in the style of Antiochus Epiphanes), he would erect his throne in the temple, circumcise himself and pretend that he was the son of God.

Prior to the coming of the Antichrist to Jerusalem, the prophets Enoch and Elijah (the two Old Testament worthies who had never died) would be sent again into the world to prepare God's faithful for battle. They would convert the sons of Israel then in the world to Christianity.[35] But when the Antichrist came to Jerusalem, all the Jews would flock to him, 'in the belief that they are receiving God, but rather they will receive the devil'.[36]

Beginning with the slaughter of Enoch and Elijah (the two witnesses of Revelation 11.3), the Antichrist would then terrorise the world for three and a half years (or 42 months). He would convert kings and princes to his cause and send messengers and preachers throughout the whole world (see Plate 20). He would attack the places where Christ walked and destroy them. His power would extend over all the world. He would also parody the work of Christ by working signs and wonders.[37]

At the end of the three and a half years of tribulation, God's judgement would finally come upon the Antichrist. Adso was unsure whether he was to be killed by Jesus Christ himself or by Michael the archangel. In either case, 'he will be killed through the power of Our Lord Jesus Christ and not through the power of any angel or archangel.'[38] Christ would not come immediately, Adso told Gerberga. Rather, the elect would have 40 days to do penance for having been led astray by the Antichrist. This is a tradition that derives from the 45 days difference in Daniel 12.12–13 between the 1,290 days of the reign of Antichrist and the 1,335 days before the end of time.[39] No one knows, declared Adso, how long it would be after this 40-day period that the Lord would come in judgement. It remained in the providence of God, 'who will judge the world in that hour in which for all eternity he predetermined it was to be judged'.[40] Only then, we can assume, would the Devil be finally sent into hell for eternity.

## The Future Binding of Satan

The final days of the Devil would however be differently configured among those who believed, not that his binding was an event that had happened in the past, but that the binding was still yet to occur in the future. The most significant revision of the Augustinian position (that the binding of Satan had occurred at the time of Christ and his loosing at the time of the Antichrist) was to be made by the Cistercian monk Joachim of Fiore (c.1135–1202). Unlike Augustine's view that the loosing of Satan was

179

contemporary with the arising of the Antichrist, Joachim aligned the binding of Satan with the defeat of the Antichrist. And further, unlike Augustine, for whom the 'thousand-year' reign of the saints was a non-earthly one, for Joachim, drawing on the tradition that there would be a period on earth between the time of Antichrist's defeat and the final judgement, the 'thousand-year' reign of the saints was an earthly one, one that began with the Antichrist's defeat and coincided with (indeed was the consequence of) the binding of Satan.

The innovative nature of Joachim's account resided in two features. The first of these was his assertion that not only were there many antichrists, but there were many Antichrists (with a capital 'A'). The second was related to this, namely, that he adopted an *historicist* approach to the book of Revelation. That is to say, he read Revelation as referring to the whole history of the Christian Church: its past, present and future.[41] The key issue thus was where exactly in the book of Revelation the account of the future began. For reasons that are not particularly clear, Joachim determined that the last chapters of Revelation, from chapter 17 onwards, referred to what was yet to come, and that this included the prediction in chapter 20 of an earthly 'millennium' following the defeat of the great Antichrist.

This historicist reading of Revelation enabled Joachim to identify the beast of Revelation 17 as the Devil, and his seven heads with seven Antichrists that were seven kings, five of whom had already fallen. In his *Liber Figurarum* (*Book of Figures*), he identified these five with Herod, Nero, Constantius II, Muhammad and the Moorish king Mesulmut. The sixth Antichrist, the one 'who is', was identified with Saladin, the then-leader of the Muslims. During the time of the sixth Antichrist, the seventh Antichrist would also arise, 'from the West', and would 'come to the aid of that king who will be the head of the pagans' – that is, the sixth Antichrist in the East.[42] The seventh Antichrist would pretend to be a king, a prophet and a priest. Unlike the tradition that the Antichrist would be a Jew, Joachim's Antichrist was the leader of a group of Christian heretics.

These two, the Western and Eastern Antichrists, would conspire to wipe the name of Christ from the face of the earth, but would be defeated by Christ. After the destruction of the Antichrist, the great dragon, Satan, would be bound and 'imprisoned in the abyss (that is, in the remaining races who will live at the ends of the earth)'.[43] Peace and justice would then reign on earth for the 'millennium', although 'God alone knows the number of the years, months, and days of that time.'[44]

Joachim's historical reading of the later chapters of Revelation led him to a further innovation. He was the first to suggest that there would be a final persecution led by Antichrist *after* an earthly 'millennium'.[45] At that time, Satan would be released once again for a final battle. As Jesus Christ would come openly in judgement at the end of the world, so too would the Devil appear openly. And yet another Antichrist, the eighth and final Antichrist, would arise, one who was identified as the tail of the seven-headed dragon. 'God's Saints', wrote Joachim, 'have specifically spoken of one Antichrist and nonetheless there will be two, one of whom will be the Greatest Antichrist,'[46] the other of whom, the final Antichrist, would be Gog (Revelation 20.8), the commander of Satan's army: 'Gog. He is the Final Antichrist,' declared Joachim in his *Liber Figurarum*.[47] For his part, Satan would appear openly with the army of Gog. God would then 'judge him and his army by fire and brimstone poured down from heaven'.[48] Both the Devil and Gog would then be cast down into the lake of fire for eternity.

For Joachim, the time was near when the Antichrist, assisted by the Devil and his demons, would bring his final onslaught against the divine forces, prior to their defeat and the establishment of the Kingdom of God. The third age of the spirit, subsequent to those of the father and the son – the earthly 'millennium' – was expected to begin in the year 1260. When this failed to happen, Joachim's followers, and notably the 'Spiritual Franciscans' – those Franciscans who were dedicated like their founder to poverty, strict observance and end-time expectations – readjusted the timetable. Peter Olivi (*c.*1248–98), for example, had the Antichrist appearing between 1320 and 1340. And in his commentary on the book of Revelation, he expressed his belief in a double Antichrist – the great or open Antichrist, the defeat of whom would precede the Kingdom of God, and preceding him, the mystical Antichrist, a false pope yet to come who would attack the Spiritual Franciscans: 'He will indeed be false, because he will heretically err against the truth of evangelical poverty and perfection.'[49]

Joachim himself had come close to identifying the Antichrist with the Pope in his commentary on the two beasts of Revelation 13. 'Just as the Beast from the Sea', he wrote,

is held to be a great king from his sect who is like Nero and almost emperor of the whole world, so the Beast ascending from the earth is held to be a great prelate [*magnum prelatum*] who will be like Simon Magus and like a universal pope [*universalis pontifex*] in the entire world. He is that Antichrist of whom Paul said he would be lifted up and opposed to everything that is said to be God, or that is worshipped, and that he would sit in God's temple showing himself as God [2 Thessalonians 2.4].[50]

Even if Joachim *had* remained somewhat ambivalent in his identification of the Antichrist with a pope, others were soon to identify him with current papal figures. And with the identification of the Antichrist with contemporary figures, the Antichrist began to play a crucial role in

European apocalyptic geopolitics. Thus, for example, much to the irritation of Pope John XXII (pope 1316–34), Peter Olivi's followers identified John XXII with the mystical Antichrist.[51] The Spiritual Franciscan Ubertino of Casale (1259–1329) went as far as to identify the mystical Antichrist with two popes, Boniface VIII (pope 1294–1303) and his successor Benedict XI (pope 1303–4).

## Apocalypse Now

It was one thing to identify the Antichrist with a particular pope. It was a much more radical step to associate the Antichrist with the institution of the papacy itself. Yet, the Antichrist was identified with the papacy in any number of radical fourteenth- and fifteenth-century commentaries on the book of Revelation. It was when one of these came to light in Wittenberg in Germany in the 1520s, in the anonymous *Commentarius in Apocalypsin ante Centum Annos Aeditus*, that Martin Luther (1483–1546) realised that he was not alone in identifying the Antichrist both with a particular pope and with the papacy as a whole. As early as 1520, the year before he was excommunicated by Pope Leo X, and no doubt detecting what the Pope had in store for him, Luther had written, 'The papacy is nothing but the kingdom of Babylon and of the true Antichrist.'[52]

In the tradition of Joachim of Fiore, Luther adopted an historicist approach to Revelation, interpreting it as a book about the future, although mostly about the past, not least because Satan was about to be unleashed and Christ to come in judgement. Thus, in his 1530 preface to the book of Revelation, he read the history of Christianity through the lens of Revelation. In so doing, he set the pattern for all Protestant readings of Revelation until the modern period. Following the Augustinian tradition, Luther had Satan bound at around the time that the book was written, early in the Christian era and, like Augustine, he did not expect the millennial period to be exactly a thousand years. Nevertheless, Luther does appear to have been convinced that Satan was about to be loosed and to bring with him Gog and Magog (the Muslims and the Red Jews – Antichrist's Jewish shock-troops).[53] The time remaining for the papal Antichrist was short, and the Last Judgement was soon to follow, after which 'Christ shall be Lord alone; all the godless will be condemned and driven to hell with the devil.'[54]

The identification of the papacy with the Antichrist also became embedded in the Calvinist tradition. John Calvin (1509–64) believed that the full and final manifestation of the Antichrist was in the papacy and among the Muslims (see Plate 21). In his commentary on Paul's letters to the Thessalonians, he rejected the tradition that the Antichrist would be the Emperor Nero returned to earth. Paul, he declared, 'is not speaking of one individual, but of a kingdom that was seized by Satan for the purpose of setting up a seat of abomination in the midst of God's temple. This we see accomplished in popery. The defection has indeed spread more widely, for since Mohammed was an apostate he turned his followers the Turks from Christ.'[55]

This identification of the papacy with the Antichrist, together with an historicist approach to the book of Revelation, became the key to Reformation Protestant readings of history and its completion. Secular and sacred history, the history of kingdoms and the Kingdom of God coalesced. As a consequence, the book of Revelation assumed an importance it had not previously had. As the English Protestant John Bale said of it, 'No one necessary point of belief is in all other Scriptures, that is not here also in one place or another. The very complete sum and whole knitting up is this heavenly book of the universal verities of the bible [...] He that knoweth not this book, knoweth not what the Church is whereof he is a member.'[56]

That the book of Revelation was about the pope and the papacy as Antichrist, and that it was the key to the understanding of history past and future, was, however, about all that Protestant commentators were agreed upon. Indeed, the most influential sixteenth- and seventeenth-century English Protestant commentators upon it – John Bale (1495–1563), John Napier (1550–1617), Thomas Brightman (1562–1607) and Joseph Mede (1586–1638) took significantly different views.

Influenced by both Augustine and Joachim of Fiore, John Bale's *The Image of Both Churches* (completed in 1547) was the first commentary in English on the book of Revelation. It was a work that set the English pattern for the interpretation of the end-times for the sixteenth century, and it viewed the history of Christianity as an ongoing struggle between the 'true' Church that remained faithful to the teachings of Christ and the 'false' Church of Rome – 'the proud church of hypocrites, the rose-coloured whore, the paramour of antichrist, and the sinful synagogue of Satan'.[57]

In the early parts of this work, Bale had followed the Joachimite tradition in surmising that the binding of Satan and the millennium were yet to occur.[58] By the third part of his commentary, however, he had changed his mind and followed Augustine, with the difference that he took the 'millennium' literally. The Antichrist, he believed, had already taken over the 'kingdoms' of Pope Boniface II (pope in 607), who had obtained a decree from the Emperor Phocas that the see of Rome should be head of all the churches and that of the Prophet Muhammad (c.570–632). But the thousand years during which Satan was bound had begun with the birth of Christ and had ended when the Devil was loosed by the magician and minor antichrist Pope Sylvester II (c.946–1003): 'This beastly antichrist, boasting himself not only to be Christ's vicar in earth, but also to be equal with him in majesty and power, set first the devil at large by his necromancy, which took from the hearts of men the living word of the Lord, lest they should be saved.'[59]

After his release, according to Bale, Satan along with the followers of the pope and Muhammad (Gog and Magog) grew in power and persecuted the faithful. Everywhere, the Catholics had 'bishops' prisons and spiritual dungeons, with plenty of ropes, stocks, and irons, and as little charity else as the devil hath in hell. Everywhere had they fagots, fire, and stakes in abundance, to consume such heretics as would not believe as holy church commanded.'[60] When Satan along with Gog and Magog had reached the pinnacle of his persecution of the true Christians, a consuming fire would come from heaven out of the mouth of God: 'That word of the Lord's indignation shall with great violence throw the devil, that wily serpent which deceived Gog and Magog with their innumerable soldiers, into a foul stinking lake, or boiling pit of wild fire and brimstone.'[61]

This modified Augustinian position can also be found in the writings of the Scot John Napier. He is mostly remembered nowadays, as the philosopher David Hume put it in his *History of England*, as 'the famous inventor of the logarithms, the person to whom the title GREAT MAN is more justly due than to any other whom this country has produced'.[62] But Hume no doubt was seriously unimpressed by the work for which Napier was most renowned in his own time, *A Plaine Discovery of the Whole Revelation of Saint John*, first published in 1593 (with a further three English editions in 1594, 1611 and 1645, two Dutch, six French and five German editions), in which Napier articulated a complex mathematics of history.[63] It was a reading of Revelation that entailed fighting the papal Antichrist in the here and now by bringing in the Reformed religion and spreading the true Gospel.

In contrast to the Augustinian alignment of the binding of Satan with the coming of Christ, Napier lined it up with the first Roman emperor to convert to Christianity 'about this 300. Yeare of Christ'. It was *'Constantine* the greate', he went on, 'who, and whose successors (except a few of short raign) maintained Christianisme and true religion, to the abolishing of *Sathans* publique kingdome: and therefore, say wee, this yeare *Sathan* is bound.'[64] And, unlike Augustine, Napier took the thousand years of his binding seriously. Thus, Satan was loosed around 1300 to stir up the armies of Gog and Magog (the papal and Muslim armies) to do battle.

It was a mistake, however, to read the thousand years of the binding of Satan as a period of peace for the true Church. Quite the contrary! The years of the Antichrist began at the same time, between 300 and 316, when the pope first became powerful.[65] So God, according to Napier, cleverly balanced the good that came from the binding of Satan with the evil that continued in the reign of Antichrist in the persons of the popes. The reign of Antichrist was expected to last, as we saw above, for some 42 months (Revelation 13.5) or 1,260 day-years (Psalms 90.4), thus bringing the end of the reign of Antichrist to around 1560 (the year in which, not coincidentally we might say, Scotland declared itself 'Reformed'), from which time Napier expected the collapse of the papacy.

Although the reign of the Antichrist was coming to an end, the return of Christ was yet some time off. Surprisingly, for one so mathematically focused, Napier gave a variety of calculated dates for the final judgement, ranging from 1688 to 1786. The Devil and his angels would on that day be cast into the fires of hell.[66] Intriguingly, and again unlike Augustine, Napier had a further millennium in mind than that during which Satan had been bound – a 'spiritual' millennium in the future. For, after the resurrection of all on the last day, the saints would reign with Christ for a thousand years (here construed only 'figuratively' since, after the end of history, 'there shall be no day, yea no year, time nor numerall distinction thereof, but aeternitie without measure').[67]

Although quite differently envisaged, we find this notion of the double millennium in the writings of the English Puritan Thomas Brightman.[68] Like John Napier, Brightman's anti-Catholicism and anti-Islamism were embedded in a complex Protestant account of cosmic history that saw the conversion of the Jews to Christianity and their restoration to Israel as a central sign of the end of history.

Agreeing with Napier again, Brightman had the binding of Satan during the reign of Constantine. And, taking the thousand years literally, he had Satan loosed around 1300 to stir up the Muslims to come against the 'true' Church that was already by then beginning its work of the reforming of Christianity. Thus, the year 1300 was both the end of one millennium and the beginning of another. From that year, Christ was spiritually ruling with his saints while yet still engaged in a battle with Satan and the Antichrist. Without detailing the algorithmic complexities by which Brightman made his calculations, suffice it to say that the conversion of the Jews and their establishment in Palestine, the final destruction of the Devil and his allies – the papacy and the Muslims – could be expected in the period 1650 to 1695.

At around the same time, with the defeat of the Antichrist, the 'heavenly' city would be established on earth for at least the remaining six hundred years of the second millennium. Brightman was in fact proposing a radical rethinking of Augustine's view that the earthly and the heavenly city were eternally opposed to each other. For Brightman, the two coalesced: 'But as touching this newe Ierusalem,' he wrote, 'it is not that Citie which the Saintes shall enjoy in the Heavens, after this life, but that Church, that is to bee looked for upon earth, the most noble and pure of all other, that ever hath beene to that tyme.'[69] In this way, he was the founder of a tradition of this-worldly utopianism based in Jerusalem, an earthly city which was to become the centre of an earth in which all men would confess Christ as their lord. In this new Jerusalem, Christ would be spiritually present, ruling through his saints. Thus, the Kingdom of God would be established, not at the end of history, but in the course of it. Only at the end of the second 'millennium' would Christ physically come in final judgement. Then the Devil 'shal be cast for ever into the lake of fire, never to goe out againe, to raise up any such newe troubles and tumults'.[70]

Like other Protestant readers of the book of Revelation, the Anglican scholar Joseph Mede was committed to the historicist approach in his *The Key of the Revelation Searched and Demonstrated* (1643).[71] He was unrelentingly critical of the papacy, identifying it with the beasts of Revelation and Daniel, the man of sin, the whore of Babylon, and of course the Antichrist.[72] Yet unlike the majority of Protestant commentators, who held to an Augustinianism of some sort or other, Mede saw the binding of Satan as an event still in the future that aligned itself with the coming of an *earthly* rather than *heavenly* millennium.

Mede dated the beginning of the millennium to 1736, some 1,260 years after the final collapse of the Western Roman Empire in 476. Christ would come in that year, and the Day of Judgement would begin. It was a 'Day of Judgement' that was to last for a thousand years.[73] During the course of that day, Antichrist would be defeated, Satan would be bound and Christ would rule from heaven over the resurrected saints, along with those Christians still alive at his coming, in a new Jerusalem on earth. Then, 'the *great Day* waxing toward evening',[74] there would follow the loosing of Satan and his final defeat along with the 'nations' of Gog and Magog, and the resurrection and judgement of all the dead: 'Which things being finished the wicked shall be cast into Hell to be tormented for ever; but the Saints shall be translated into Heaven to live with Christ for ever.'[75]

With the renewed Protestant interest in the book of Revelation, and the identification of the Antichrist with the papacy, it is no matter for surprise that Catholic scholars also became engaged with the interpretation of that book. Catholics knew that the historicist reading of Revelation had turned upside down the transcendent meaning of the Catholic Church: 'Was the Church divine or demonic? Was it the bride of Christ or the whore of Satan?' The key Catholic strategies were to divest the present of any apocalyptic significance either by locating the Antichrist in the past or by projecting his arrival well into the future.[76] In the face of Protestant 'historicism', Catholics thus adopted either 'preterism', which found most of the prophecies in Revelation (apart from the few to do with the *very* end of history) to have been fulfilled within a short time following the composition of the book, or 'futurism', which viewed most of the prophecies in Revelation as referring to events yet to occur.

It was the futurism of the Spanish Jesuit Francisco Ribera (1537–91) and of the Italian Jesuit Robert Bellarmine (1542–1621) that were to dominate Catholic readings of Revelation.[77] According to Ribera, only the first few chapters of Revelation had to do with the past. For him, it was a book pre-eminently about the future. Far from covering the period from the early Church to the second coming, the book of Revelation was concerned totally (or almost so) with events in the future – and particularly the (now literally construed) three-and-a-half-year reign of the Antichrist prior to the end of the world. Thus, Antichrist was neither the papacy nor the pope but an individual who would reign in Jerusalem immediately before the end of history, would rebuild the temple, abolish Christianity, deny Christ, be accepted by the Jews, pretend to be God and conquer the world. The millennium was not to be understood literally as a thousand years but only (following Augustine) spiritually, and signifying the whole period between the death of Christ and the coming of Antichrist.

Similarly, Bellarmine followed the biography of the Antichrist initiated by Adso in the middle of the tenth century. Bellarmine argued that the Antichrist was a single individual, that he was not yet come, that he would be a Jew from the tribe of Dan who would come chiefly for and be received by the Jews, that he would become king of the Jews and rule from Jerusalem for three and a half years; he would be the monarch of the whole world and would persecute the Christians throughout the world in a great war (the war of Gog and Magog), before being finally defeated.

## Satan and the Fires of Hell

The problem of when Satan was bound and loosed was not easy to resolve. That man had been redeemed through the life and death of Christ suggested that *then* was the time when Satan had been bound for a thousand years. And yet the obvious objection to any binding of Satan at a point in the past was that no period as long as a thousand years could be found in which it could be claimed that evil had ceased and the Church had enjoyed a long period of undisturbed peace and spiritual well-being. This drove many to locate the binding of Satan in the future. The just as obvious objection to any assertion that Satan was not yet bound, and that therefore he was just as active after the life and death of Christ as he had been before it, was that it brought into doubt the victory over Satan, sin and death that Christ was *already* supposed to have accomplished.

Still, all, whether Catholic or Protestant, were agreed that the work of Christ would *eventually* result in a victory over Satan, sin and death. After the Day of Judgement, sin would be no more, the good would be rewarded with eternal happiness in heaven, and the Devil and his fallen angels, the Antichrist and the wicked would be punished with eternal misery in hell (see Plate 24). 'We have heard', wrote the Presbyterian John Shower (*c*.1657–1715), of some who have endured breaking on the Wheel, ripping up of their Bowels, fleaing alive, racking of Joynts, burning of Flesh, pounding in a Mortar, tearing in pieces with Flesh-hooks, boyling in Oyl, roasting on hot fiery Grid-irons, etc. And yet all these, tho' you should superad thereto all Diseases, such as the Plague, Stone, Gout, Stragury, or whatver else you can name most torturing to the Body [...] thet would all come short [...] of that Wrath, that Horror, that unconceivable Anguish which the Damned must inevitably suffer every Moment, without any Intermission of their Pains, in Hellish Flames.[78]

The punishments of the damned reflected those with which Shower's contemporaries were all too familiar in their everyday lives – infinitely intensified for an infinite time. It was an assault on all the senses. Thus, the eyes would be affronted by horrible sights. 'Did lust enter at the Eye from corporeall Beauties?' asked the clergyman Robert Sharrock of Winchester Cathedral (1630–84). 'In Hell', he declared, 'Horror shall more abundantly enter there from ghastly sights.'[79] The nose would be assaulted by awful smells: 'Your dainty delicate persons', wrote the Anglican William Gearing (c.1625–90), 'that now cannot brook the least savoury smell, shall lie down in a stinking dungeon, in a loathsome lake, that burns with fire and brimstone forever.'[80] The ears were assaulted by the crying of the damned, who 'shall ever be whining, pining, weeping, mourning, ever tormented without ease', wrote John Bunyan (1628–88).[81] The terrors of hell were multiplied by the shrieking and wailing of one's companions, by children crying out against their parents, husbands against wives and wives against husbands, masters and servants, ministers and people, magistrates and subjects, cursing and recriminating against each other into the infinite future.

Moreover, the horrors of this eternal cacophony of misery and blame were augmented by the screams of demons. The damned, imagined William Gearing, would be affronted by the horrid noise of damned spirits, 'crying and roaring out with doleful shriekings'.[82] In our current life, suggested John Bunyan, the very thought of demons appearing was sufficient to make the flesh tremble and the hair stand on end. But the spirits of the wicked would be daunted by hobgoblin and foul fiend. What will you do, he asked, 'when not onely the supposition of the devils appearing, but the reall society of all the devils in hell to be with thee howling and roaring, screeching and yelling in such a hideous manner, that thou wilt be even at thy wits end, and be ready to run starke madde again for anguish and torment'.[83]

The Devil's roles in hell reflected the conceptual ambivalence at the heart of the Christian tradition. As we have seen, on the one hand, the Devil was God's implacable enemy and deserving of God's infinite wrath and his eternal punishment. Yet on the other hand, the Devil and his minions were God's servants in the divine punishment of the damned. They were both tormented and tormenting (see Plate 25). According to the Cambridge Platonist Henry More (1614–87), wicked souls would be exposed to grim and remorseless officers of justice, as devoid of any sense of good as those that they would punish. These demons 'satiate their lascivient cruelty with all manner of abuses and torments they can imagine', while the people's souls would be tortured in ways far above 'what the cruellest Tyranny has inflicted here, either upon the guilty or innocent'.[84] The somewhat unfortunately named Puritan Christopher Love (1618–51) made the analogy between the sadism of devils in hell and the mercy of earthly executioners:

Beloved, it would somewhat lessen a mans torments, though a man were condemned to endure some punishment, if the man that was to be his executioner, were a mercifull man; if he would spare him what he might: If a man were to be burnt in the hand, if the man that was to burn him would spare him, and hardly touch him, he would count it a great happiness: it would somewhat lessen your torments were they but mercifull creatures in hell. But who are your tormenters? Your tormenters are Divels, in whom is no pity, who will not spare, but will torment you as much as they are able to inflict, or you to bear: Be sure your tormenters will have no mercy; but they will load you with rivers of brimstone, and mountaines of fire to the utmost.[85]

Thus, the punishments inflicted by the Devil and his angels upon the damned in hell manifested the glory and justice of God. They were tormenters and executioners to wicked men, wrote Thomas Bromhall in his *Treatise of Specters* (1658), 'so that his Justice might shine the more glorious, to the comfort of the Godly, and of his Elect'.[86]

If in the course of history the Devil could be said to have sufficient autonomy in his actions against mankind to absolve God from the responsibility for them, it was otherwise after his final defeat. The Devil had at last been rendered powerless. And for the sufferings inflicted upon the damned in hell by him and his evil angels only God could now be held responsible. Let no man imagine, declared the Calvinist Thomas Goodwin in his *Discourse of the Punishment of Sin in Hell* (1680), 'that Devils are the greatest Tormenters of Men, or of their consciences in Hell: or if any would affirm it, I would demand, who it is that torments the Consciences of Devils themselves? Certainly none but God.'[87]

Within seventeenth-century Protestant orthodoxy, the wrath of God had replaced both Satanic hate *and* divine love. In Catholic orthodoxy of the same period, the justice of God overpowered his goodness. For the Catholic Angelo Maria da San Filippo (1670–1703), the temptation to privilege love over justice was of the Devil; and part of God's happiness consisted in the sufferings of the damned in hell:

If God were to look at those reprobates with a displeased eye, it might be hoped that, so as not to cause himself eternal regret, he might let a drop of his infinite mercy fall and put out that vast fire; but since the torture of the condemned souls forms part of the sovereign happiness, it is not possible to hope for mercy unless one believes that God wishes to deprive himself of a part of his glory for all eternity and reduce the beatitude which he receives from their suffering by half.[88]

Before the end of history, the Satanic paradox provided a way to mitigate God's responsibility for evil. With the Devil's final defeat at the end of history, the paradox was removed. The Devil was no longer God's powerful enemy, but his defeated servant. Although the Devil punished the damned in hell, God alone was responsible for their sufferings. His all-powerfulness was no longer in doubt. His goodness, on the other hand, appeared to have been overtaken by his wrathful justice.

# CHAPTER NINE

# The 'Death' of the Devil

The fool hath said in his heart, There is no God

Psalms 14.1 (KJV)

## Satan and Superstition

In 1550, it was as impossible not to believe in the Devil as it was impossible not to believe in God. By the middle of the eighteenth century, intellectual conditions had changed sufficiently for at least some among the 'literate' elite, both religious and non-religious, to contemplate the non-existence of the Devil, or at the very least to question whether he any longer had a role in history or could act in the world.

This relegation of Satan to the distant corners of the educated European mind is exemplified by William Hogarth in his print *Credulity, Superstition, and Fanaticism*, first published in April 1762 (see Plate 26). In this print, what had been core components of religious belief in the middle of the sixteenth century are now decried as superstition, to be believed only by the credulous and the fanatical. The domain of superstition had increased considerably, as that of religion correspondingly decreased.

Hogarth's print depicts a tonsured Jesuit priest disguised as a Methodist preaching on the text 'I speak as a fool' (2 Corinthians 11.21). Under his clerical garb, he is wearing a harlequin jacket. In his left hand he holds the puppet of a witch, being suckled by an animal familiar; in his other, that of the Devil with a forked tail, holding a gridiron.

The three figures around the pulpit each bear a candle. They reference three of the period's most famous ghosts: the ghost of Sir George Villiers who warned a servant of the impending assassination of his son George the Duke of Buckingham; the ghost of the murdered Julius Caesar appearing before Brutus; and the ghost of Mrs Veale of whom Daniel Defoe wrote in his *A True Relation of the Apparition of One Mrs Veal the Next Day after her Death to One Mrs Bargrave at Canterbury the 8th of September, 1705.*

In a pew at the foot of the pulpit, another minister pushes a statue of the Cock Lane ghost down the dress front of a young woman, while a demon whispers in the ear of another congregant. The thermometer to the right of the pulpit that measures human emotions and mental disorders (from the depths of despair to the heights of lust, ecstasy and madness) is topped by another image of the Cock Lane ghost and the ghost known as the Drummer of Tedworth. Before the pulpit lies the figure of Mary Toft, a woman from Godalming in Surrey, who was reputed to give birth to live rabbits. Next to her, a shoe black, probably the demoniac William Perry, the Boy of Bilson, vomits nails. He holds a bottle of urine in which the evil spirit possessing him has been confined, although the cork has popped out, allowing the spirit to escape.

For Hogarth, credulity, superstition and fanaticism rested (literally) on several books depicted in the print. Pre-eminent among these was Joseph Glanvill's famous book in defence of spirits, demons and witches, *Saducismus Triumphatus: Or, Full and Plain Evidence Concerning Witches and Apparitions* (1681), edited after his death by the Platonist Henry More. Next to the Boy of Bilson there appeared that most influential of English demonologies, the 1597 *Daemonologie* of King James.

What had previously been an accepted part of the intellectual world had now become the subject of satire and ridicule. What then were the intellectual conditions that had made possible the relegation of the Devil from the central position within Christian thought that he had occupied up until that time? In the broadest terms, it was the gradual exclusion of the spiritual – both the supernatural (miracles worked by God) and the preternatural (wonders, often worked by demons) – from the domain of the natural. It signalled the development of new forms of Christian spirituality that grounded personal faith and religion not in divine revelation, Scripture or the presence of the divine or the demonic in the world, but in the rational contemplation of a disenchanted world.

The beginning point for this was the early sixteenth century, that period shortly before the Reformation in which the medieval Thomist account of the link between miracles and wonders, dominant since the early fifteenth century, still held sway. In his *Summa contra Gentiles* (*The Summa against the Gentiles*), Aquinas had distinguished between three kinds of physical events or occurrences. The first were natural – that which *is* always or *is* for the most part. This natural order could be violated in either of two ways. It could be disrupted by miracles (*miracula*) – acts performed directly by God without the mobilisation of secondary causes (the supernatural). Or it could be interrupted by wonders (*miranda*) – unusual events that depended on secondary causes alone and required no suspension of God's ordinary providence (the preternatural).[1] This category of wonders could be further subdivided into wonders that were caused by spiritual agents (such as Satan and his minions) and those that came about without agents through natural (though often hidden or occult) causes.

The distinction between the divinely miraculous and the demonically wondrous was made most clearly by the Dominican theologian Jacopo Passavanti (d. 1357) in his *Lo Specchio della vera Penitenzia* (*The Mirror of True Penitence*). Because the Devil 'knows every science and every art,' he wrote, he is able to join one thing to another, because all things must obey him, as far as concerns local motion. And he is able to do and to simulate marvelous things. I do not say, of course, that the devil is able to perform true miracles, but marvelous things, understanding by true miracles properly those things which we know to be above or outside of the true order of nature, such as raising a dead man or creating something out of nothing, or restoring sight to the blind, and things like these. And such miracles only God can perform.[2]

It was a distinction that, while limiting the powers of the Devil, nonetheless gave him ample scope for his activities.

## The Cessation of Miracles

By 1651, when Thomas Hobbes (1588–1679) published his *Leviathan*, the doctrine of the cessation of miracles had become commonplace, sufficiently so for Hobbes to be able to set out the rights of governors and the duties of subjects without recourse to anything beyond the Holy Scriptures. 'Seeing therefore Miracles now cease,' declared Hobbes, 'we have no sign left, whereby to acknowledge the pretended Revelations, or Inspirations of any private man; nor obligation to give ear to any Doctrine, farther than it is conformable to the Holy Scriptures, which since the time of our Saviour, supply the place, and sufficiently recompense the want of all other Prophecy.'[3]

In so saying, Hobbes was declaring divine revelation closed from the time of the Scriptures. He was also precluding the necessity of taking any notice of any religious truths delivered since New Testament times, particularly any claiming to be true as the result of accompanying miracles. It was not a doctrine that went so far as to say that God could no longer work miracles. But it was claiming that, at least since the time of Christ (or within some few centuries after that), God chose not to do so (or only rarely did). It was a doctrine which both reinforced and arose out of the Protestant principle of *sola Scriptura* (by Scripture alone). And it was as much a critique of Catholicism's claims to extend the range of Christian doctrine beyond the Biblical as it was a declaration that God no longer intervened supernaturally in the affairs of men.

The claim that miracles had ceased was the most important of an array of arguments against miracles in sixteenth-century English Protestant theology which were intended to criticise the claims of the Catholic Church to sole religious truth and legitimacy, and to establish the identity of English Protestantism. Claims that apparent miracles were the fraudulent acts of a charlatan priesthood, the works of Satan, or part of the eschatological activities of the papal Antichrist, were all marshalled against miracles as legitimating the truth of Catholicism. As D.P. Walker has noted, 'The aim of this doctrine of the cessation of miracles is plainly to demolish at one blow all modern Catholic miracles, presented as divinely given marks of the true Church, instead of having to show that each single one is fraudulent or produced by superstitious magic, and at the same time to prove that the Roman Church is Antichrist.'[4]

But arguments to this effect were more than this. They were central to English Protestantism's aligning of itself with 'rationality' against a fraudulent Catholic priesthood and an ignorant and credulous laity. Thus, these were the first shots in a war against Catholicism which had the unintended consequence of setting in play the establishment of new rational spiritualities, ones which by the middle of the eighteenth century were to become part of a general critique of supernaturalism in religion as the domain of the irrational and the superstitious and the refuge of both charlatans and gullible fools.

Although English Protestant theologians could be ambivalent about the cessation of miracles, they were to a man committed to view them critically. They would have looked in vain to the major European reformers for much support. The European reformers, though recognising the value of a critique of miracles in their cause against Catholicism, were similarly ambivalent. Martin Luther accepted that God did miracles to establish Christianity and that, as faith became established, miracles gradually ceased. While he accepted that the 'miracle' of the soul transformed by faith would continue until the Last Day, the much more rare miracles of the body, as exemplified in Christ's healing miracles, were no longer needed since the Christian faith came to rest securely on the Scriptures. This excused the absence of miracles within Protestantism, though it did not go as far as disparaging their apparent continuation in Catholicism.[5]

More than Luther, Calvin engaged directly with the Catholic claim that miracles validated Catholicism and their absence falsified Protestantism. Against this, Calvin mounted a counter-argument from Scripture that miracles, far from indicating the truth of doctrines, pointed far more to false prophets and antichrists.[6] Miracles, he declared, nourished idolatry, drawing people away from the true worship of God. Their miracles are 'so foolish and ridiculous, so vain and false'.[7] And he hinted that Catholic doctrine, rather than being confirmed by miracles, was disconfirmed by illusory Satanic wonders.[8] Still, Calvin's considered opinion was that miracles had probably ceased in the time of the early Church. No doubt he thought it better to criticise all Catholic miracles as fraudulent on the basis of their cessation than to argue for the possibility of Protestant ones. Thus, he declared,

> Though Christ does not expressly state whether he intends this gift to be temporary, or to remain perpetually in his Church, yet it is more probable that miracles were promised only for a time, in order to give lustre to the

gospel, while it was new and in a state of obscurity [...].
And certainly we see that the use of them ceased not long
afterwards, or at least, that instances of them were so rare
as to entitle us to conclude that they would not be equally
common in all ages.[9]

All this is not to imply that, from the time of the
Reformation, the miraculous disappeared from Protestant
modes of thinking. But what we can say is that, from this
time on, 'miracle' had become a contested category within
elite Protestant theological discussions; it remained so even
when, in the eighteenth century, the debate shifted from
the issue of when God may have ceased to work miracles to
that of whether (as in the case of Spinoza) God *could* work
miracles, or (as in the case of David Hume) whether there
could ever be sufficient evidence to demonstrate that he had
done so. Crucially, the doctrine of the cessation of miracles
entailed that, in the absence of the everyday miraculous
intervention of God, the world was a much more 'orderly'
place than had previously been conceived. And that which
had previously been conceived as miraculous could now
be construed as superstitious.

## The Devil De-skilled

The debate on the possibility of miracles did not affect the
Devil directly. As we know, he had never had *supernatural*
powers and could only work within the domain of the
'natural' or rather the 'preternatural'. He was, after all,
the master of the 'preternatural', a creator of wonders, the
exemplary practitioner of 'natural magic'. As the Puritan
theologian William Perkins (1558–1602) put it, the Devil
had his own 'exquisite knowledge of all naturall things;
as of the influences of the starres, the constitutions of men
and other creatures, the kinds, vertues, and operations of

plants, rootes, hearbs, stones, &c. which knowledge of his, goeth many degrees beyond the skill of all men, yea even of those that are most excellent in this kind, as Philosophers, and Physicians'.[10]

In effect, then, the activity of the Devil was part of the domain of 'nature', and demonology part of 'natural philosophy'. This was why Joseph Glanvill (1636–80), along with other fellows of the Royal Society, saw no contradiction between his commitment to the emerging experimental method in science, his support of natural magic and his belief in the activities of spirits, demons and witches. '*Indeed*, as things are for the present,' he wrote to the Royal Society,

> The LAND of ESPIRITS is a kinde of *America*, and not well discover'd *Region*; yea, it stands in the *Map of humane Science* like *unknown Tracts*, fill'd up with *Mountains, Seas, and Monsters* [...] For we know not any thing of the world we live in, but by *experiment* and the *Phaenomena*; and there is the same way of *speculating immaterial* nature by *extraordinary Events* and *Apparitions*, which possibly might be improved to *notices* not *contemptible*, were there a *Cautious*, and *Faithful History* made of those *certain* and *uncommon appearances*.[11]

In short, between early modern science and demonology, no contradiction was perceived. The consequence of this was that, in practice, it was difficult for both natural philosophers and demonologists to distinguish between wonders naturally caused and those in which demons had played a role. The only difference between the work of demons and unassisted natural wonders was the active agency of a free will in the former case.

So it is perhaps unsurprising that there was a growing tendency among philosophers, if not among their demonological brethren, to see the presence of the demonic as theoretically redundant. Even Joseph Glanvill, for example, in spite of his intentions to support the reality of spirits and witchcraft, set out to provide by means of his doctrine of 'poisonous ferment' a 'naturalistic' explanation of key themes in demonology. According to Glanvill, the witch's familiar not only sucks from the witch but also infuses a 'poisonous ferment' into her. It is plain to see, he continued, 'that the *evil spirit* having *breath'd* some *vile vapour* into the *body* of the *Witch*, it may *taint* her *bloud* and *spirits* with a *noxious quality*, by which her *infected imagination*, heightned by *melancholy*, and this *worse cause* may do much hurt'.[12] It was this poisonous ferment that was primarily responsible for the capacity of the witch to do evil, 'so that I am apt to think there may be a *power* of *real fascination* in the *Witch's eyes* and *imagination*, by which for the most part she acts upon *tender* bodies.'[13] And it enabled the witch to transform her terrestrial body into one more suitable for travel to the sabbath, and one more pliable for transformation into animal forms.

Still, during the seventeenth century, in spite of a growing scepticism about his role as the cause of wonders, the Devil was well served by the intellectual fascination with those events. In contrast to the apparently shrunken domain of miracles, the seventeenth century began with an expansion of wonders preternatural, both spiritual and natural, of special divine providences, apocalyptic expectations and demonic possessions. However that may be, over the course of the century, the domain of preternatural wonders *caused by spiritual agents* shrank as wonders lost their evidential value as signs of divine or demonic activities. The world of 'natural wonders' not caused by spiritual agents became the dominant province of natural philosophy, and natural philosophers the arbiters of what was to be conceived as the domain of the natural.

If the Devil had lost intellectual purchase in the natural philosopher's mind as the consequence of the demise of the relation between wonders and spiritual agents as causes of them, he further lost his grip when wonders themselves became intellectually marginalised. And in the early part of the eighteenth century, there was a loss of interest in wonders more generally. They too became intellectually redundant as the result of a shift away from the scientific investigation of nature through its *disorderliness* to a focus on its *orderliness*, its *simplicity* and its *uniformity*. A world of wonders, whether natural or demonic, was a world insubordinate to God. A world subordinate to God as creator was not one of wondrous disruptions, but of order, decorum, regularity and uniformity. The 'order of nature', its regularity and uniformity evidencing its divine designer, now excluded the preternatural, and wonders were relegated to the domain of superstition and vulgarity. As Lorraine Daston and Katherine Park put it,

> The learned rejection of wonder and wonders in the early eighteenth century partook of metaphysics and snobbery. The 'order of nature,' like 'enlightenment' was defined largely by what or who was excluded. Marvels and vulgarity played symmetrical and overlapping roles in this process of exclusion: the order of nature was the anti-marvellous; the enlightened were the anti-vulgar; and, [...] marvels were vulgar.[14]

And 'the Devil', no longer occupying a viable intellectual space, was relegated to the domain of credulity and superstition.

Something similar may be said to have happened to magical effects, considered as a subset of 'the wondrous'. As we saw at the end of Chapter Four, Renaissance magic attempted to incorporate natural magic into the broadening domain of natural philosophy. This project of incorporating natural magic into natural philosophy more generally was effectively a denial that natural magic was magical at all. Put another way, it was an attempt to move magic (or at least some parts of it) from the realm of the preternatural to that of the purely natural. In effect, the more magic became identified by the Church with witchcraft, sorcery and demonology, the more concerned were proponents of natural magic to identify it purely with the natural. The more it could be naturalised by natural philosophers, the less it could be demonised by the demonologists.

Thus, during the period from the Renaissance at the beginning of the sixteenth century to the rise of science at the end of the seventeenth, the boundaries of magic were continually debated and finally redrawn. In the latter part of the seventeenth century, those parts of natural magic that were congenial to natural philosophy were eventually incorporated into emerging early modern science. In the eighteenth century, those parts of magic that were not capable of being absorbed – necromancy, ritual magic, angelic and demonic magic, sorcery and witchcraft – were relegated to the domain of superstition. Thus, the preternaturally magical became either naturalised or rejected as superstitious. The Devil had lost his modus operandi. Theology reacted accordingly: natural theology became a theology of nature. As Daston and Park note, 'The quiet exit of demons from respectable theology coincides in time and corresponds in structure almost exactly with the disappearance of the preternatural in respectable natural philosophy.'[15]

## The Devil Disembodied

The doctrine of the cessation of miracles entailed that all causation within the world was natural, by virtue of its denial of any supernatural incursion of the divine into the natural realm. In short, all events within the world were deemed to have been only naturally caused. Preternatural events came to be seen as occurring independently of the activity of any spiritual agents such as the Devil and his minions. The Devil became a victim of changing understandings of 'the natural' that excluded his having any role therein.

The Devil also came under attack from the other direction, not from shifts in the understandings of nature, but from assaults on the nature of spiritual beings and their ability to have a physical existence or even a physical presence. Thus, alongside the debates about the boundaries of the natural, there was from the late part of the sixteenth century a debate about the nature of the demonic, more specifically, about the possibility of demonic embodiment. The denial of its possibility was at the core of Reginald Scot's critique of demonology in his *The Discoverie of Witchcraft* in 1584.

As we have seen in Chapter Four, witchcraft as imagined by the demonologists was fundamentally dependent on the assumption of the corporeality of demons and the possibility of their corporeal interaction with humans. Sex with the Devil was the ultimate form of such interaction. And it was here that Scot's key argument against demonology was to be found, for Scot opposed demonology with physiology. Sex was only possible, he argued, among beings *essentially* corporeal. Spirits by nature incorporeal were incapable of the desires of the flesh: 'Item, where the genitall members want, there can be no lust of the flesh: neither dooth nature give anie desire of generation, where there is no propagation or succession required. And as spirits cannot be greeved with hunger, so can they not be inflamed with lusts.'[16]

Scot was not unaware of the subtle arguments of the demonologists that led to the possibilities of sex in 'virtual' bodies. But his rhetorical strategy was to restrict all talk of sexuality to physiological processes in real and not assumed bodies, and thus to rule out on principle any corporeal interactions between the Devil and human beings. The assaults of Satan, he declared, are spirituall, and not temporall. In which respect *Paule* wisheth us not to provide a corselet of steele to defend us from his clawes; but biddeth us to put on the whole armour of God [...]. For we wrestle not against flesh and bloud; but against principalities and powers, and spirituall wickednesse. And therefore he adviseth us to be sober and watch: for the divell goeth about like a roring lion, seeking whome he may devoure. He meaneth not with carnall teeth [...]. Why then should we thinke that a divell, which is a spirit, can be knowne, or made tame and familiar unto a naturall man; or contrarie to nature, can be by a witch made corporall, being by God ordeined to a spirituall proportion.[17]

Scot did not deny the existence of the Devil, nor of demons or spirits in general. Rather he restricted the activity of the Devil solely to the spiritual realm – to spirit on spirit: 'sathan or the divell while we feed, allureth us with gluttonie: he thrusteth lust into our generation; and sloth into our exercise; into our conversation envie; into our traffike avarice; into our correction wrath; into our government pride; [...] When we wake, he mooveth us to evill works; when we sleepe, to evill and filthie dreames.'[18]

Scot's rejection of the 'external' operations of spirits in the world was a radical one. But his locating of the activities of the 'spiritual realm' within the 'internal' world of the mind was of a piece with mainstream Protestant theology. The demonism embedded in the liturgy, in sermons, conduct books, pulp press pamphlets, in diaries and commonplace books, and in autobiographies and popular lives centred above all on the notion of the 'internal temptation' of the Protestant soul. As Nathan Johnstone notes, 'Whereas the medieval remit of the Devil had included temptation as one of a variety of activities with which he might afflict mankind, Protestants elevated it into the single most important aspect of his agency, which virtually eclipsed all others.'[19] And for Scot, it was, to all intents and purposes, Satan's *only* activity.

Moreover, the internalisation of the Devil's work was crucial in the development of Protestant self-regulation, for it problematised the origin of the individual's innermost thoughts. Were they of the spirit of God or of the Devil? Thus was relief from the demonic only possible through the most rigorous introspection, self-regulation and examination of the conscience. In this way, the disembodied Devil of Reginald Scot was no longer an exotic 'other' in the outer world of compacts with Satan, witches' sabbaths and the demonically possessed. The norms of Satanism were no longer to be found in the Devil hidden in thunderstorms, or appearing in the shape of a black dog, or as an incubus. The Devil in Scot, as in Protestantism more generally, was normalised. He was present in the inner life of all Christians. For Scot, the Devil was no longer the inverter (à la Stuart Clark) of the external physical world,[20] but, more crucially, the subverter of the internal spiritual world of the individual.[21] He was no longer a player in cosmic history, only in the personal history of the individual Christian.

It was Thomas Hobbes who took Reginald Scot's analysis that one step further. For Scot, incorporeal beings could not interact with humans. For Thomas Hobbes, the notion that there could be beings who were by nature incorporeal substances was contradictory. According to Hobbes, the word 'body' denoted a something that filled or occupied a particular place. The terms 'substance' and 'body', he argued in his *Leviathan*, signified the same thing. And therefore, '*Substance incorporeall* are words, which when they are joined together, destroy one another, as if a man should say, an *Incorporeall Body*.'[22]

On the face of it, and to many of his readers, this appeared to be a denial of the existence of spirits, and thus of angels and demons. Certainly, Hobbes did argue that, in many instances, spirits were the products of the human imagination. This, he claimed, was the result of a misunderstanding of the true nature of vision, namely, the taking of objects that appeared to the imagination as if they were objects that really existed outside us, objects that, because they often vanished from view, were also taken to be essentially incorporeal. Not knowing that 'vision' could be misleading, 'it was hard for men to conceive of those Images in the Fancy, and in the Sense, otherwise, than of things really without [outside] us: Which some will have to be absolutely Incorporeall.'[23]

As far as angels were concerned, Hobbes was convinced that there was no mention of them in the Old Testament where they could not be interpreted as 'supernaturall apparitions of the Fancy, raised by the speciall and extraordinary operation of God, thereby to make his presence and commandements known to mankind'.[24] He was forced to a change of mind by his reading of the New Testament, which 'extorted from my feeble Reason, an acknowledgement, and beleef, that there be also Angels substantiall and permanent'.[25] And what applied to Angels applied also to demons – they could be figments of the imagination, but they could also be creatures that had a *real* existence outside of us.

Thus, in keeping with his materialist philosophy, and with his belief in the Scriptures, Hobbes was forced to an acknowledgement that, in so far as they existed outside of us, and because the notion of incorporeal bodies was a contradictory one, spirits did exist, but as naturally *embodied* beings located in space. 'By the name of *Spirit*,' he wrote in *Of Humane Nature*, 'we understand a *body natural*, [...] that filleth up the place which the image of a visible body might fill up [...] and consequently, to conceive a Spirit, is to conceive something that hath dimension.'[26]

On the face of it, this ought to have opened up demonology to the domain of natural philosophy, in the same way as the demonologists' assumption that demons could *assume* bodies did. Naturally embodied demons, as Hobbes constructed them, were assuredly part of the natural realm and capable of interacting with humans. But this was a conclusion that Hobbes wished to avoid. He did so by denying that spirits could be perceived by the senses. As such, they could not be naturally known and therefore could not be part of any natural philosophy. To have 'natural evidence' of the existence of angels, good and evil, was impossible, for Spirits, he declared, 'we suppose to be those substances which work *not* upon the *Sense*; and therefore not conceptible.'[27] In short, demonology could not be a science.

As for demonic possession, Hobbes ruled out on principle the possibility of an embodied demon physically entering the body of a person. Bodies could not 'intermix'. So, when Jesus commanded Spirits to depart the possessed, he was merely speaking figuratively to those who suffered, not from possession by demons, but from the natural diseases of madness, lunacy, frenzy or epilepsy. Both demonology and exorcism were, for Hobbes, merely means by which Catholic priests attempted to keep possession of their prestige and 'the People more in awe of their Power',[28] thus lessening the proper dependence of subjects on their sovereign power.

It was one thing to deny the capacity of the Devil to interact with humans, a denial viewed as the first step on the slippery slope towards atheism; it was quite another to deny his existence altogether. Thus, it was a significant moment both in the history of demonology and in theology when Benedict de Spinoza (1632–77) denied the Devil's existence. In a brief chapter entitled 'Of Devils' in his short treatise *God, Man, and his Well Being* around 1660, Spinoza concluded that Demons 'cannot possibly exist'.[29] It was the inevitable consequence of a philosophy that there was only one substance – a God who was identified with Nature. For some, this identification of God and Nature was viewed as a divinisation of nature, for most a naturalisation of the divine. In either case, there could be nothing contrary to

God: 'If the Devil is a thing contrary to God and has nothing from God, then he agrees completely with Nothing.'[30] Moreover, as an answer to the problem of evil within the human emotions, Satan was unnecessary. 'For we have no need, as others do,' he wrote, 'to posit Devils in order to find causes of hate, envy, anger, and such passions. We have come to know them sufficiently without the aid of such fictions.'

Spinoza had noticed the demonic paradox at the heart of Christianity. Thus, he singled out for particular criticism the idea of the Devil as both God's ally and his opponent. He saw it as absurd that God both allowed the Devil to ensnare men and then punished them eternally for being so ensnared. Thus, in 1675, Spinoza responded to a letter from Alfred Burgh accusing him of being entrapped by the Devil:

[N]ow you dream of a Prince, God's enemy, who against God's will ensnares most men (for the good are few) and deceives them, whom God therefore delivers over to this master of wickedness for everlasting torture. So divine justice permits the Devil to deceive men with impunity, but does not permit men, haplessly deceived and ensnared by the Devil, to go unpunished.[31]

To Hugo Boxtel, Spinoza wrote that Satan and his minions were, like spirits and ghosts in general, merely the product of human imagination, the result of the desire that 'men commonly have to narrate things not as they are but as they would like them to be'.[32] To the same correspondent, he teasingly remarked that he was puzzled why believers were uncertain about the existence of female as well as male demons, in particular, why 'those who have seen naked spirits have not cast their eyes on the genital parts; perhaps they were too afraid, or ignorant of the difference'.[33] Arguments in favour of spirits, together with any apparent evidence to their existence, he concluded, 'will not convince anyone that ghosts and spectres of all kinds exist, except those who, shutting their ears to the voice of reason, suffer themselves to be led astray by superstition which is so hostile to right reason that, so as to lower the prestige of philosophers, it prefers to believe old wives' tales.'[34]

## Bodies, Platonic and Demonic

To Joseph Glanvill and his Cambridge Platonist colleague Henry More, the denial of spirits was, if not tantamount to atheism, then the direct route to it. 'Atheism is begun in Sadducism [the denial of spirits],' wrote Glanvill, 'And those that dare not bluntly say, There is NO GOD, content themselves […] to deny there are SPIRITS or WITCHES.'[35] As early as 1653, Henry More was convinced 'that a contemptuous misbelief of suchlike Narratives concerning *Spirits*, and an endeavour of making them all ridiculous and incredible is a dangerous Prelude to *Atheisme* it self, or else a more close and crafty Profession or Insinuation of it. For assuredly that Saying was nothing so true in Politics, *No Bishop, no King*; as in Metaphysicks, *No Spirit, no God.*'[36]

Atheism, materialism and the moral libertinism which, it was believed, necessarily accompanied these, help to explain the passion with which many in the later part of the seventeenth century sought out credible stories of the activities of deceased witches, angels and demons. The credibility of these 'Relations' was perceived as the strongest bulwark against the atheist: 'if there be once any visible ghosts or spirits acknowledged as things permanent, it will not be easy for any to give reason why there might not be one supreme ghost also, presiding over them all and the whole world,' wrote the Cambridge Platonist Ralph Cudworth in 1678.[37] Joseph Glanvill, for his part, as we noted earlier, was convinced that the empirical approach in natural philosophy could be used to verify the reality of soul and spirit. This was the preferred weapon against the onslaught of materialism, and the key to the defence of the coexistence of spirit and matter. Robert Boyle, Glanvill's colleague in the Royal Society, wrote to him in 1677 exhorting him to examine all accounts meticulously, 'for we live in an age, and a place, wherein all stories of witchcrafts, or other magical feats, are by many, even of the wise, suspected; and by too many, that would pass for wits, derided and exploded'.[38] Followers of Hobbes and Spinoza were especially suspected. Thus, Henry More in a letter to his friend Joseph Glanvill exclaimed,

> And forasmuch as such course-grain'd Philosophers as those *Hobbians* and *Spinozians*, and the rest of that Rabble, slight Religion and the Scriptures, because there is such express mention of Spirits and Angels in them, [...] I look upon it as a special piece of Providence that there are ever anon such fresh examples of Apparitions and Witchcrafts as may rub up and awaken their benummed and lethargick Mindes into a suspicion at least, if not assurance that there are other intelligent Beings besides those that are clad in heavy Earth or Clay.[39]

At the centre of More and Glanvill's defence of the existence of spirits was the Platonic doctrine of the 'vehicles' of the soul. In keeping with their commitment to the pre-existence of souls, the journey of souls, demons and angels, from the time of creation until eternity, was a temporal one. All human souls, like demons and angels, had been in existence since the time of creation. But the journey of souls and spirits was also a spatial one. Spirits had been, and always would be, located in this spatio-temporal realm, whether in ethereal, aerial or (in the case of human souls) terrestrial bodies, each spirit connected with a body appropriate to the heavens, the air or the earth.

The belief that spirits were necessarily connected to bodies was an inheritance from the third-century philosophy known as Neoplatonism. As Ralph Cudworth summed it up, the ancient philosophers generally conceived the soul in its pre-existent state to 'have had a lucid and ethereal body [...] as its chariot or vehicle; which being incorruptible, did always inseparably adhere to the soul, in its after-lapses and descents, into an aereal first, and then a terrestrial body'.[40] By ensuring that spirits were always *physically* located, the Platonic notion of the embodiment of spirits angelic or demonic in ethereal or aerial bodies ensured their role in natural philosophy, against those who, like Reginald Scot and Thomas Hobbes, had excluded them from the domain of 'the natural' or the perceptible, and against those who, like Spinoza, denied their existence.

The doctrine of the vehicles of the soul also provided Henry More with his key argument against the French philosopher René Descartes (1596–1650). Descartes had defined 'spirit' or 'soul' as an incorporeal substance that was unextended in space. For More, to deny the possibility of anything's being extended was to deny the possibility of its being *anywhere at all*; it was thus tantamount to a denial of its existence, 'it being the very essence of whatever is, to have parts or extension in some manner or other'. To take away all extension, he continued, 'is to reduce a thing onely to a Mathematical point, which is nothing else but pure Negation or Non-entity; and there being no *medium* betwixt *extended* and *not-extended*, no more then there is betwixt Entity and Non-entity, it is plain that if a thing *be* at all, it must be *extended*.'[41]

Thus, More's concept of the soul as extended in space did entail that the realm of spirit and soul could not be removed from natural philosophy. As *essentially* extended, spirit was inextricably located in the world of space and time. Yet, while the notion of the spirit's extension ensured that it was somewhere in the universe, it failed to allow for the possibility of its being at any *specific location*. The implication of its being *extended* was that it was, like God, everywhere at the one time – that is, coextensive with the universe – and that was clearly not desirable. The theory of the vehicles of the soul allowed More to avoid this outcome for it allowed for a *specific* location of spirit. The vehicle of the spirit, whether ethereal, aerial or terrestrial, limited the spirit's potentially infinite extension. The spirit was 'contained' in and by the vehicle, *its* shape and form, by virtue of its innate capacity to penetrate the body it possessed (its 'essential spissitude'), determined by the shape and form of its vehicle. Thus could a plurality of spirits – demonic, angelic and human – coexist within the same universe and be available to empirical observation.

The hopes of More and Glanvill to maintain the Devil within the domain of natural philosophy were, however, forlorn. Their proposal entailed the adoption of a Neoplatonism far too philosophically extravagant for some, too theologically unorthodox for most. Their efforts to ensure that spirits remained empirically observable through the Platonic doctrine of the vehicles of the soul was the last significant attempt to retain the demonic within the domain of natural philosophy.

## Disenchanting the World

The moments in the disenchantment of the world that we have examined so far in this chapter were to come together in the Dutch Protestant theologian Balthasar Bekker's (1634–98) four-volume work *De Betoverde Weereld* (*The World Bewitched*), published in Dutch between 1691 and 1693, and in a summarised form in English in 1700 as *The World Turn'd Upside Down*.[42] As Jonathan Israel notes, measured in terms of publications generated, the controversy created by *The World Bewitched* 'was assuredly the biggest controversy of

Early Enlightenment Europe, producing a stupendous 300 publications for and against'.[43]

Bekker was accused of being a follower of Hobbes and Spinoza, and thus of atheism, although he did not read *Leviathan* until after he had completed the first two volumes of *The World Bewitched*, and he took pains explicitly to reject Spinoza's identification of God and Nature.[44] Still, while he did not deny the existence of the Devil, he denied him any power at all: 'I banish from the Universe that abominable Creature to chain him in Hell, that *Jesus*, our Supream King, may more powerfully and securely reign.'[45] The Devil, he believed had been accorded so much power that monotheism had been replaced by dualism or ditheism, 'or such as believe two Gods'.[46]

According to Bekker, demonology was an illicit incursion by paganism into Judaism and early Christianity. Matters became worse in Medieval Catholicism, he claimed, ascribing to the Devil all the miracles that the pagans attributed to the demons, devils and inferior gods. Protestant Christianity, he believed, had improved matters somewhat, but much of the common Catholic opinion about demons remained.

In the four volumes of *The World Bewitched*, a comprehensive array of matters Satanic came under critical scrutiny – demonology, spirits, ghosts, apparitions, spectres, magic, witchcraft, divination, soothsaying, curses, charms, haunted houses and demonic possession. While not denying the existence of angels or demons, Bekker denied the central premise of all demonology, namely, that Satan, demons, angels or spirits could act within the domain of nature and have any influence upon the lives of men. The removal of demons from nature enabled Bekker to distinguish true faith from superstition, in the belief that true faith made everything in nature subject not to the caprices of the demonic, but to the providence of God. And it was a consequence of his Calvinist belief in the sovereignty of God that Bekker disallowed the activities of demons or other spirits in nature.

His scepticism was not only (ironically, perhaps) the result of his Calvinism. In his conviction that incorporeal beings could not interact within nature, he was a direct descendant of Reginald Scot, a copy of the 1606 Dutch edition of whose *The Discoverie of Witchcraft* was to be found in his library, and whose influence Bekker attested. But it was Reginald Scot now filtered through the body–soul dualism of Descartes. Bekker stayed firmly within the Cartesian dichotomy between 'thought' and 'extension'. Reason tells us that it is possible that spirits, angels and demons can exist independently of body. Man, on the other hand, is a compound of both. From our own experience, he argued, we know that without a body our souls cannot affect other souls or bodies. In short, embodiment is crucial for acting in the world. Consequently, a disembodied spirit cannot interact with anything apart from itself. Contact between demons and humans is, as a result, impossible, and demonology is based upon a false premise.

Still, committed as he was to the truth of Scripture, Bekker needed to make sense of those passages in Scripture that suggested the interaction of the demonic and the human. He did so by reading the relevant Scriptures, not as referring to the Satanic so much as to the evil inclinations within men. Thus, he saw no reason to read the story of the serpent in the Garden of Eden as involving the Devil tempting Eve and bringing about the fall, nor to read the story of the temptation of Christ as anything but a visionary experience. Similarly with the stories in the New Testament of the casting out of spirits from the possessed: 'so that the cure of *Daemonia*, was not properly an expulsion of Devils, but a miraculous cure of incurable Diseases.'[47] The Devil, he argued, has no knowledge, natural, civil or spiritual. 'I rest as yet', he wrote, 'upon the same foundation of Scripture and Reason, to prove the Empire of the Devil is but a Chimera, and that he has neither such a Power, nor such an Administration as is ordinarily ascribed to him.'[48] Neither reason, nor revelation, nor experiments 'give us cause,' Bekker concluded, 'to ascribe to wicked Spirits, all the Operations and effects that are generally supposed to proceed from the Devil or from Men, his Confederates'.[49] In sum, the world of Balthasar Bekker was the first to be completely and comprehensively disenchanted. It was only a short step from Balthasar Bekker to William Hogarth and the relegation of the Devil to the domain of credulity, superstition and fanaticism.

Thus, by the early part of the eighteenth century, as a being now disembodied, the Devil no longer had a literal existence within nature and outside of man. To Daniel Defoe (1660–1731), all the Devil's old emissaries – witches, warlocks, magicians, conjurers, astrologers – seemed to be out of work. Satan had merely a 'spiritual' or even only a metaphorical existence within the mind of man. As Defoe put in his *History of the Devil* in 1726,

No wonder then that he has chang'd Hands too, and that he has left of pawawing in these Parts of the World; that we don't find our Houses disturb'd as they used to be, and the Stools and Chairs walking about out of one Room into another, as formerly; that Children don't vomit crooked Pins and rusty stub Nails, as of old, the Air is not full of Noises, nor the Church-Yard full of Hobgoblins; Ghosts don't walk about in Winding-Sheets, and the good old scolding Wives visit and plague their Husbands after they are dead, as they did when they were alive. The Age is grown too wise to be agitated by these dull scare-crow Things which their Fore-Fathers were tickled with; *Satan* has been obliged to lay by his Puppet-shews and his Tumblers, those things are grown stale; his morrice-dancing Devils, his mountebanking and quacking won't do now.[50]

# Epilogue

For some forms of modern conservative Christianity, marginalised within modern Western 'secular' thought, the belief remains that the Devil is active and will remain so until finally consigned to an eternity in hell at the end of history. The existence of the Devil, and his capacity to act in history, nature and in human lives, remains for many Christians, both Protestant and Catholic, a satisfactory explanation of natural misfortune and human suffering, mitigated by the paradoxical conviction that, at the end of the day, Satan is carrying out God's will, *and* that, at the end of history, he will be defeated and eternally punished for doing so.

This was a story that had lost its central and paradigmatic role in Western intellectual life by the middle of the eighteenth century. By then, for an educated elite at least, the Devil had become a figure *of* history – one of the past rather than the present or the future – and not a participant *within* it. The biography of the Devil had become fiction, not fact. The history of the Devil had become merely the history of an idea. As a result, it became intellectually possible to write 'quasi-secular' histories of the Devil such as Daniel Defoe's *The History of the Devil* in 1726, or 'secular' histories of witchcraft like Francis Hutchinson's (1660–1739) *Historical Essay Concerning Witchcraft* in 1718 – histories that recognised the significance of 'the Devil' for Western intellectual history, while not endorsing any actual role in history that he was traditionally understood to have had.

Thus, it is only from that time on that it becomes possible to tell two stories. One is the traditional Christian story that sees Satan as a key player in cosmic history from creation, through fall and redemption, to Last Judgement, followed by the consignment of the Devil along with the damned to hell for eternity. The other is the secular history of how the idea of the Devil within that theological context has been historically created, constructed and reconstructed over a period that stretches from the 'birth' of that idea in the centuries before the Christian era, to its elaboration in the story of the fall and redemption in the early and medieval Church, to its central role in magic, witchcraft and possession in the classical demonology of the medieval and early modern periods, to its place in the history of Christian apocalypticism and finally to the 'death' of the idea in the first half of the eighteenth century.

Ironically, it was the rise of the secular history of the idea of the Devil that made possible his effective elimination from liberal Christian theologies, his relegation to theological irrelevance being the most importance consequence of the growth of liberal Protestantism from the beginning of the nineteenth century. As the Protestant theologian Friedrich Schleiermacher put it in his *The Christian Faith* (1830–1), 'The idea of the Devil, as developed among us, is so unstable that we cannot expect anyone to be convinced of its truth.'[1]

Ironically, too, the marginalisation of the orthodox Christian story of the Devil in the modern West has allowed for a proliferation of 'lives' of the Devil in popular culture. The Devil still exists within the Christian story, but also beyond it, an objectification of the oft-times incomprehensible evil that lies within us and around us, threatening to destroy us. The spell of disenchantment has been broken. The Devil now has new domains and new borders. Hedged in by the traditional Christian story on the one side, on the other by modern secular agnosticism, he 'prowls around, looking for someone to devour' yet again, both delectable and dangerous, fascinating and terrifying, familiar and alien, in a newly enchanted world.

As a secular history of the idea of the Devil, this work is one that can only have been thought and written after the middle of the eighteenth century. But it is also one that is sensitive to the depth and breadth of the Christian history of salvation within which Satan lived, moved and had his being. It is to be hoped that this new biography of the Devil will go some way to restoring him to the central place that he has occupied in Western intellectual history for the better part of the last two thousand years, and to the recognition of the pivotal role that he has had and still continues to play in the history of all of us.

# Notes

## Chapter One: The Devil is Born

1 Unless annotated KJV (King James Version), all Biblical quotations are from the New Revised Standard Version.

2 Unless otherwise indicated, all dates are AD.

3 Quotations from *Enoch* taken from George W.E. Nickelsburg, *A Commentary on the Book of 1 Enoch, Chapters 1–36; 81–108* (Minneapolis: Fortress Press, 2001).

4 Elaine Pagels, 'The Social History of Satan, the "Intimate Enemy": A Preliminary Sketch', *Harvard Theological Review* 84 (1991), p. 116.

5 James C. Vander Kam (trans.), *The Book of Jubilees* (Louvain: E. Peeters, 1989); James C. Vander Kam, *The Book of Jubilees* (Sheffield: Sheffield Academic Press, 2001).

6 'The First Apology of Justin', in Marcus Dods, George Reith and B.P. Pratten (trans.), *The Writings of Justin Martyr and Athenagoras*, Ante-Nicene Christian Library, Vol. 2 (Edinburgh: T. & T. Clark, 1879), ch. 5. Justin used the same word δαίμωνες here to refer to both gods and demons.

7 'The Second Apology of Justin', in ibid., ch. 5. In Justin's version, the demons are the offspring of the angels rather than the spirits of the dead giants.

8 Annette Yoshiko Reed, 'The Trickery of the Fallen Angels and the Demonic Mimesis of the Divine: Aetiology, Demonology, and Polemics in the Writings of Justin Martyr', *Journal of Early Christian Studies* 12 (2004), p. 171.

9 'A Plea for the Christians', in Dods, Reith and Patten (trans.), *The Writings of Justin Martyr and Athenagoras*, ch. 24.

10 Anthony Bowen and Peter Garnsey (trans.), *Lactantius: Divine Institutes* (Liverpool: Liverpool University Press, 2003), 2.14–17.

11 Ibid., 2.14.2–5.

12 Ibid., 2.14.12-13.

13 Ibid., 2.14.14.

14 Ibid., 2.14.5.

15 'The Extant Fragments of the Five Books of the Chronography of Julius Africanus', in Alexander Roberts and James Donaldson (eds), *Fathers of the Third Century, Ante-Nicene Fathers*, Vol. 6 (Peabody, MA: Hendrickson Publishers, 2004), ch. 2.

16 Augustine, *The City of God*, in Philip Schaff (ed.), *St. Augustine's City of God and Christian Doctrine* (Buffalo: The Christian Literature Co., 1887), 15.22.

17 Augustine, *The City of God*, 15.23.

18 Ibid.

19 'Satan', in Karel Van der Toorn, Bob Becking and Pieter W. Van der Horst, *Dictionary of Deities and Demons in the Bible* (Leiden: Brill, 1995); and Stefan Schreiber, 'The Great Opponent: The Devil in Early Jewish and Formative Christian Literature', in Friedrich V. Reiterer et al. (eds), *The Concept of Celestial Beings: Origins, Development and Reception* (Berlin: Walter de Gruyter, 2007), pp. 437–57.

20 Pagels, 'The Social History of Satan', p. 114.

21 Maxwell J. Davidson, *Angels at Qumran: A Comparative Study of 1 Enoch 1–36, 72–108 and Sectarian Writings from Qumran* (Sheffield: Sheffield Academic Press, 1992).

22 Florentino Garcia Martinez, *The Dead Sea Scrolls Translated: The Qumran Texts in English* (Leiden: Brill, 1994); and Devorah Dimant, 'Between Qumran Sectarian and Non-Sectarian Texts: The Case of Belial and Mastema', in A.D. Roitman, L.H. Schiffman and S. Tzoref (eds), *The Dead Sea Scrolls and Contemporary Culture* (Leiden: Brill, 2011), pp. 235–56.

23 Schreiber, 'The Great Opponent', p. 440. On an earlier dating for Chronicles, and therefore concerns about 'Satan' being a personal name, see 'Satan', in Van der Toorn, Becking and Van der Horst, *Dictionary of Deities and Demons in the Bible*.

24 'Devil', in Van der Toorn, Becking and Van der Horst, *Dictionary of Deities and Demons in the Bible*. I am especially indebted to Van der Toorn et al. for this discussion.

25 See also Matthew 8.28–34 and Luke 8.26–39.

26 On Jesus as an exorcist, Graham H. Twelftree, *Jesus the Exorcist: A Contribution to the Study of the Historical Jesus* (Tübingen: J.C.B. Mohr (Paul Siebeck), 1993).

27 See also Mark 1.12–13 and Luke 4.1–13.

28 See also Mark 3.22–7 and Luke 11.14–23.

29 The traditional reading of this verse is that the Devil put it then into the heart of Judas that he should betray Jesus. I follow here the reading of Henry Ansgar Kelly, *Satan: A Biography* (Cambridge: Cambridge University Press, 2006), p. 109.

## Chapter Two: The Fall of the Devil

1 Adam is not an important figure in the Hebrew Bible. Indeed, apart from the story of the fall of Adam and Eve in the book of Genesis, there is only one unambiguous reference to Adam in the Hebrew Bible (1 Chronicles 1.1).

2 Jacob Neusner, *Genesis Rabbah: The Judaic Commentary to the Book of Genesis: A new American Translation* (Atlanta, GA: Scholars Press, 1985).

3 Philip C. Almond, *Adam and Eve in Seventeenth-Century Thought* (Cambridge: Cambridge University Press, 1999), p. 18.

4 Almond, *Adam and Eve in Seventeenth-Century Thought*, ch. 3.
5 On Justin, see Jeffrey Burton Russell, *Satan: The Early Christian Tradition* (Ithaca, NY, and London: Cornell University Press, 1987), pp. 63–72; and Robert Alan King, *Justin Martyr on Angels, Demons, and the Devil* (Casa Grande, AZ: King and Associates, 2011). For Justin's writings, see Dods, Reith and Pratten (trans.), *The Writings of Justin Martyr and Athenagoras*.
6 'Dialogue with Trypho', 79, in Dods, Reith and Pratten (trans.), *The Writings of Justin Martyr and Athenagoras*.
7 Ibid., 124.
8 Ibid.
9 'The Second Apology of Justin,' 7, in Dods, Reith and Pratten (trans.), *The Writings of Justin Martyr and Athenagoras*.
10 'The First Apology of Justin', 28, in Dods, Reith and Pratten (trans.), *The Writings of Justin Martyr and Athenagoras*.
11 'Tatian's Address to the Greeks', 7, in B.P. Pratten, Marcus Dods and Thomas Smith (trans.), *The Writings of Tatian and Theophilus; and The Clementine Recognitions*, Ante-Nicene Christian Library, Vol. 3 (Edinburgh: T. & T. Clark, 1883).
12 Ibid., 16.
13 Ibid., 7.
14 Ibid., 12.
15 Ibid., 15.
16 'The Three Books of Theophilus of Antioch to Autolycus', 2.28, in Pratten, Dods and Smith (trans.), *The Writings of Tatian and Theophilus*. The Greek for 'dragon' (δράκων) allows for a play on the word for 'revolting' (ἀποδεδρακέναι, *apodedrakenai*).
17 'Irenaeus against Heresies', in Alexander Roberts and W.H. Rambaut (trans.), *The Writings of Irenaeus, Vol. 2*, Ante-Nicene Christian Library, Vol. 9 (Edinburgh: T. & T. Clark, 1883).
18 'Of Patience', in V. Thelwall (trans.), *The Writings of Quintus Sept. Flor. Tertullianus, Vol. 1*, Ante-Nicene Christian Library, Vol. 11 (Edinburgh: T. & T. Clark, 1882).
19 Peter Holmes (trans.), *The Five Books of Quintus Sept. Flor. Tertullianus against Marcion*, Ante-Nicene Christian Library, Vol. 7 (Edinburgh: T. & T. Clark, 1878), 2.10.
20 Ibid.
21 'On the Spectacles', 8, in Thelwall (trans.), *The Writings of Quintus Sept. Flor. Tertullianus, Vol. 1*.
22 Holmes (trans.), *The Five Books of Quintus Sept. Flor. Tertullianus against Marcion*, 2.10.
23 'Apology', 22, in Thelwall (trans.), *The Writings of Quintus Sept. Flor. Tertullianus, Vol. 1*.
24 Ibid.
25 Tertullian, 'The Prescription against Heretics', ch. 40, in Alexander

Roberts and James Donaldson (eds), *Latin Christianity: Its Founder, Tertullian*, Ante-Nicene Fathers, Vol. 3 (Grand Rapids, MI: Eerdmans, 1980). See also Elaine Pagels, *The Origin of Satan* (New York: Random House, 1995), ch. 6.

26 For a comparative synopsis of these versions, see Gary A. Anderson and Michael E. Stone, *A Synopsis of the Books of Adam and Eve* (Atlanta, GA: Scholars Press, 1994). See also Gary Anderson, Michael Stone and Johannes Tromp (eds), *Literature on Adam and Eve: Collected Essays* (Leiden: Brill, 2000).

27 Brian Murdoch, *The Apocryphal Adam and Eve in Medieval Europe* (Oxford: Oxford University Press, 2009).

28 'Life of Adam and Eve', 13–16, in James H. Charlesworth, *The Old Testament Pseudepigrapha, Vol. 2* (New York: Doubleday, 1985).

29 'The Apocalypse of Moses', 16, in Charlesworth, *The Old Testament Pseudepigrapha, Vol. 2*.

30 G.W. Butterworth (trans.), *Origen: On First Principles* (Gloucester, MA: Peter Smith, 1973), 1.5.5. Except for some passages from the original Greek, we know this work mostly through the Latin translation of Rufinus of Aquileia under the title *De Principiis*.

31 Origen, *Homilies*, 12.4.4, in Thomas P. Scheck (trans.), *Homilies on Numbers: Origen* (Downers Grove, IL: IVP Academic, 2009).

32 Augustine, *City of God*, 11.15, in Schaff (ed.), *St. Augustine's City of God and Christian Doctrine*.

33 Butterworth (trans.), *Origen: On First Principles*, 1.8.1.

34 Ibid.

35 Ibid., 2.9.6.

36 Henry Chadwick (trans.), *Origen: Contra Celsum* (Cambridge: Cambridge University Press, 1953), 7.35.

37 Ibid., 4.66. See also Russell, *Satan: The Early Christian Tradition*, p. 135.

38 In this sense, he is the binary opposite of Christ who, though having the freedom to choose evil, never does so as the result of his desire to do good.

39 Henri Crouzel, *Origen* (Edinburgh: T. & T. Clark, 1989), p. 263. See also Lisa R. Holliday, 'Will Satan be Saved? Reconsidering Origen's Theory of Volition in *Peri Archon*', *Vigiliae Christianae* 63 (2009), pp. 1–23.

40 Augustine, *The City of God*, 21.17, in Schaff (ed.), *St. Augustine's City of God and Christian Doctrine*.

41 Quoted by Crouzel, *Origen*, p. 267.

42 George Rust, *A Letter of Resolution Concerning Origen and the Chief of his Opinions* (London, 1661), p. 131. On Origenism in seventeenth-century England, see Philip C. Almond, *Heaven and Hell in Enlightenment England* (Cambridge: Cambridge University Press, 1994), ch. 1. See also. C.A. Patrides, 'The Salvation of Satan', *Journal of the History of Ideas* 28 (1967), pp. 467–78.

43 Richard Montagu, *The Acts and Monuments of the Church before Christ Incarnate* (London, 1642), p. 7.

44 I ignore here the possibility that God could have created people such that they always freely chose to do good (which is not as logically incoherent as it may first appear).

## Chapter Three: Hell's Angel

1 Frances M. Young, 'Insight or Incoherence? The Greek Fathers on God and Evil', *Journal of Ecclesiastical History* 24 (1973), pp. 113–14.

2 Irenaeus, *Against Heresies*, 3.23.1, in Philip Schaff (ed.), *Ante-Nicene Fathers*, Vol. 1 (Grand Rapids, MI: Christian Classics Ethereal Library, 1993). On Irenaeus, see Gustaf Aulén, *Christus Victor: An Historical Study of the Three Main Types of the Idea of Atonement* (Eugene, OR: Wipf & Stock, 2003).

3 Irenaeus, *Against Heresies*, 5.1.1.

4 Quoted by Hastings Rashdall, *The Idea of Atonement in Christian Theology* (London: Macmillan, 1919), p. 259.

5 Gregory of Nyssa, *The Great Catechism*, 24, in Philip Schaff (ed.), *A Select Library of the Nicene and Post-Nicene Fathers*, Series 2, Vol. 5 (Grand Rapids, MI: Eerdmans, 2005).

6 Ibid., 25.

7 Ibid., 22.

8 Ibid., 23.

9 J.N.D. Kelly, *Early Christian Doctrines* (London: A. & C. Black, 1985), p. 384.

10 Augustine, *On the Holy Trinity*, 4.13, in Philip Schaff (ed.), *A Select Library of the Nicene and Post-Nicene Fathers*, Vol. 3 (Grand Rapids, MI: Eerdmans, 2005). See also C.W. Marx, *The Devil's Rights and the Redemption in the Literature of Medieval England* (Cambridge: D.S. Brewer, 1995).

11 Augustine, *Sermon 263*, in John E. Rotelle (ed.), *The Works of Saint Augustine: A Translation for the 21st Century* (Charlottesville, VA: InteLex Corporation, 2001).

12 James Bliss (trans.), *Morals on the Book of Job by St. Gregory the Great, Translated with Notes and Indices. In Three Volumes* (Oxford and London: John Henry Parker and J.G.F. and J. Rivington, 1844), 32.23.47. See also Carole Straw, *Gregory the Great: Perfection in Imperfection* (Berkeley, CA: University of California Press, c.1988).

13 Bliss (trans.), *Morals on the Book of Job*, 1.36.52.

14 Ibid., 23.30.58.

15 Ibid., 4.3.8.

16 Ibid., 32.24.51.

17 Gregory the Great, 'Homily 25', in Santha Bhattacharji, *Reading the Gospels with Gregory the Great: Homilies on the Gospels 21–26* (Petersham, MA: St Bede's Publications, 2001).

18 Bliss (trans.), *Morals on the Book of Job*, 17.30.46.

19 Ibid., 4.10.16.

20 Ibid., 23.20.37.

21 Ibid., 18.41.67.

22 Ibid., 32.24.50.

23 Odo John Zimmerman (trans.), *Saint Gregory the Great: Dialogues* (Washington, DC: Catholic University of America, 1959), 4.59. Gregory does believe, however, that there will be a purgatorial fire after death for minor sins.

24 J.A. MacCulloch, *The Harrowing of Hell: A Comparative Study of an Early Christian Doctrine* (Edinburgh: T. & T. Clark, 1930).

25 Ralph V. Turner, 'Descendit ad Inferos: Medieval Views on Christ's Descent into Hell and the Salvation of the Ancient Just', *Journal of the History of Ideas* 27 (1966), pp. 173–94.

26 The dating of *The Gospel of Nicodemus*, from the first century onwards, has been historically much disputed. See G.C. O'Ceallaigh, 'Dating the Commentaries of Nicodemus', *Harvard Theological Review* 56 (1963), pp. 21–58.

27 Montague R. James, *The Apocryphal New Testament* (Oxford: Clarendon, 1953), p. 95.

28 *The Gospel of Nicodemus*, Greek, 20.1, in ibid.

29 Ibid., Greek, 20.3.

30 Ibid.

31 Ibid., Greek, 22.2.

32 Ibid., Greek, 23.

33 *The Gospel of Nicodemus*, Latin A, 20.3, in James, *The Apocryphal New Testament*.

34 *The Gospel of Nicodemus*, Latin B, 24, in ibid.

35 Jeffrey A. Trumbower, *Rescue for the Dead: The Posthumous Salvation of Non-Christians in Early Christianity* (Oxford: Oxford University Press, 2001), ch. 5.

36 Jacques Le Goff, *The Birth of Purgatory* (Chicago: University of Chicago Press, 1986).

37 Quoted in ibid., pp. 251–2.

38 Ibid., p. 257.

39 Fathers of the English Dominican Province (trans.), *St. Thomas Aquinas: Summa Theologica* (New York: Benziger Bros, 1947), suppl., appendix 1.2.3 (subsequently referred to as *S.T.*).

40 F.S. Ellis (ed.), *The Golden Legend or Lives of the Saints Compiled by Jacobus de Voragine, Archbishop of Genoa* (Edinburgh: Edinburgh University Press, 1900), 6.61.

41 Alex Bugnolo (trans.), *Master Peter Lombard's Book of Sentences* (2006), 2.6.2. Available at http://www.franciscan-archive.org/lombardus/index.html (accessed 20 November 2013).

42 Ibid., 2.6.3.

43 Bugnolo (trans.), *Master Peter Lombard's Book of Sentences*, 2.6.4.

44 Ibid., 2.6.5.

45 Ibid.

46 Ibid., 2.6.6.

47 Alex Bugnolo (trans.), *St. Bonaventure's Commentaries on the Four Books of Sentences of Master Peter Lombard* (2006–7), 2.6.2.1. Available at http://www.franciscan-archive.org/bonaventura/sent.html (accessed 20 November 2013).

48 Ibid.

49 Ibid.

50 *S.T.* 1.63.2.

51 Ibid., 1.63.5.

52 Ibid., 1.64.2. Earlier I argued that Origen's position is in fact quite close to that of Aquinas.

53 Ibid., 1.114.1.

54 Jeffrey Burton Russell, *Lucifer: The Devil in the Middle Ages* (Ithaca, NY, and London: Cornell University Press, 1984), p. 203. I am indebted to Russell for his account of Aquinas and the Devil.

55 *S.T.* 1.114.3.

56 Ibid., 3.8.7.

57 Ibid., 1.64.4.

58 Ibid., 1.64.4.

59 Ibid., suppl. 89.4.

60 Ibid., 3.49.2. The passage is from Augustine's *De Trinitate*, 13.14.

61 Ibid., 3.49.3. See also Anselm, 'Why God Became Man', in Eugene R. Fairweather (ed. and trans.), *A Scholastic Miscellany: Anselm to Ockham* (London: SCM Press, 1956).

62 *S.T.* 3.49.2.

63 Quoted by Alain Boureau, *Satan the Heretic: The Birth of Demonology in the Mediaeval West* (Chicago and London: Chicago University Press, 2006), p. 25.

## Chapter Four: The Devil Rides Out

1 Quoted by Boureau, *Satan the Heretic*, p. 17.

2 Ibid., p. 27.

3 Lynn Thorndike, *A History of Magic and Experimental Science* (New York: Columbia University Press, 1923–58), 3.18.

4 *The Secret Supper*, in Walter P. Wakefield and Austin P. Evans, *Heresies of the High Middle Ages: Selected Sources Translated and Annotated* (New York and London: Columbia University Press, 1969), p. 460.

5 Ibid.

6 Ibid., 7.

7 Ibid., 12.

8 *The Book of the Two Principles*, 1.8, in Wakefield and Evans, *Heresies of the High Middle Ages*.

9 Ibid., 5.4.

10 *The Summa of Rainerius Sacconi*, 21, in Wakefield and Evans, *Heresies of the High Middle Ages*.

11 *Summa against the Cathars and Waldensians*, 1, in Wakefield and Evans, *Heresies of the High Middle Ages*.

12 Ibid., 22.

13 Ibid., 21.

14 Ibid., 22.

15 David Keck, *Angels and Angelology in the Middle Ages* (Oxford: Oxford University Press, 1998). On the recognition of the pseudonymous origin of these works, see Karlfried Froehlich, 'Pseudo-Dionysius and the Reformation of the Sixteenth Century', in Colm Luibheid (trans.), *Pseudo-Dionysius: The Complete Works* (New York: Paulist Press, 1987), pp. 33–46.

16 Brian Davies (ed.) and Richard Regan (trans.), *The De Malo of Thomas Aquinas* (Oxford: Oxford University Press, 2001).

17 See Chapter Five, 'Devilish Bodies'.

18 Davies and Regan (trans.), *The De Malo of Thomas Aquinas*, 16.9.

19 Ibid.

20 Ibid. See also Augustine, *The Divination of Demons*, 3, in Roy Deferrari (ed.), *Saint Augustine: Treatises on Marriage and Other Subjects* (New York: Fathers of the Church, 1955).

21 Richard Kieckhefer, *Magic in the Middle Ages* (Cambridge: Cambridge University Press, 2000), chs 4, 6. David Pingree, 'The Diffusion of Arabic Magical Texts in Western Europe', in Charles S.F. Burnett et al. (eds), *La Diffusione delle Scienze Islamiche nel Medioevo Europeo* (Rome: Accademia Nazionale dei Lincei, 1987), pp. 57–102.

22 Technically, 'necromancy' involved the conjuring of the dead, but since the dead were believed to be spirits in disguise, it came to mean the invoking of spirits in general.

23 Kieckhefer, *Magic in the Middle Ages*, ch. 7. Benedek Láng, *Unlocked Books: Manuscripts of Learned Magic in the Medieval Libraries of Central Europe* (University Park, PA: The Pennsylvania State University Press, 2008) has developed a fivefold classification – natural, image, ritual (daemonic), divination and alchemy.

24 On the history of the legends about Simon Magus, see Alberto Ferreiro, 'Simon Magus: The Patristic-Medieval Traditions and Historiography', *Apocrypha* 7 (1996), pp. 147–65.

25 M.B. Riddle (trans.), *Acts of the Apostles Peter and Paul*, in Alexander Roberts and James Donaldson (eds), *The Ante-Nicene Fathers*, Vol. 8 (Grand Rapids: William B. Eerdmans, 1951), p. 484.

26 Ibid.

27 Ibid.

28 Riddle (trans.), *Acts of the Apostles Peter and Paul.*

29 Augustine, *On Christian Doctrine*, 2.23.36, in Schaff (ed.), *St. Augustine's City of God and Christian Doctrine.*

30 Augustine, *City of God*, 10.9, in Schaff (ed.), *St. Augustine's City of God and Christian Doctrine.*

31 Augustine, *On Christian Doctrine*, 2.20–3, in Schaff (ed.), *St. Augustine's City of God and Christian Doctrine.*

32 Stephen A. Barney et al., *The* Etymologies *of Isidore of Seville* (Cambridge: Cambridge University Press, 2006), p. 3.

33 William E. Klingshirn, 'Isidore of Seville's Taxonomy of Magicians and Diviners', *Traditio* 58 (2006), p. 59.

34 Barney et al., *The* Etymologies *of Isidore of Seville*, 8.9.3.

35 Ibid., 8.9.31.

36 The nine were necromancy, geomancy, hydromancy, aeromancy, pyromancy (belonging to hell, earth, water, air and fire), soothsaying, augury, horoscopy and fortune-telling.

37 Jerome Taylor (trans.), *The* Didascalicon *of Hugh of St. Victor* (New York: Columbia University Press, 1991), p. 155.

38 Ibid., p. 154.

39 Alighieri Dante, *Divine Comedy*, *Inferno*, 20.116–17. Translated by Richard Kay, 'The Spare Ribs of Dante's Michael Scot', *Dante Studies* 103 (1985), p. 2. I am especially indebted to Kay for this discussion of Scot.

40 On Michael Scot, see Thorndike, *A History of Magic and Experimental Science*, 2.307–37; and Charles Homer Haskins, *Studies in the History of Mediaeval Science* (New York: Frederick Ungar Publishing, 1960), pp. 272–98.

41 Kay, 'The Spare Ribs of Dante's Michael Scot', pp. 4–7.

42 Thorndike, *A History of Magic and Experimental Science*, 2.319.

43 As paraphrased in Lynn Thorndike, *Michael Scot* (London: Nelson, 1965), p. 78. See also Thorndike, *A History of Magic and Experimental Science*, 2.324.

44 Catherine Rider, *Magic and Impotence in the Middle Ages* (Oxford: Oxford University Press, 2006), p. 77.

45 Jean-Pierre Brach, 'Magic IV', in Wouter J. Hanegraaff (ed.), *Dictionary of Gnosis and Western Esotericism* (Leiden: Brill, 2006), p. 732. On William of Auvergne, see Steven P. Marrone, 'William of Auvergne on Magic in Natural Philosophy and Theology', in Jan Aertsen and Andreas Speer (eds), 'Was ist Philosophie im Mittelalter', *Miscellania Medievalia* 26 (1998), pp. 741–8.

46 Thorndike, *A History of Magic and Experimental Science*, 2.338–71.

47 'Proem', *Speculum Astronomiae*, in Paola Zambelli, *The* Speculum Astronomiae *and its Enigma* (Dordrecht: Kluwer Academic, 1992).

48 *Speculum Astronomiae*, ch. 11, in Zambelli, *The* Speculum Astronomiae *and its Enigma.*

49 *Speculum Astronomiae*, ch. 11.

50 Ibid.

51 Ibid., ch. 17.

52 Richard C. Dales (trans.), *The* Opus Maius *of Roger Bacon*, in Richard C. Dales, *The Scientific Achievements of the Middle Ages* (Philadelphia: University of Pennsylvania Press, 1973), p. 163.

53 Claire Fanger, 'Things Done Wisely by a Wise Enchanter: Negotiating the Power of Words in the Thirteenth Century', *Esoterica* 1 (1999), pp. 97–132. I am indebted to Fanger for her analysis of Bacon's views on magic.

54 Jeremiah Hackett, 'Roger Bacon on Astronomy-Astrology: The Sources of the *Scientia Experimentalis*,' in Jeremiah Hackett (ed.), *Roger Bacon and the Sciences: Commemorative Essays* (Leiden: Brill, 1997), pp. 175–98; and William R. Newman, 'An Overview of Roger Bacon's Alchemy', in Jeremiah Hackett (ed.), *Roger Bacon and the Sciences: Commemorative Essays*, pp. 317–36.

55 Robert Belle Burke (trans.), *The Opus Maius of Roger Bacon* (Philadelphia: University of Pennsylvania Press, 1928), 1.113.

56 R.A. Markus, 'Augustine on Magic: A Neglected Semiotic Theory', *Revue des Études Augustiniennes* 40 (1994), pp. 375–88.

57 Fanger, 'Things Done Wisely by a Wise Enchanter', p. 99.

58 Claire Fanger (trans.), *Opus Tertium*, in Fanger, 'Things Done Wisely by a Wise Enchanter', p. 111.

59 Dales (trans.), *The* Opus Maius *of Roger Bacon*, in Dales, *The Scientific Achievements of the Middle Ages*, pp. 162–3.

60 Fanger (trans.), *Opus Maius*, in Fanger, 'Things Done Wisely by a Wise Enchanter', pp. 117–18.

61 Láng, *Unlocked Books*; and Frank Klaasen, 'English Manuscripts of Magic, 1300–1500: A Preliminary Survey', in Claire Fanger (ed.), *Conjuring Spirits: Texts and Traditions of Medieval Ritual Magic* (Stroud: Sutton Press, 1998), pp. 3–31.

62 Richard Kieckhefer, *Forbidden Rites: A Necromancer's Manual of the Fifteenth Century* (University Park, PA: Pennsylvania State University Press, 1998), p. 26. See also Fanger (ed.), *Conjuring Spirits*, p. viii. Fanger includes both demonic and angelic magic under the rubric 'ritual magic'.

63 Kieckhefer, *Forbidden Rites*. This work contains both an analysis of the text and the Latin text.

64 There are various forms of scrying: catoptromancy (divination by means of a mirror), crystallomancy (by a crystal), cyclicomancy or lecanomancy (by a cup or basin filled with liquid), onychomancy (by an anointed fingernail), hydromancy (by water in a natural body). Kieckhefer, *Forbidden Rites*, p. 97.

65 Ibid., chs 2–5.

66 Ibid., p. 128.

67 'Determination made by the Faculty of Theology at Paris in the Year of our Lord 1398 Regarding Certain Newly Arisen Superstitions', in Brian P. Levack (ed.), *The Witchcraft Sourcebook* (New York: Routledge, 2004), p. 49.

68 Kieckhefer, *Forbidden Rites*, pp. 165–6.

69 Ibid., p. 155.

70 'Determination made by the Faculty of Theology at Paris in the Year of our Lord 1398 Regarding Certain Newly Arisen Superstitions,' in Levack (ed.), *The Witchcraft Sourcebook*, p. 50.

71 Ibid.

72 Robert Mathiesen, 'A Thirteenth-Century Ritual to Attain the Beatific Vision from the *Sworn Book* of Honorius of Thebes', in Fanger (ed.), *Conjuring Spirits*, pp. 143–62. Mathiesen dates this work to the first half of the thirteenth century. I follow Kieckhefer in dating it a century later. See Richard Kieckhefer, 'The Devil's Contemplatives: The *Liber Iuratus*, the *Liber Visionum* and Christian Appropriation of Jewish Occultism', in Fanger (ed.), *Conjuring Spirits*, pp. 250–65; and Katelyn Mesler, 'The *Liber Iuratus Honorii* and the Christian Reception of Angel Magic', in Claire Fanger (ed.), *Invoking Angels: Theurgic Ideas and Practices, Thirteenth to Sixteenth Centuries* (University Park, PA: Pennsylvania State University Press, 2012), pp. 113–50.

73 Daniel J. Driscoll (ed.), *The Sworn Book of Honourius the Magician, As Composed by Honourius through Counsel with the Angel Hocroel* (Gillette, New Jersey: Heptangle Press, 1977), p. 67, quoted by Mathiesen, 'A Thirteenth-Century Ritual', p. 155.

74 For a possible connection to Jewish mysticism, see Kieckhefer, 'The Devil's Contemplatives', pp. 250–65.

75 Driscoll (ed.), *The Sworn Book of Honourius the Magician*, p. 7, quoted by Mathiesen, 'A Thirteenth-Century Ritual', p. 151.

76 Ibid.

77 Ibid.

78 Ibid.

79 Kieckhefer, 'The Devil's Contemplatives', pp. 253–4.

80 Driscoll (ed.), *The Sworn Book of Honourius the Magician*, p. 1, quoted by Mathiesen, 'A Thirteenth-Century Ritual', pp. 147–8 (with variations in square brackets by Mathiesen). In spite of the concerns of Honorius, six manuscripts of the *Sacred or Sworn Book* were to survive the ecclesiastical and scholarly attacks upon it, five in Latin, one of which from the fourteenth century came into the possession of the Elizabethan Magus John Dee (whence it passed into the hands of the dramatist Ben Jonson) and another of which was a sixteenth-century partially English version.

81 Claire Fanger and Nicholas Watson (trans.), 'The Prologue to the *Liber Visionum* of John of Morigny', 1, in Claire Fanger and Nicholas Watson (eds), 'John of Morigny, Prologue to *Liber Visionum* (c.1304–1318),

Translated, Edited, and Introduced', *Esoterica* 3 (2001), pp. 108–217. I am especially indebted to Fanger and Watson for this account.

82 For a blending of natural, angelic and demonic magic in Elizabethan England, see Frank Klaasen, 'Ritual Invocation and Early Modern Science: The Skrying Experiments of Humphrey Gilbert', in Fanger (ed.), *Invoking Angels*, pp. 341–66.

## Chapter Five: Devilish Bodies

1 Alan Charles Kors and Edward Peters, *Witchcraft in Europe, 400–1700: A Documentary History* (Philadelphia: University of Pennsylvania Press, 2001), p. 154.

2 Peter Brown, *Religion and Society in the Age of Augustine* (London: Faber and Faber, 1972), p. 132. See also p. 137.

3 Michael D. Bailey, 'From Sorcery to Witchcraft: Clerical Conceptions of Magic in the Later Middle Ages', *Speculum* 76 (2001), pp. 960–90. I am especially indebted to Bailey for this discussion.

4 Wakefield and Evans, *Heresies of the High Middle Ages*, pp. 444–5.

5 Ibid., p. 444.

6 Ibid., pp. 154–5.

7 G.B. Harrison (ed.), *King James the First: Daemonologie* (London: John Lane, 1924), p. 9.

8 Norman Cohn, *Europe's Inner Demons* (St Albans: Paladin, 1976).

9 Michael D. Bailey and Edward Peters, 'A Sabbat of Demonologists: Basel, 1431–1440', *The Historian* 65 (2003), pp. 1375–95.

10 *Errores Gazariorum*, in Kors and Peters, *Witchcraft in Europe, 400–1700*, p. 161.

11 Ibid., p. 160.

12 Ibid., p. 161.

13 Wakefield and Evans, *Heresies of the High Middle Ages*, pp. 78–9.

14 Claude Tholosan, *Ut Magorum et Maleficiorum Errores …*, in Kors and Peters, *Witchcraft in Europe, 400–1700*, p. 164.

15 Ibid., p. 165.

16 Michael D. Bailey, *Battling Demons: Witchcraft, Heresy, and Reform in the Late Middle Ages* (University Park, PA: Pennsylvania State University Press, 2003); and Michael D. Bailey, 'The Medieval Concept of the Witches' Sabbath', *Exemplaria* 8 (1996), pp. 420–39.

17 Michael D. Bailey, 'The Feminization of Magic and the Emerging Idea of the Female Witch in the Late Middle Ages', *Essays in Medieval Studies* 19 (2002), p. 123.

18 Henry Charles Lea, *Materials toward a History of Witchcraft* (New York: Thomas Yoselhoff, 1957), 1.268. See also Bailey, *Battling Demons*, ch. 2.

19 John Stearne, *The Discoverie of Witchcraft* (London, 1648), p. 15.

20 Alexander Roberts, *A Treatise of Witchcraft* (London, 1616), p. 43.

21 Christopher S. Mackay (ed. and trans.), *Malleus Maleficarum* (Cambridge: Cambridge University Press, 2006), 1.6.45A.

22 Mackay (ed. and trans.), *Malleus Maleficarum*, 2.1.4.3B–C.
23 Walter Stephens, *Demon Lovers: Witchcraft, Sex, and the Crisis of Belief* (Chicago: University of Chicago Press, 2002), p. 42.
24 Quoted by ibid., p. 21. For the original, see Lea, *Materials toward a History of Witchcraft*, 1.276.
25 Quoted by Stephens, *Demon Lovers*, p. 97. On *Strix*, see Peter Burke, 'Witchcraft and Magic in Renaissance Italy: Gianfrancesco Pico and his *Strix*', in Sydney Anglo (ed.), *The Damned Art: Essays in the Literature of Witchcraft* (London: Routledge & Kegan Paul, 1977), pp. 32–52.
26 Montague Summers (ed.), *An Examen of Witches (Discours Des Sorciers) by Henri Boguet* (Warrington: Portrayer Publishers, 2002), pp. 31–2.
27 Susanna Burghartz, 'The Equation of Women and Witches: A Case Study of Witchcraft Trials in Lucerne and Lausanne in the Fifteenth and Sixteenth Centuries', in Richard J. Evans (ed.), *The German Underworld: Deviants and Outcasts in German History* (London: Routledge, 1988), pp. 57–74; and Lara Apps and Andrew Gow, *Male Witches in Early Modern Europe* (Manchester: Manchester University Press, 2003).
28 Mackay (ed. and trans.), *Malleus Maleficarum*, 2.16.147A.
29 Ibid., 1A–1B.
30 Dyan Elliott, *Fallen Bodies: Pollution, Sexuality, and Demonology in the Middle Ages* (Pennsylvania: University of Pennsylvania Press, 1999), p. 153.
31 *S.T.* 2.2.154.11.
32 Mackay (ed. and trans.), *Malleus Maleficarum*, 1.6.45A.
33 Hans Peter Broedel, *The* Malleus Maleficarum *and the Construction of Witchcraft: Theology and Popular Belief* (Manchester: Manchester University Press, 2003), p. 182.
34 William of Auvergne, *De Universo*, 2.3.25, cited in Mackay (ed. and trans.), *Malleus Maleficarum*, 1.6.45A, n.343.
35 Lea, *Materials toward a History of Witchcraft*, 1.161.
36 Tamar Herzig, 'The Demons' Reaction to Sodomy: Witchcraft and Homosexuality in Gianfrancesco Pico della Mirandola's "Strix"', *Sixteenth Century Journal* 34 (2003), p. 62.
37 Summers (ed.), *An Examen of Witches*, p. 32.
38 Mackay (ed. and trans.), *Malleus Maleficarum*, 1.3.24B.
39 Harriet Stone and Gerhild Scholz Williams (trans.), *On the Inconstancy of Witches: Pierre de Lancres* Tableau de l'Inconstance des Mauvais Anges et Demons *(1612)* (Tempe, AZ: Arizona Center for Medieval and Renaissance Studies with Brepols, 2006), 3.5.4.
40 Ibid., 3.5.5.
41 Ibid., 3.4.4.
42 Ibid.

43 Stone and Williams (trans.), *On the Inconstancy of Witches*, 3.4.4.

44 Ibid., 3.5.8.

45 Ibid., 3.5.1.

46 Porphyry, *De Abstinentia*, 2.39, cited in Gregory A. Smith, 'How Thin is a Demon?', *Journal of Early Christian Studies* 16 (2008), p. 486. I am particularly indebted to Smith for this discussion of early Christian notions of embodied demons.

47 Butterworth (trans.), *Origen: On First Principles*, preface, 8; and Smith, 'How Thin is a Demon?', p. 488.

48 *Life of St. Anthony*, 9, in Roy J. Deferrari (ed.), *Early Christian Biographies* (Washington, DC: Catholic University of America Press, 1952), p. 144. Traditionally, the work is ascribed to Athanasius (*c*.296–373). The notion of the Devil as a black man or an Ethiopian weaves through the history of the Devil. See David Brakke, 'Ethiopian Demons: Male Sexuality, the Black-skinned Other, and the Monastic Self', *Journal of the History of Sexuality* 10 (2001), pp. 501–35.

49 *Life of St. Anthony*, 28, in Deferrari (ed.), *Early Christian Biographies*, p. 161.

50 Ibid., 40, p. 171.

51 Ibid., 40, p. 172.

52 Ibid., 31, p. 164.

53 Derwas J. Chitty (trans.), *The Letters of St Antony the Great* (Fairacres: SLG Press, 1975), letter 6, p. 19. My italics.

54 Smith, 'How Thin is a Demon?', p. 509.

55 Ibid., p. 512. And see Robert E. Sinkewicz, *Evagrius of Pontus: The Greek Ascetic Corpus* (Oxford: Oxford University Press, 2003), pp. 200–1. This work also contains Evagrius' *On the Eight Thoughts*, the seventh of which was vainglory. When it was translated by John Cassian into Latin, Pope Gregory the Great refined the list to produce the seven deadly sins (lust, gluttony, avarice, sloth, wrath, envy and pride), thence into Dante's *Divine Comedy*.

56 Augustine, *Divination of Demons*, 3.7, in Deferrari (ed.), *Saint Augustine: Treatises on Marriage and Other Subjects*, p. 426.

57 Ibid., 5.9, p. 430.

58 David L. Mosher (trans.), *Saint Augustine: Eight-Three Different Questions* (Washington, DC: Catholic University of America Press, 1982), 12, p. 43.

59 Barney et al., *The* Etymologies *of Isidore of Seville*, 8.11.16–17.

60 H. von E. Scott and C.C. Swinton Bland (trans.), *The Dialogue on Miracles: Caesarius of Heisterbach (1220–1235)* (London: George Routledge & Sons, 1929), 3.6. See also Elliott, *Fallen Bodies*, ch. 6.

61 Scott and Bland (trans.), *The Dialogue on Miracles*, 5.15.

62 Ibid.

63 Ibid.

64 Bugnolo (trans.), *Master Peter Lombard's Book of Sentences*, 2.8.1.1.

65 Bugnolo (trans.), *Master Peter Lombard's Book of Sentences*, 2.8.1.1.
66 Ibid., 2.8.2.4.
67 Bugnolo (trans.), *St. Bonaventure's Commentaries on the Four Books of Sentences of Master Peter Lombard*, 2.8.1.1. My italics.
68 Ibid., 2.8.1.2.2.
69 Ibid., 2.3.1.1, and Keck, *Angels and Angelology in the Middle Ages*, pp. 93–9.
70 Bugnolo (trans.), *St. Bonaventure's Commentaries on the Four Books of Sentences of Master Peter Lombard*, 16.1.
71 *S.T.* 1.51.1.
72 *S.T.* 1.51.2.
73 Ibid.
74 Ibid.
75 Bugnolo (trans.), *St. Bonaventure's Commentaries on the Four Books of Sentences of Master Peter Lombard*, 2.8.1.3.1.
76 Mackay (ed. and trans.), *Malleus Maleficarum*, 2.1.4.109B.
77 Ibid., 2.1.4.109A.

## Chapter Six: The Devil and the Witch

1 Thomas Potts, *The Wonderfull Discoverie of Witches in the Countie of Lancaster* (London, 1613), sig. L.2.v.
2 Ibid., sig.L.2.v. See Philip C. Almond, *The Lancashire Witches: A Chronicle of Sorcery and Death on Pendle Hill* (London: I.B.Tauris, 2012).
3 Potts, *The Wonderfull Discoverie of Witches in the Countie of Lancaster*, sig. L.2.r.
4 Ibid., sig. M.4.v.
5 Nazarena Orlandi (ed.), Helen Josephine Robins (trans.), *Saint Bernardino of Siena, Sermons* (Siena: Tipografia Sociale, 1920), pp. 166–7, quoted by Richard Kieckhefer, 'Avenging the Blood of Children: Anxiety over Child Victims and the Origins of the European Witch Trials', in Alberto Ferreira (ed.), *The Devil, Heresy and Witchcraft in the Middle Ages: Essays in Honour of Jeffrey B. Russell* (Leiden: Brill, 1998), p. 95.
6 Kieckhefer, 'Avenging the Blood of Children', pp. 101–2. See also Lyndal Roper, *Witch Craze: Terror and Fantasy in Baroque Germany* (New Haven, CT, and London: Yale University Press, 2004), pp. 67–81.
7 Mackay (ed. and trans.), *Malleus Maleficarum*, 2.1.2.97C–D.
8 Ibid., 2.1.3.104A.
9 *Errores Gazariorum*, in Kors and Peters, *Witchcraft in Europe, 400–1700*, p. 160.
10 *Bericht des Luzerner Chronisten Johann Fründ über die Hexenverfolgung im Wallis*, in Joseph Hansen, *Quellen und Untersuchungen zur Geschichte des Hexenwahns und der Hexenverfolgung im Mittelalter*

(Bonn: Carl Georgi, Universitäts-Buchdruckerei und Verlag, 1901), p. 536.

11 Lea, *Materials toward a History of Witchcraft*, 1.178–80. The phrases in square brackets are additions to the canon *Episcopi* in the *Decretum*.

12 Wakefield and Evans, *Heresies of the High Middle Ages*, p. 444. See also Hansen, *Quellen*, p. 48.

13 Levack (ed.), *The Witchcraft Sourcebook*, p. 46.

14 Quoted by Matthew Champion, 'Crushing the Canon: Nicolas Jacquier's Response to the Canon *Episcopi* in the *Flagellum Haereticorum Fascinariorum*', *Magic, Ritual, and Witchcraft* 6 (2011), p. 186.

15 Bartolomeo della Spina, *Quaestio de Strigibus* (Venice, 1523), chs 21–6. See also Lea, *Materials toward a History of Witchcraft*, 1.390–1.

16 Granger Ryan and Helmut Ripperger (trans.), *The Golden Legend of Jacobus de Voragine* (New York: Arno Press, 1969), p. 397.

17 Mackay (ed. and trans.), *Malleus Maleficarum*, 2.1.3.105C.

18 Ibid., 1.1.10C–D.

19 Ibid., 2.1.3.105C (my italics).

20 P.G. Maxwell-Stuart, *Martín del Rio: Investigations into Magic* (Manchester and New York: Manchester University Press, 2000), p. 92. See also Randy A. Scott (trans.), *On the Demon-Mania of Witches* (Toronto: Centre for Reformation and Renaissance Studies, 1995), pp. 114–17.

21 George Mora (ed.), *Witches, Devils, and Doctors in the Renaissance: Johann Weyer, De Praestigiis Daemonum* (Binghamton, NY: Medieval and Renaissance Texts and Studies, 1991), pp. 225–6.

22 Reginald Scot, *The Discoverie of Witchcraft* (London, 1584), p. 185.

23 Ibid., p. 185.

24 Summers (ed.), *An Examen of Witches*, p. 45.

25 Ibid., pp. 48–9.

26 Kors and Peters, *Witchcraft in Europe, 400–1700*, p. 154.

27 *Errores Gazariorum*, in ibid., p. 162.

28 William Perkins, *A Discourse of the Damned Art of Witchcraft* (Cambridge, 1608), pp. 41–2.

29 Ibid., pp. 44–5.

30 Levack (ed.), *The Witchcraft Sourcebook*, p. 48.

31 E.A. Ashwin (trans.), *Francesco Maria Guazzo: Compendium Maleficarum* (New York, Dover Publications, 1988), pp. 13–16. For the pact in the last of the classical demonologies, see Montague Summers (ed.), *Demoniality by Ludovico Maria Sinistrari Friar Minor* (New York: Benjamin Blom, 1972), pp. 8–11.

32 For an English translation, Philip Mason Palmer and Robert Pattison More, *The Sources of the Faust Tradition from Simon Magus to Lessing* (New York: Oxford University Press, 1936), pp. 60–75.

33 Ibid., p. 61.

34 Ibid., p. 62.

35 Ibid.

36 Palmer and More, *The Sources of the Faust Tradition*, p. 63.

37 This was the first use of the term 'mediatrix' in the West to signify her mediating role between God and the sinner.

38 John Henry Jones (ed.), *The English Faust Book: A Critical Edition Based on the Text of 1592* (Cambridge: Cambridge University Press, 1994).

39 Ibid., p. 93.

40 Ibid., p. 95.

41 Ibid., pp. 98–9.

42 Ibid., p. 180.

43 Ibid.

44 Lambert Daneau, *A Dialogue of Witches* (London, 1575), sig. F.4.v.

45 Ibid., sig. F.4.v.

46 Jeffrey Burton Russell, *Witchcraft in the Middle Ages* (Ithaca, NY, and London: Cornell University Press, 1972), pp. 242–3.

47 Summers (ed.), *An Examen of Witches*, p. 129.

48 Ibid., p. 130.

49 Christina Larner, *Enemies of God: The Witch-Hunt in Scotland* (London: Blackwell, 1981), pp. 110–12.

50 Levack (ed.), *The Witchcraft Sourcebook*, p. 114.

51 Ibid., p. 115.

52 Michael Dalton, *The Countrey Justice Containing the Practice of the Justices of the Peace out of their Sessions* (London, 1630), p. 273.

53 Thus, the nipple was often sought for in the genital regions. For an early example of this at the popular level, see Anon., *The Most Strange and Admirable Discoverie of the Three Witches of Warboys, Arraigned, Convicted, and Executed at the Last Assises at Huntington* (London, 1593), sigs O.3.v–O.4.r. See also Philip C. Almond, *The Witches of Warboys: An Extraordinary Story of Sorcery, Sadism and Satanic Possession* (London: I.B.Tauris, 2008).

54 Anon., *The Examination and Confession of Certaine Wytches at Chensforde in the Countie of Essex* (n.p., 1566), sig. 2.A.7.v.

55 Michael Dalton, *The Countrey Justice* (London, 1697), p. 384.

56 Harrison (ed.), *King James the First: Daemonologie*, p. 80.

57 Anon., *The Witches of Northamptonshire* (London, 1612), sig. C.2.r (my italics).

58 Scot, *The Discoverie of Witchcraft*, p. 47.

## Chapter Seven: A Very Possessing Devil

1 Anon., *A True and Fearefull Vexation of One Alexander Nyndge* (London, 1615), sig. A.3.v. For a more detailed elaboration of the materials in this chapter, see Philip C. Almond, *Demonic Possession and Exorcism in Early Modern England: Contemporary Texts and their Cultural Contexts* (Cambridge: Cambridge University Press, 2004).

2 Anon., *A True and Fearefull Vexation of One Alexander Nyndge*, sigs A.3.r–v.

3 Anon., *A True and Fearefull Vexation of One Alexander Nyndge*, sig. B.1.r.

4 H.C. Erik Midelfort, 'The Devil and the German People: Reflections on the Popularity of Demon Possession in Sixteenth-Century Germany', in Steven E. Ozment (ed.), *Religion and Culture in the Renaissance and Reformation* (Kirksville, MO: Sixteenth Century Publishers, 1989), p. 105.

5 Daniel P. Walker, *Unclean Spirits: Possession and Exorcism in France and England in the Late Sixteenth and Early Seventeenth Centuries* (Philadelphia: University of Pennsylvania Press, 1981), p. 4.

6 Summers (ed.), *An Examen of Witches*, p. 12.

7 Levinus Lemnius, *The Secret Miracles of Nature* (London, 1658), p. 385.

8 Ashwin (trans.), *Francesco Maria Guazzo*, pp. 170–1.

9 P.G. Maxwell-Stuart, *The Occult in Early Modern Europe: A Documentary History* (New York: St Martin's Press, 1999), p. 57.

10 Walker, *Unclean Spirits*, p. 21.

11 Anon., *The Most Wonderful and True Storie, of a Certaine Witch Named Alse Gooderidge* (London, 1597), p. 34.

12 Anon., *The Disclosing of a Late Counterfeyted Possession by the Devyl in Two Maydens within the Citie of London* (London, 1574), sig. A.4.v.

13 F.W. Brownlow, *Shakespeare, Harsnett, and the Devils of Denham* (Newark, DE: University of Delaware Press), pp. 243–53.

14 John Deacon and John Walker, *A Summarie Answere to al the Material Points in any of Master Darel his Bookes More Especiallie to that One Booke of his, Intituled, the Doctrine of the Possession and Dispossession of Demoniaks out of the Word of God* (London, 1601), p. 16.

15 Alan C. Kors and Edward Peters, *Witchcraft in Europe, 1100–1700: A Documentary History* (London: J.M. Dent and Sons, 1973), pp. 346–7.

16 Stephen Bradwell, 'Mary Glovers Late Woeful Case, Together with her Joyfull Deliverance' (1603), in Michael MacDonald (ed.), *Witchcraft and Hysteria in Elizabethan London* (London: Routledge, 1991), pp. 26ff.

17 Edward Jorden, *A Briefe Discourse of a Disease Called the Suffocation of the Mother* (London, 1603), in MacDonald (ed.), *Witchcraft and Hysteria in Elizabethan London*, sigs C.1.r–v.

18 Ibid., title page.

19 Ibid., 'The Epistle Dedicatorie'.

20 Bradwell, 'Mary Glovers Late Woeful Case, Together with her Joyfull Deliverance', p. 57.

21 For a comprehensive analysis of the case of Anne Gunter, see James Sharpe, *The Bewitching of Anne Gunter* (London: Profile, 1999).

22 Brownlow, *Shakespeare, Harsnett, and the Devils of Denham*, pp. 223, 349, 381, 386, 401, 409.

23 Ibid., p. 225.

24 Anon., *The Most Wonderful and True Storie, of a Certaine Witch Named Alse Gooderidge*, p. 1.

25 For a contemporary list of symptoms of epilepsy, see Thomas Willis, *The London Practice of Physick* (London, 1685), p. 239.

26 E.g., James Mason, *The Anatomie of Sorcerie* (London, 1612), pp. 41f.

27 Lemnius, *The Secret Miracles of Nature*, pp. 86–9.

28 Carol Karlsen, *The Devil in the Shape of a Woman: Witchcraft in Colonial New England* (New York: Vintage Books, 1989), p. 234.

29 Ibid., p. 233.

30 Richard Baxter, *The Certainty of the World of Spirits* (London, 1691), p. 173.

31 Thomas C. Faulkner et al., *Robert Burton: The Anatomy of Melancholy* (Oxford: Clarendon Press, 1989–), 1.135–6.

32 James O. Halliwell, *The Private Diary of John Dee* (London: Camden Society, 1842), pp. 35–6.

33 Konrad Gesner, *The Treasure of Euonymus*, 1559, p. 331, quoted by Paul H. Kocher, 'The Idea of God in Elizabethan Medicine', *Journal of the History of Ideas* 51 (1950), p. 21.

34 John Deacon and John Walker, *Dialogicall Discourses of Spirits and Divels* (London, 1601), pp. 206–8. See also Walker, *Unclean Spirits*, pp. 69–70.

35 Brownlow, *Shakespeare, Harsnett, and the Devils of Denham*, p. 304.

36 Ibid., pp. 308–9.

37 Deacon and Walker, *Dialogicall Discourses of Spirits and Divels*, p. 206.

38 John Darrell, *The Doctrine of the Possession and Dispossession of Demoniakes* (England [?], 1600), p. 10.

39 C. l'Estrange Ewen, *Witchcraft and Demonianism* (London: Heath Cranton, 1933), p. 191.

40 Levack (ed.), *The Witchcraft Sourcebook*, p. 257.

41 Ashwin (trans.), *Francesco Maria Guazzo*, pp. 167–9.

42 Maxwell-Stuart, *The Occult in Early Modern Europe*, p. 46.

43 Anon., *A Breife Narration of the Possession, Dispossession, and, Repossession of William Sommers* (London, 1598), sigs E.3.r–v.

44 John Darrell, *An Apologie, or Defence of the Possession of William Sommers* (Amsterdam[?], 1599[?]), p. 9.

45 Anon., *A Breife Narration of the Possession, Dispossession, and, Repossession of William Sommers*, sig. B.3.v.

46 Anon., *A Strange and True Relation of a Young Woman Possest with the Devill by Name Joyce Dovey* (London, 1647), p. 2.

47 John E. Cox, *The Works of Thomas Cranmer* (Cambridge: Cambridge University Press, 1844), p. 243.

48 Anon., *A Breife Narration of the Possession, Dispossession, and, Repossession of William Sommers*, sig. D.1.r.

49 Francis Grant [Lord Cullen], *Sadducismus Debellatus* (London, 1698), p. 17.

50 Anon., *A Breife Narration of the Possession, Dispossession, and, Repossession of William Sommers*, sig. B.1.v.

51 James O. Halliwell, *Letters of the Kings of England* (London: H. Colburn, 1848), p. 124.

52 Bradwell, 'Mary Glovers Late Woeful Case, Together with her Joyfull Deliverance', p. 21.

53 Anon., *The Most Strange and Admirable Discoverie of the Three Witches of Warboys*, sig. C.4.v.

54 Bradwell, 'Mary Glovers Late Woeful Case, Together with her Joyfull Deliverance', p. 4.

55 Midelfort, 'The Devil and the German People', p. 99.

56 John Cotta, *The Triall of Witch-craft*, p. 76.

57 William Drage, *Daimonomageia* (London, 1665), p. 5.

58 Sharpe, *The Bewitching of Anne Gunter*, pp. 44, 172, 184.

59 Grant, *Sadducismus Debellatus* pp. 3ff., 15, 33.

60 George More, *A True Discourse Concerning the Certain Possession and Dispossession of 7 Persons in one Family in Lancashire* (London, 1600), p. 29.

61 Anon., *The Most Strange and Admirable Discoverie of the Three Witches of Warboys*, sig. C.4.r.

62 Scott (trans.), *On the Demon-Mania of Witches*, p. 169.

63 Lemnius, *The Secret Miracles of Nature*, p. 385.

64 Ibid., p. 386.

65 Anon., *A True and Fearefull Vexation of one Alexander Nyndge*, sig. A.3.r.

66 Samuel Harsnett, *A Discovery of the Fraudulent Practices of John Darrel* (London, 1599), p. 117.

67 Michel de Certeau, *The Possession at Loudun* (Chicago: University of Chicago Press, 2000).

68 Anon., *Wonderfull Newes from the North* (London, 1650); and [John Barrow], *The Lord's Arm Stretched Out* (London, 1664).

69 Sarah Ferber, *Demonic Possession and Exorcism in Early Modern France* (London: Routledge, 2004), p. 67.

70 Gaetano Paxia (trans.), *The Devil's Scourge: Exorcism during the Italian Renaissance* (Boston: Weiser Books, 2002), p. 128.

71 Ibid., p. 185.

72 Quoted by MacDonald (ed.), *Witchcraft and Hysteria in Elizabethan London*, p. 28.

73 Anon., *The Most Strange and Admirable Discoverie of the Three Witches of Warboys*, sig. B.3.r. See also sig. N.3.r.

74 Clarke, *The Lives of Two and Twenty English Divines* (London, 1660), pp. 189–90.

75 Harsnett, *A Discovery of the Fraudulent Practices of John Darrel*, p. 288.

76 Anon., *The Most Wonderful and True Storie, of a Certaine Witch Named Alse Gooderidge*, pp. 13, 17, 19, 22.

77 Drage, *Daimonomageia*, p. 33.

78 Darrell, *An Apologie, or Defence of the Possession of William Sommers*, sig. F.3.r.

79 Harsnett, *A Discovery of the Fraudulent Practices of John Darrel*, p. 35.
80 Abraham Hartwell (trans.), *A True Discourse upon the Matter of Martha Brossier of Romorantin* (London, 1599). On Brossier, see Ferber, *Demonic Possession and Exorcism in Early Modern France*.
81 Walker, *Unclean Spirits*, pp. 34–5.
82 Brownlow, *Shakespeare, Harsnett, and the Devils of Denham*, pp. 226–7, 368.
83 Ibid., p. 386.
84 Ibid., p. 332.
85 Darrell, *An Apologie, or Defence of the Possession of William Sommers*, sig. G.1.v.
86 George Gifford, *A Dialogue Concerning Witches and Witchcraftes* (London, 1593), sig. I.2.v.
87 Cotta, *The Triall of Witch-craft*, p. 126.
88 Richard Bernard, *A Guide to Grand-Jury Men* (London, 1627), p. 208.
89 Harsnett, *A Discovery of the Fraudulent Practices of John Darrel*, p. 231.
90 Ibid., p. 189.
91 Stephen Greenblatt, 'Loudun and London', *Critical Inquiry* 12 (1985–6), p. 337.

## Chapter Eight: The Devil Defeated

1 Harrison (ed.), *King James the First: Daemonologie*, p. 81.
2 Stuart Clark, *Thinking with Demons: The Idea of Witchcraft in Early Modern Europe* (Oxford: Oxford University Press, 1997), p. 419.
3 Anon., *The Most Wonderful and True Storie, of a Certaine Witch Named Alse Gooderidge*, sig. A.2.r.
4 Ibid., sigs. E.1.v–E.2.v.
5 Thomas Jollie, *The Surey Demoniack* (London, 1697), p. 18.
6 Darrell, *An Apologie, or Defence of the Possession of William Sommers*, sig. D.4.v.
7 Ibid., sig. G.1.v.
8 Brownlow, *Shakespeare, Harsnett, and the Devils of Denham*, pp. 331–2.
9 More, *A True Discourse Concerning the Certain Possession and Dispossession of 7 Persons in one Family in Lancashire*, p. 62.
10 John Swan, *A True and Breife Report, of Mary Glovers Vexation* (London, 1603), p. 21.
11 Augustine, *City of God*, 20.7 in Schaff (ed.), *St. Augustine's City of God and Christian Doctrine*. On Augustine's eschatology, see Brian E. Daley, *The Hope of the Early Church* (Cambridge: Cambridge University Press, 1991), pp. 131–50.
12 Augustine, *City of God*, 20.8 in Schaff (ed.), *St. Augustine's City of God and Christian Doctrine*.
13 Ibid., 20.7.
14 Ibid., 20.30.
15 Ibid., 20.8.

16 Augustine, *City of God*, 20.8.
17 Ibid., 20.19.
18 I am particularly indebted here to Richard Kenneth Emmerson, *Antichrist in the Middle Ages: A Study of Medieval Apocalypticism, Art, and Literature* (Seattle: University of Washington Press, 1981), pp. 38–9.
19 John Jewel, *Exposition upon the Two Epistles of St. Paul to the Thessalonians*, quoted by Emmerson, *Antichrist in the Middle Ages*, p. 8.
20 Steven R. Cartwright, 'Thietland's Commentary on the Antichrist and the End of the Millennium', in Richard Landes, Andrew Gow and David C. van Meter, *The Apocalyptic Year 1000: Religious Expectation and Social Change* (Oxford: Oxford University Press, 2003), pp. 93–108. See also Steven R. Cartwright (trans.), 'Thietland of Einsiedeln on 2 Thessalonians', in Steven R. Cartwright and Kevin L. Hughes (trans.), *Second Thessalonians: Two Early Medieval Commentaries* (Kalamazoo, MI: Medieval Institute Publications, 2001), pp. 41–76.
21 Cartwright (trans.), 'Thietland of Einsiedeln on 2 Thessalonians', p. 51.
22 Ibid., p. 51.
23 Ibid., p. 52.
24 Ibid., p. 56.
25 Ibid., p. 58.
26 Ibid., p. 57.
27 Daniel Verhelst, 'Adso of Montier-en-Der and the Fear of the Year 1000', in Landes, Gow and van Meter, *The Apocalyptic Year 1000*, pp. 81–92.
28 Bernard McGinn, *Anti-Christ: Two Thousand Years of the Human Fascination with Evil* (San Francisco: Harper, 1996), p. 101. For a translation of the *Epistola*, Bernard McGinn, *Apocalyptic Spirituality* (London: SPCK, 1979), pp. 89–96.
29 Adso, *Letter on the Origin and Time of the Antichrist*, in McGinn, *Apocalyptic Spirituality*, p. 90.
30 Ibid., p. 91.
31 Ibid., p. 93.
32 Ibid., p. 91.
33 Ibid.
34 Ibid., p. 92.
35 On the conversion of the Jews to Christianity prior to Christ's return, see Philip C. Almond, 'Thomas Brightman and the Origins of Philo-Semitism: An Elizabethan Theologian and the Restoration of the Jews to Israel', *Reformation and Renaissance Review* 9 (2007), pp. 4–25.
36 Adso, *Letter on the Origin and Time of the Antichrist*, in McGinn, *Apocalyptic Spirituality*, p. 94.
37 Ibid., p. 92. His capacity to perform miracles such as raising the dead or if he only seemed to (in the mode of a magician) was a matter of

much debate. See Augustine, *City of God*, 20.19, in Schaff (ed.), *St. Augustine's City of God and Christian Doctrine*.

38 Adso, *Letter on the Origin and Time of the Antichrist*, in McGinn, *Apocalyptic Spirituality*, p. 96. That the Antichrist would be killed attested his being human rather than his being the Devil in incarnate form who, as a fallen angel, was immortal.

39 Adso took the notion of the period of time after the death of the Antichrist from the mid-ninth-century commentator Haimo of Auxerre. 'It should be noted', said Haimo, 'that the Lord will not come immediately to judge when Antichrist has been killed, but, as we learn from the Book of Daniel, after his death the elect will be given forty-five days for penance. Indeed, it is completely unknown how long the span of time may be before the Lord comes.' See Kevin L. Hughes (trans.), 'Haimo of Auxerre: Exposition of the Second Letter to the Thessalonians', in Cartwright and Hughes (trans.), *Second Thessalonians: Two Early Medieval Commentaries*, pp. 28–9. It is not clear why Adso shortened Daniel's, Haimo's and initially Jerome's period of 45 days (though it would match the period of Christ's time in the wilderness). But, like Haimo, he did leave a possible gap between the end of the 45 days and the coming of Christ, the length of which only God knew. See Robert E. Lerner, 'Refreshment of the Saints: The Time after Antichrist as a Station for Earthly Progress in Medieval Thought', *Traditio* 32 (1976), pp. 97–144.

40 Adso, *Letter on the Origin and Time of the Antichrist*, in McGinn, *Apocalyptic Spirituality*, p. 96.

41 Robert E. Lerner, 'Antichrists and Antichrist in Joachim of Fiore', *Speculum* 60 (1985), pp. 553–70.

42 McGinn, *Apocalyptic Spirituality*, p. 138.

43 Ibid., p. 140.

44 Ibid.

45 Lerner, 'Antichrists and Antichrist in Joachim of Fiore', p. 566.

46 McGinn, *Apocalyptic Spirituality*, pp. 140–1.

47 Ibid., p. 136.

48 Ibid., p. 140.

49 Bernard McGinn, *Visions of the End: Apocalyptic Traditions in the Middle Ages* (New York: Columbia University Press, 1979), p. 211. In the bull *Sancta Romana et Universa Ecclesia* in 1318, the pope excommunicated them, and he condemned Olivi's commentary on the book of Revelation in 1326.

50 Quoted by Bernard McGinn, *Antichrist: Two Thousand Years of the Human Fascination with Evil* (San Francisco: Harper, 1996), pp. 141–2.

51 Bernard Gui, *Practica Inquisitionis Heretice Pravitatis*, 5.4.5, in Wakefield and Evans, *Heresies of the High Middle Ages*.

52 Quoted by Robert Rusconi, 'Antichrist and Antichrists' in Bernard Mc Ginn (ed), *The Encyclopedia of Apocalypticism: Volume 2:*

*Apocalypticism in Western History and Culture* (New York/London: Continuum, 2000), p. 312.

53 Philip D.W. Krey and Peter D.S. Krey (eds), *Luther's Spirituality* (Mahwah, NJ: Paulist Press, 2007), p. 55.

54 Ibid.

55 Quoted by Katharine R. Firth, *The Apocalyptic Tradition in Reformation Britain 1530–1645* (Oxford: Oxford University Press, 1979), pp. 34–5.

56 John Bale, *The Image of Bothe Churches after the Moste Wonderfull and Heavenly Revelation of Sainct John the Evangelist*, in Henry Christmas (ed.), *Select Works of John Bale, D.D. Bishop of Ossory. Containing the Examinations of Lord Cobham, William Thorpe, and Anne Askewe, and The Image of Both Churches* (Cambridge: Cambridge University Press, 1849), p. 252.

57 Ibid., p. 251. See also Richard Bauckham, *Tudor Apocalypse: Sixteenth Century Apocalypticism, Millennarianism and the English Reformation: From John Bale to John Foxe and Thomas Brightman* (Oxford: Sutton Courtenay Press, 1978); and Firth, *The Apocalyptic Tradition in Reformation Britain 1530–1645*.

58 Bale, *The Image of Bothe Churches*, in Christmas, *Select Works of John Bale*, p. 341.

59 Ibid., p. 561.

60 Ibid., p. 574.

61 Ibid., p. 575.

62 David Hume, *The History of England* (London: T. Cadell, 1792), 7.44.

63 Philip C. Almond, 'John Napier and the Mathematics of the "middle future" Apocalypse', *Scottish Journal of Theology* 63 (2010), pp. 54–69.

64 John Napier, *A Plaine Discovery of the Whole Revelation of Saint John* (Edinburgh, 1593), p. 62.

65 Ibid.

66 Ibid., p. 243.

67 Ibid., p. 240.

68 Almond, 'Thomas Brightman and the Origins of Philo-Semitism'.

69 Thomas Brightman, *A Revelation of the Revelation* (Amsterdam, 1615), p. 121.

70 Ibid., p. 860.

71 The original Latin version, *Clavis Apocalyptica*, was published in 1632.

72 Jeffrey K. Jue, *Heaven upon Earth: Joseph Mede (1586–1638) and the Legacy of Millenarianism* (Dordrecht: Springer, 2006).

73 Quoted ibid., p. 131.

74 Joseph Mede, *The Key of the Revelation Searched and Demonstrated* (London, 1643), part 2, p. 123.

75 Ibid.

76 On Catholic responses, Kenneth G.C. Newport, *Apocalypse and Millennium: Studies in Biblical Eisegesis* (Cambridge: Cambridge University Press, 2000), ch. 4.

77 Ironically, modern Evangelical Protestant interpretations of Revelation favour the Catholic futurist reading. Brightman was familiar with both Ribera and Bellarmine, though the latter was his main target. In his commentary on Revelation, Brightman devoted an excursus of 140 pages to refuting Bellarmine's account.

78 John Shower, *Heaven and Hell: Or, The Unchangeable State of Happiness or Misery for all Mankind in Another World* (London, 1700), pp. 17–18.

79 Robert Sharrock, *De Finibus Virtutis Christianae* (Oxford, 1673), p. 41.

80 William Gearing, *A Prospect of Heaven: Or, A Treatise of the Happiness of the Saints in Glory* (London, 1673), p. 226.

81 Roger Sharrock (ed.), *The Miscellaneous Works of John Bunyan* (Oxford: Clarendon Press, 1976–), 1.300.

82 Gearing, *A Prospect of Heaven*, p. 226.

83 Sharrock (ed.), *The Miscellaneous Works of John Bunyan*, 1.274–5.

84 Henry More, *The Immortality of the Soul, so Farre forth as it is Demonstrable from the Knowledge of Nature and the Light of Reason* (London, 1659), pp. 441, 434.

85 Christopher Love, *Hell's Terror, Or, A Treatise of the Torments of the Damned as a Preservative against Security* (London, 1653), pp. 46–7.

86 Thomas Bromhall, *A Treatise of Specters. Or, An History of Apparitions, Oracles, Prophecies, and Predictions, with Dreams, Visions, and Revelations. And the Cunning Delusions of the Devil* (London, 1658), p. 350.

87 Thomas Goodwin, *A Discourse of the Punishment of Sin in Hell: Demonstrating the Wrath of God to be the Immediate Cause Thereof* (London, 1680), p. 98.

88 Quoted by Piero Camporesi, *The Fear of Hell: Images of Damnation and Salvation in Early Modern Europe* (Cambridge: Polity Press, 1990), p. 93.

## Chapter Nine: The 'Death' of the Devil

1 Lorraine Daston and Katherine Park, *Wonders and the Order of Nature, 1150–1750* (New York: Zone, 2001).

2 Kors and Peters, *Witchcraft in Europe, 400–1700*, p. 108.

3 Thomas Hobbes, *Leviathan*, 32, in Noel Malcolm (ed.), *Thomas Hobbes: Leviathan* (Oxford: Clarendon, 2012), 3.584.

4 Walker, *Unclean Spirits*, p. 67.

5 D.P. Walker, 'The Cessation of Miracles', in I. Merkel and A.G. Debus, *Hermeticism and the Renaissance: Intellectual History and the Occult in Early Modern Europe* (Washington, DC: Folger, 1988), pp. 111–12.

6 William Pringle (trans.), *Commentary on a Harmony of the Evangelists, Matthew, Mark, and Luke by John Calvin* (Grand Rapids, MI: Baker Book House, 1984), 3.140.

7 John T. McNeill (ed.), *Calvin: Institutes of the Christian Religion* (Louisville, KT: Westminster John Knox Press, 2006), p. 16.

8 Ibid., p. 17.

9 Pringle (trans.), *Commentary on a Harmony of the Evangelists, Matthew, Mark, and Luke by John Calvin*, 3.389.

10 Perkins, *A Discourse of the Damned Art of Witchcraft*, p. 59.

11 Joseph Glanvill, *A Blow at Modern Sadducism in some Philosophical Considerations about Witchcraft* (London, 1668), pp. 115-17.

12 Joseph Glanvill, *A Philosophical Endeavour towards the Defence of Witches and Apparitions* (London, 1666), p. 18. See also Julie A. Davies, 'Poisonous Vapours: Joseph Glanvill's Science of Witchcraft', *Intellectual History Review* 22 (2012), pp. 163–79.

13 Glanvill, *A Philosophical Endeavour*, p. 24.

14 Daston and Park, *Wonders and the Order of Nature, 1150–1750*, p. 350.

15 Ibid., p. 361.

16 Scot, *The Discoverie of Witchcraft*, p. 87.

17 Ibid., p. 508.

18 Ibid.

19 Nathan Johnstone, *The Devil and Demonism in Early Modern England* (Cambridge: Cambridge University Press, 2006), p. 16. I am indebted to Johnstone for his analysis of Protestant demonism.

20 Stuart Clark, 'Inversion, Misrule and the Meaning of Witchcraft', *Past and Present* 87 (1980), pp. 98–127.

21 This remains the dominant image of the role of the Devil within those forms of modern liberal Christianity that still accord to the Devil a role in the spiritual lives of persons.

22 Hobbes, *Leviathan*, 34, in Malcolm (ed.), *Thomas Hobbes: Leviathan*, 3.610.

23 Ibid., 45, in Malcolm (ed.), *Thomas Hobbes: Leviathan*, 3.1012.

24 Ibid., 34, in Malcolm (ed.), *Thomas Hobbes: Leviathan*, 3.630.

25 Ibid.

26 Thomas Hobbes, *Humane Nature: Or, The Fundamental Elements of Policy* (London, 1651), pp. 133–4.

27 Ibid., p. 135.

28 Hobbes, *Leviathan*, 47, in Malcolm (ed.), *Thomas Hobbes: Leviathan*, 3.1110.

29 Levack (ed.), *The Witchcraft Sourcebook* , p. 306.

30 Ibid., p. 306.

31 Samuel Shirley (trans.), *Spinoza: The Letters* (Indianapolis and Cambridge: Hackett Publishing Company, 1995), ep. 76, p. 341.

32 Ibid., ep. 52, pp. 262–3.

33 Ibid., ep. 54, pp. 267–8.

34 Shirley (trans.), *Spinoza*, ep. 54, p. 270.

35 Joseph Glanvill, *Saducismus Triumphatus* (London, 1681), sig. F.3.r.

36 Henry More, *An Antidote against Atheisme* (London, 1652), p. 164.

37 Thomas Birch (ed.), *The True Intellectual System of the Universe ... by Ralph Cudworth* (Andover: Gould and Newman, 1838), 2.115.

38 Thomas Birch (ed.), *The Works of the Honourable Robert Boyle* (London, 1744–72), 6.57–8.

39 Glanvill, *Saducismus Triumphatus*, sig. B.8.v.

40 Birch, *The True Intellectual System of the Universe ... by Ralph Cudworth*, 3.270.

41 Henry More, *The Immortality of the Soul*, in Henry More, *A Collection of Several Philosophical Writings* (London, 1662), p. 3.

42 Volume 1 of this work was also published in England in 1695 under the title *The World Bewitch'd*. The 1700 publication also includes a translation of volume 1.

43 Jonathan I. Israel, *Radical Enlightenment: Philosophy and the Making of Modernity 1650–1750* (Oxford: Oxford University Press, 2001), p. 382. I am indebted to Israel for this discussion of Bekker.

44 B[althasar] B[ekker], *The World Turn'd Upside Down* (London, 1700), preface.

45 Ibid.

46 Ibid.

47 Ibid., 'An Abridgement of the Whole Work'.

48 Ibid.

49 Ibid.

50 Daniel Defoe, *The History of the Devil* (London, 1727), pp. 388–9.

## Epilogue

1 Friedrich Schleiermacher, *The Christian Faith* (Edinburgh: T. & T. Clark, 1928), p. 161. See also Kelly, *Satan: A Biography*, pp. 308–15.

# Bibliography

Almond, Philip C., *Heaven and Hell in Enlightenment England* (Cambridge: Cambridge University Press, 1994).

—— *Adam and Eve in Seventeenth-Century Thought* (Cambridge: Cambridge University Press, 1999).

—— *Demonic Possession and Exorcism in Early Modern England: Contemporary Texts and their Cultural Contexts* (Cambridge: Cambridge University Press, 2004).

—— 'Thomas Brightman and the Origins of Philo-Semitism: An Elizabethan Theologian and the Restoration of the Jews to Israel', *Reformation and Renaissance Review* 9 (2007), pp. 4–25.

—— *The Witches of Warboys: An Extraordinary Story of Sorcery, Sadism and Satanic Possession* (London: I.B.Tauris, 2008).

—— 'John Napier and the Mathematics of the "Middle Future" Apocalypse', *Scottish Journal of Theology* 63 (2010), pp. 54–69

—— *The Lancashire Witches: A Chronicle of Sorcery and Death on Pendle Hill* (London: I.B.Tauris, 2012)

Anderson, Gary A. and Michael E. Stone, *A Synopsis of the Books of Adam and Eve* (Atlanta, GA: Scholars Press, 1994).

—— —— and Johannes Tromp (eds), *Literature on Adam and Eve: Collected Essays* (Leiden: Brill, 2000).

Anon., *A Breife Narration of the Possession, Dispossession, and, Repossession of William Sommers* (London, 1598).

Anon., *A Strange and True Relation of a Young Woman Possest with the Devill by Name Joyce Dovey* (London, 1647).

Anon., *A True and Fearefull Vexation of One Alexander Nyndge* (London, 1615).

Anon., *The Disclosing of a Late Counterfeyted Possession by the Devyl in Two Maydens within the Citie of London* (London, 1574).

Anon., *The Examination and Confession of Certaine Wytches at Chensforde in the Countie of Essex* (n.p., 1566).

Anon., *The Most Strange and Admirable Discoverie of the Three Witches of Warboys, Arraigned, Convicted, and Executed at the Last Assises at Huntington* (London, 1593).

Anon., *The Most Wonderful and True Storie, of a Certaine Witch Named Alse Gooderidge* (London, 1597).

Anon., *The Witches of Northamptonshire* (London, 1612).

Anon., *Wonderfull Newes from the North* (London, 1650).

Apps, Lara and Andrew Gow, *Male Witches in Early Modern Europe* (Manchester: Manchester University Press, 2003).

# Bibliography

Ashwin, E.A. (trans.), *Francesco Maria Guazzo: Compendium Maleficarum* (New York: Dover Publications, 1988).

Augustine, *Sermon 263*, in John E. Rotelle (ed.), *The Works of Saint Augustine: A Translation for the 21st Century* (Charlottesville, VA: InteLex Corporation, 2001).

—— *On the Holy Trinity*, in Philip Schaff (ed.), *A Select Library of the Nicene and Post-Nicene Fathers*, Vol. 3 (Grand Rapids, MI: Eerdmans, 2005).

Aulén, Gustaf, *Christus Victor: An Historical Study of the Three Main Types of the Idea of Atonement* (Eugene, OR: Wipf & Stock, 2003).

Bailey, Michael D., 'The Medieval Concept of the Witches' Sabbath', *Exemplaria* 8 (1996), pp. 420–39.

—— 'From Sorcery to Witchcraft: Clerical Conceptions of Magic in the Later Middle Ages', *Speculum* 76 (2001), pp. 960–90.

—— 'The Feminization of Magic and the Emerging Idea of the Female Witch in the Late Middle Ages', *Essays in Medieval Studies* 19 (2002), pp. 120–34.

—— *Battling Demons: Witchcraft, Heresy, and Reform in the Late Middle Ages* (University Park, PA: Pennsylvania State University Press, 2003).

—— and Edward Peters, 'A Sabbat of Demonologists: Basel, 1431–1440', *The Historian* 65 (2003), pp. 1375–95.

Barber, Malcolm, *The Cathars: Dualist Heresies in Languedoc in the High Middle Ages* (Harlow: Pearson Education, 2000).

Barney, Stephen A. et al., *The Etymologies of Isidore of Seville* (Cambridge: Cambridge University Press, 2006).

[Barrow, John], *The Lord's Arm Stretched Out* (London, 1664).

Bauckham, Richard, *Tudor Apocalypse: Sixteenth-Century Apocalypticism, Millennarianism and the English Reformation: From John Bale to John Foxe and Thomas Brightman* (Oxford: Sutton Courtenay Press, 1978).

Baxter, Richard, *The Certainty of the World of Spirits* (London, 1691).

B[ekker], B[althasar], *The World Turn'd Upside Down* (London, 1700).

Bernard, Richard, *A Guide to Grand-Jury Men* (London, 1627).

Bhattacharji, Santha, *Reading the Gospels with Gregory the Great: Homilies on the Gospels 21–26* (Petersham, MA: St Bede's Publications, 2001).

Birch, Thomas (ed.), *The Works of the Honourable Robert Boyle* (London, 1744–72).

—— (ed.), *The True Intellectual System of the Universe … by Ralph Cudworth* (Andover: Gould and Newman, 1838).

Blagrave, Joseph, *Blagraves Astrological Practice of Physick* (London, 1672).

Blenkinsopp, Joseph, *Creation, Un-creation, Re-creation: A Discursive Commentary on Genesis 1–11* (London: T. & T. Clark International, 2011).

Bliss, James (trans.), *Morals on the Book of Job by St. Gregory the Great, Translated with Notes and Indices. In Three Volumes* (Oxford and London: John Henry Parker and J.G.F. and J. Rivington, 1844).

Boureau, Alain, *Satan the Heretic: The Birth of Demonology in the Mediaeval West* (Chicago and London: Chicago University Press, 2006).

Bowen, Anthony and Peter Garnsey (trans.), *Lactantius: Divine Institutes* (Liverpool: Liverpool University Press, 2003).

Bradwell, Stephen, 'Mary Glovers Late Woeful Case, Together with her Joyfull Deliverance' (1603), in Michael MacDonald (ed.), *Witchcraft and Hysteria in Elizabethan London* (London: Routledge, 1991).

Brakke, David, 'Ethiopian Demons: Male Sexuality, the Black-skinned Other, and the Monastic Self', *Journal of the History of Sexuality* 10 (2001), pp. 501–35.

Brightman, Thomas , *A Revelation of the Revelation* (Amsterdam, 1615).

Broedel, Hans Peter, *The* Malleus Maleficarum *and the Construction of Witchcraft: Theology and Popular Belief* (Manchester: Manchester University Press, 2003).

Bromhall, Thomas, *A Treatise of Specters; Or, An History of Apparitions, Oracles, Prophecies, and Predictions, with Dreams, Visions, and Revelations. And the Cunning Delusions of the Devil* (London, 1658).

Brown, Peter, *Religion and Society in the Age of Augustine* (London: Faber and Faber, 1972).

Brownlow, F.W., *Shakespeare, Harsnett, and the Devils of Denham* (Newark, DE: University of Delaware Press, 1993).

Bugnolo, Alex (trans.), *Master Peter Lombard's Book of Sentences* (2006). Available at http://www.franciscan-archive.org/lombardus/index. html (accessed 20 November 2013).

—— (trans.), *St. Bonaventure's Commentaries on the Four Books of Sentences of Master Peter Lombard* (2006–7). Available at http://www. franciscan-archive.org/bonaventura/sent.html (accessed 20 November 2013).

Burke, Peter, 'Witchcraft and Magic in Renaissance Italy: Gianfrancesco Pico and his *Strix'*, in Sydney Anglo (ed.), *The Damned Art: Essays in the Literature of Witchcraft* (London: Routledge & Kegan Paul, 1977).

Burke, Robert Belle (trans.), *The Opus Maius of Roger Bacon* (Philadelphia: University of Pennsylvania Press, 1928).

Burghartz, Susanna, 'The Equation of Women and Witches: A Case Study of Witchcraft Trials in Lucerne and Lausanne in the Fifteenth and Sixteenth Centuries', in Richard J. Evans (ed.), *The German Underworld: Deviants and Outcasts in German History* (London: Routledge, 1988).

Butterworth, G.W. (trans.), *Origen: On First Principles* (Gloucester, MA: Peter Smith, 1973).

Camporesi, Piero, *The Fear of Hell: Images of Damnation and Salvation in Early Modern Europe* (Cambridge: Polity Press, 1990).

Cartwright, Steven R. and Kevin L. Hughes (trans.), *Second Thessalonians: Two Early Medieval Commentaries* (Kalamazoo, MI: Medieval Institute Publications, 2001).

# Bibliography

Certeau, Michel de, *The Possession at Loudun* (Chicago: University of Chicago Press, 2000).

Chadwick, Henry (trans.), *Origen: Contra Celsum* (Cambridge: Cambridge University Press, 1953).

Champion, Matthew, 'Crushing the Canon: Nicolas Jacquier's Response to the Canon *Episcopi* in the *Flagellum Haereticorum Fascinariorum*', *Magic, Ritual, and Witchcraft* 6 (2011), pp. 183–211.

Charlesworth, James H., *The Old Testament Pseudepigrapha*, Vol. 2 (New York: Doubleday, 1985).

Chitty, Derwas J. (trans.), *The Letters of St Antony the Great* (Oxford: SLG Press, 1975).

Christmas, Henry (ed.), *Select Works of John Bale, D.D. Bishop of Ossory. Containing the Examinations of Lord Cobham, William Thorpe, and Anne Askewe, and The Image of Both Churches* (Cambridge: Cambridge University Press, 1849).

Clark, Stuart, 'Inversion, Misrule and the Meaning of Witchcraft', *Past and Present* 87 (1980), pp. 98–127.

—— *Thinking with Demons: The Idea of Witchcraft in Early Modern Europe* (Oxford: Oxford University Press, 1997).

Clarke, Samuel, *The Lives of Two and Twenty English Divines* (London, 1660).

Cohn, Norman, *Europe's Inner Demons* (St Albans: Paladin, 1976).

Cotta, John, *The Triall of Witch-craft* (London, 1616).

Cox, John E., *The Works of Thomas Cranmer* (Cambridge: Cambridge University Press, 1844).

Crouzel, Henri, *Origen* (Edinburgh: T. & T. Clark, 1989).

Cudworth, Ralph, *The True Intellectual System of the Universe* (London: Thomas Tegg, 1845).

Dales, Richard C., *The Scientific Achievements of the Middle Ages* (Philadelphia: University of Pennsylvania Press, 1973).

Daley, Brian E., *The Hope of the Early Church* (Cambridge: Cambridge University Press, 1991).

Dalton, Michael, *The Countrey Justice Containing the Practice of the Justices of the Peace out of their Sessions* (London, 1630).

—— *The Countrey Justice* (London, 1697).

Daneau, Lambert, *A Dialogue of Witches* (London, 1575).

Danielou, Jean, *Origen* (London: Sheed and Ward, 1955).

Darrell, John, *An Apologie, or Defence of the Possession of William Sommers* (Amsterdam[?], 1599[?]).

—— *A True Narration of the Strange and Grevous Vexation by the Devil, of 7. Persons in Lancashire* (England[?], 1600).

—— *The Doctrine of the Possession and Dispossession of Demoniakes* (England[?], 1600).

Daston, Lorraine and Katherine Park, *Wonders and the Order of Nature, 1150–1750* (New York: Zone, 2001).

Davidson, Maxwell J., *Angels at Qumran: A Comparative Study of 1 Enoch 1–36, 72–108 and Sectarian Writings from Qumran* (Sheffield: Sheffield Academic Press, 1992).

Davies, Brian (ed.) and Richard Regan (trans.), *The De Malo of Thomas Aquinas* (Oxford: Oxford University Press, 2001).

Davies, Julie A., 'Poisonous Vapours: Joseph Glanvill's Science of Witchcraft', *Intellectual History Review* 22 (2012), pp. 163–79.

Deacon, John and John Walker, *A Summarie Answere to al the Material Points in any of Master Darel his Bookes More Especiallie to that One Booke of his, Intituled, the Doctrine of the Possession and Dispossession of Demoniaks out of the Word of God* (London, 1601).

—— —— *Dialogicall Discourses of Spirits and Divels* (London, 1601).

Deferrari, Roy (ed.), *Saint Augustine: Treatises on Marriage and Other Subjects* (New York: Fathers of the Church, 1955).

Defoe, Daniel, *The History of the Devil* (London, 1727).

Della Spina, Bartolomeo, *Quaestio de Strigibus* (Venice, 1523).

Dimant, Devorah, 'Between Qumran Sectarian and Non-Sectarian Texts: The Case of Belial and Mastema,' in A.D. Roitman, L.H. Schiffman and S. Tzoref (eds), *The Dead Sea Scrolls and Contemporary Culture* (Leiden: Brill, 2011).

Dods, Marcus, George Reith and B.P. Pratten (trans.), *The Writings of Justin Martyr and Athenagoras*, Ante-Nicene Christian Library, Vol. 2 (Edinburgh: T. & T. Clark, 1879).

Drage, William, *Daimonomageia* (London, 1665).

Driscoll, Daniel J. (ed.), *The Sworn Book of Honourius the Magician, as Composed by Honourius through Counsel with the Angel Hocroel* (Gillette, NJ: Heptangle Press, 1977).

Elliott, Dyan, *Fallen Bodies: Pollution, Sexuality, and Demonology in the Middle Ages* (Pennsylvania: University of Pennsylvania Press, 1999).

Ellis, F.S. (ed.), *The Golden Legend or Lives of the Saints Compiled by Jacobus de Voragine, Archbishop of Genoa* (Edinburgh: Edinburgh University Press, 1900).

Emmerson, Richard Kenneth, *Antichrist in the Middle Ages: A Study of Medieval Apocalypticism, Art, and Literature* (Seattle: University of Washington Press, 1981).

Ewen, C. l'Estrange, *Witchcraft and Demonianism* (London: Heath Cranton, 1933).

Fairfax, Edward, *Daemonologia: A Discourse on Witchcraft* (London: Muller, 1971).

Fairweather, Eugene R. (ed. and trans.), *A Scholastic Miscellany: Anselm to Ockham* (London: SCM Press, 1956).

Fanger, Claire, 'Plundering the Egyptian Treasure: John the Monk's *Book of Visions* and its Relation to the Ars Notoria of Solomon', in Claire Fanger (ed.), *Conjuring Spirits: Texts and Traditions of Medieval Ritual Magic* (Stroud: Sutton Press, 1998).

—— 'Things Done Wisely by a Wise Enchanter: Negotiating the Power of Words in the Thirteenth Century', *Esoterica* 1 (1999), pp. 97–132.

—— (ed.), *Conjuring Spirits: Texts and Traditions of Medieval Ritual Magic* (Stroud: Sutton Press, 1998).

—— (ed.), *Invoking Angels: Theurgic Ideas and Practices, Thirteenth to Sixteenth Centuries* (University Park, PA: Pennsylvania State University Press, 2012).

—— and Nicholas Watson (eds), 'John of Morigny, Prologue to *Liber Visionum* (*c.*1304–1318), Translated, Edited, and Introduced', *Esoterica* 3 (2001), pp. 108–217.

Fathers of the English Dominican Province (trans.), *St. Thomas Aquinas: Summa Theologica* (New York: Benziger Bros, 1947).

Faulkner, Thomas C. et al., *Robert Burton: The Anatomy of Melancholy* (Oxford: Clarendon Press, 1989–).

Ferber, Sarah, *Demonic Possession and Exorcism in Early Modern France* (London: Routledge, 2004).

Ferreiro, Alberto, 'Simon Magus: The Patristic-Medieval Traditions and Historiography', *Apocrypha* 7 (1996), pp. 147–65.

Firth, Katharine R., *The Apocalyptic Tradition in Reformation Britain 1530–1645* (Oxford: Oxford University Press, 1979).

Flint, Valerie, 'The Demonisation of Magic and Sorcery in Late Antiquity: Christian Redefinitions of Pagan Religions,' in Bengt Ankarloo and Stuart Clark (eds), *Witchcraft and Magic in Europe: Ancient Greece and Rome* (London: Athlone Press, 1999), pp. 279–348.

Froehlich, Karlfried, 'Pseudo-Dionysius and the Reformation of the Sixteenth Century', in Colm Luibheid (trans.), *Pseudo-Dionysius: The Complete Works* (New York: Paulist Press, 1987).

Froom, Le Roy Edwin, *The Prophetic Faith of our Fathers* (Washington, DC: Review and Herald Publishing Association, 1946–54).

Gearing, William, *A Prospect of Heaven: Or, A Treatise of the Happiness of the Saints in Glory* (London, 1673).

Gibson, Marion, *Possession, Puritanism and Print: Harsnett, Shakespeare and the Elizabethan Exorcism Controversy* (London: Pickering & Chatto, 2006).

Gifford, George, *A Dialogue Concerning Witches and Witchcraftes* (London, 1593).

Glanvill, Joseph , *A Philosophical Endeavour towards the Defence of Witches and Apparitions* (London, 1666).

—— *A Blow at Modern Sadducism in some Philosophical Considerations about Witchcraft* (London, 1668).

—— *Saducismus Triumphatus* (London, 1681).

Goodwin, Thomas, *A Discourse of the Punishment of Sin in Hell; Demonstrating the Wrath of God to be the Immediate Cause Thereof* (London, 1680).

Grant, Francis [Lord Cullen], *Sadducismus Debellatus* (London, 1698).

Greenblatt, Stephen, 'Loudun and London', *Critical Inquiry* 12 (1985–6), pp. 326–46.

Gregory of Nyssa, *The Great Catechism*, in Philip Schaff (ed.), *A Select Library of the Nicene and Post-Nicene Fathers*, Series 2, Vol. 5 (Grand Rapids, MI: Eerdmans, 2005).

Haar, Stephen, *Simon Magus: The First Gnostic?* (Berlin: Walter de Gruyter, 2003).

Hackett, Jeremiah, 'Roger Bacon on Astronomy-Astrology: The Sources of the *Scientia Experimentalis*', in Jeremiah Hackett (ed.), *Roger Bacon and the Sciences: Commemorative Essays* (Leiden: Brill, 1997).

Halliwell, James O., *The Private Diary of John Dee* (London: Camden Society, 1842).

— *Letters of the Kings of England* (London: H. Colburn, 1848).

Hamilton, Bernard, 'The Cathars and Christian Perfection', in Peter Biller and Barrie Dobson (eds), *The Medieval Church: Universities, Heresy, and the Religious Life* (Woodbridge: Boydell Press, 1999).

Hanegraaff, Wouter J. (ed.), *Dictionary of Gnosis and Western Esotericism* (Leiden: Brill, 2006).

Hansen, Joseph, *Quellen und Untersuchungen zur Geschichte des Hexenwahns und der Hexenverfolgung im Mittelalter* (Bonn: Carl Georgi, Universitäts-Buchdruckerei und Verlag, 1901).

Harrison, G.B. (ed.), *King James the First: Daemonologie* (London: John Lane, 1924).

Harsnett, Samuel, *A Discovery of the Fraudulent Practices of John Darrel* (London, 1599).

— *A Declaration of Egregious Popish Impostures* (London, 1603), in F.W. Brownlow, *Shakespeare, Harsnett, and the Devils of Denham* (Newark, DE: University of Delaware Press, 1993).

Hart, John, *The Firebrand Taken out of the Fire* (London, 1654).

Hartwell, Abraham (trans.), *A True Discourse upon the Matter of Martha Brossier of Romorantin* (London, 1599).

Haskins, Charles Homer, *Studies in the History of Mediaeval Science* (New York: Frederick Ungar Publishing, 1960).

Hendel, Ronald, 'The Nephilim Were on the Earth: Genesis 6: 1–4 and its Ancient Near Eastern Context', in Christopher Auffarth and Loren T. Stuckenbruck (eds), *The Fall of the Angels* (Leiden and Boston, MA: Brill, 2004).

Henry, John, 'The Fragmentation of Renaissance Occultism and the Decline of Magic', *History of Science* 46 (2008), pp. 1–48.

Herzig, Tamar 'The Demons' Reaction to Sodomy: Witchcraft and Homosexuality in Gianfrancesco Pico della Mirandola's "Strix"', *Sixteenth Century Journal* 34 (2003), pp. 53–72.

Hill, W. Speed, *Richard Hooker: Of the Laws of Ecclesiastical Polity* (Cambridge, MA: Belknap Press, 1977–).

# Bibliography

Hobbes, Thomas , *Humane Nature: Or, The Fundamental Elements of Policy* (London, 1651).

Holliday, Lisa R., 'Will Satan be Saved? Reconsidering Origen's Theory of Volition in *Peri Archon*', *Vigiliae Christianae* 63 (2009), pp. 1–23.

Holmes, Peter (trans.), *The Five Books of Quintus Sept. Flor. Tertullianus against Marcion*, Ante-Nicene Christian Library, Vol. 7 (Edinburgh: T. & T. Clark, 1878).

Hume, David, *The History of England* (London: T. Cadell, 1792).

Irenaeus, *Against Heresies*, in Philip Schaff (ed.), *The Ante-Nicene Fathers*, Vol. 1 (Grand Rapids, MA: Christian Classics Ethereal Library, 1993).

Israel, Jonathan I., *Radical Enlightenment: Philosophy and the Making of Modernity 1650–1750* (Oxford: Oxford University Press, 2001).

James, Montague R., *The Apocryphal New Testament* (Oxford: Clarendon, 1953).

Jeffrey, David Lyle (ed.), 'Adam', in *Dictionary of Biblical Tradition in English Literature* (Grand Rapids, MI: Eerdmans, 1992).

Johnstone, Nathan, *The Devil and Demonism in Early Modern England* (Cambridge: Cambridge University Press, 2006).

Jollie, Thomas, *The Surey Demoniack* (London, 1697).

—— *A Vindication of the Surey Demoniack* (London, 1698).

Jones, John Henry (ed.), *The English Faust Book: A Critical Edition Based on the Text of 1592* (Cambridge: Cambridge University Press, 1994).

Jorden, Edward, *A Briefe Discourse of a Disease Called the Suffocation of the Mother* (London, 1603), in Michael MacDonald (ed.), *Witchcraft and Hysteria in Elizabethan London* (London: Routledge, 1991).

Jue, Jeffrey K., *Heaven upon Earth: Joseph Mede (1586–1638) and the Legacy of Millenarianism* (Dordrecht: Springer, 2006).

Karlsen, Carol, *The Devil in the Shape of a Woman: Witchcraft in Colonial New England* (New York: Vintage Books, 1989).

Kay, Richard, 'The Spare Ribs of Dante's Michael Scot', *Dante Studie* 103 (1985), pp. 1–14.

Keck, David, *Angels and Angelology in the Middle Ages* (Oxford: Oxfor University Press, 1998).

Kelly, Henry Ansgar, *Satan: A Biography* (Cambridge: Cambri University Press, 2006).

Kelly, J.N.D., *Early Christian Doctrines* (London: A. & C. Black, 1985'

Kieckhefer, Richard, 'Avenging the Blood of Children: Anxiety Child Victims and the Origins of the European Witch Trial Alberto Ferreira (ed.), *The Devil, Heresy and Witchcraft in the I Ages: Essays in Honour of Jeffrey B. Russell* (Leiden: Brill, 1998).

—— *Forbidden Rites: A Necromancer's Manual of the Fifteenth (* (University Park, PA: Pennsylvania State University Press, 1°

—— 'The Devil's Contemplatives: The *Liber Iuratus*, the *Liber* and Christian Appropriation of Jewish Occultism', in Clair

(ed.), *Conjuring Spirits: Texts and Traditions of Medieval Ritual Magic* (Stroud: Sutton Press, 1998).

—— *Magic in the Middle Ages* (Cambridge: Cambridge University Press, 2000).

King, Robert Alan, *Justin Martyr on Angels, Demons, and the Devil* (Casa Grande, AZ: King and Associates, 2011).

Klaasen, Frank, 'English Manuscripts of Magic, 1300–1500: A Preliminary Survey', in Claire Fanger (ed.), *Conjuring Spirits: Texts and Traditions of Medieval Ritual Magic* (Stroud: Sutton Press, 1998).

—— 'Ritual Invocation and Early Modern Science: The Skrying Experiments of Humphrey Gilbert', in Claire Fanger (ed.), *Invoking Angels: Theurgic Ideas and Practices, Thirteenth to Sixteenth Centuries* (University Park, PA: Pennsylvania State University Press, 2012).

Klingshirn, William E., 'Isidore of Seville's Taxonomy of Magicians and Diviners', *Traditio* 58 (2006), pp. 59–90.

Kocher, Paul H., 'The Idea of God in Elizabethan Medicine', *Journal of the History of Ideas* 51 (1950), pp. 3–29.

Kors, Alan C. and Edward Peters, *Witchcraft in Europe, 1100–1700: A Documentary History* (London: J.M. Dent and Sons, 1973).

—— —— *Witchcraft in Europe, 400–1700: A Documentary History* (Philadelphia: University of Pennsylvania Press, 2001).

Krey, Philip D.W. and Peter D.S. Krey (eds), *Luther's Spirituality* (Mahwah, NJ: Paulist Press, 2007).

Landes, Richard, Andrew Gow and David C. van Meter, *The Apocalyptic Year 1000: Religious Expectation and Social Change* (Oxford: Oxford University Press, 2003).

Láng, Benedek, *Unlocked Books: Manuscripts of Learned Magic in the Medieval Libraries of Central Europe* (University Park, PA: Pennsylvania State University Press, 2008).

Larner, Christina, *Enemies of God: The Witch-Hunt in Scotland* (London: Blackwell, 1981).

Lea, Henry Charles, *Materials toward a History of Witchcraft* (New York: Thomas Yoselhoff, 1957).

Le Goff, Jacques, *The Birth of Purgatory* (Chicago: University of Chicago Press, 1986).

Lemnius, Levinus, *The Secret Miracles of Nature* (London, 1658).

Lerner, Robert E., 'Refreshment of the Saints: The Time after Antichrist as a Station for Earthly Progress in Medieval Thought', *Traditio* 32 (1976), pp. 97–144.

—— 'Antichrists and Antichrist in Joachim of Fiore', *Speculum* 60 (1985), pp. 553–70.

Levack, Brian P. (ed.), *The Witchcraft Sourcebook* (New York: Routledge, 2004).

*Life of St. Anthony*, in Roy J. Deferrari (ed.), *Early Christian Biographies* (Washington, DC: Catholic University of America Press, 1952).

# Bibliography

Love, Christopher, *Hells Terror: Or, A Treatise of the Torments of the Damned as a Preservative against Security* (London, 1653).

MacCulloch, J.A., *The Harrowing of Hell: A Comparative Study of an Early Christian Doctrine* (Edinburgh: T. & T. Clark, 1930).

MacDonald, Michael (ed.), *Witchcraft and Hysteria in Elizabethan London: Edward Jorden and the Mary Glover Case* (London: Tavistock, 1991).

McGinn, Bernard, *Apocalyptic Spirituality* (London: SPCK, 1979).

— *Visions of the End: Apocalyptic Traditions in the Middle Ages* (New York: Columbia University Press, 1979).

— *Antichrist: Two Thousand Years of the Human Fascination with Evil* (San Francisco: Harper, 1996).

— (ed.), *The Encyclopedia of Apocalypticism, Vol. 2: Apocalypticism in Western History and Culture* (New York and London: Continuum, 2000).

Mackay, Christopher S. (ed. and trans.), *Malleus Maleficarum* (Cambridge: Cambridge University Press, 2006).

McNeill, John T. (ed.), *Calvin: Institutes of the Christian Religion* (Louisville, KT: Westminster John Knox Press, 2006).

Malcolm, Noel (ed.), *Thomas Hobbes: Leviathan* (Oxford: Clarendon, 2012).

Markus, R.A., 'Augustine on Magic: A Neglected Semiotic Theory', *Revue des Études Augustiniennes*, 40 (1994), pp. 375–88.

Marrone, Steven P., 'William of Auvergne on Magic in Natural Philosophy and Theology', in Jan Aertsen and Andreas Speer (eds), 'Was ist Philosophie im Mittelalter,' *Miscellania Medievalia* 26 (1998), pp. 741–8.

Martinez, Florentino Garcia, *The Dead Sea Scrolls Translated: The Qumran Texts in English* (Leiden: Brill, 1994).

— and Eibert J.C. Tigchelaar, *The Dead Sea Scrolls Study Edition* (Leiden: Brill, 1997).

Marx, C.W., *The Devil's Rights and the Redemption in the Literature of Medieval England* (Cambridge: D.S. Brewer, 1995).

Mason, James, *The Anatomie of Sorcerie* (London, 1612).

Mathiesen, Robert, 'A Thirteenth-Century Ritual to Attain the Beatific Vision from the *Sworn Book* of Honorius of Thebes', in Claire Fanger (ed.), *Conjuring Spirits: Texts and Traditions of Medieval Ritual Magic* (Stroud: Sutton Press, 1998).

Maxwell-Stuart, P.G., *The Occult in Early Modern Europe: A Documentary History* (New York: St Martin's Press, 1999).

— *Martín del Rio: Investigations into Magic* (Manchester and New York: Manchester University Press, 2000).

Mede, Joseph, *The Key of the Revelation Searched and Demonstrated* (London, 1643).

Mesler, Katelyn, 'The *Liber Iuratus Honorii* and the Christian Reception of Angel Magic', in Claire Fanger (ed.), *Invoking Angels: Theurgic Ideas and Practices, Thirteenth to Sixteenth Centuries* (University Park, PA: Pennsylvania State University Press, 2012).

Midelfort, H.C. Erik, 'The Devil and the German People: Reflections on the Popularity of Demon Possession in Sixteenth-Century Germany', in Steven E. Ozment (ed.), *Religion and Culture in the Renaissance and Reformation* (Kirksville, MO: Sixteenth Century Publishers, 1989).

Montagu, Richard, *The Acts and Monuments of the Church before Christ Incarnate* (London, 1642).

Monter, E. William, *Witchcraft in France and Switzerland: The Borderlands during the Reformation* (Ithaca, NY, and London: Cornell University Press, 1976).

Mora, George (ed.), *Witches, Devils, and Doctors in the Renaissance: Johann Weyer, De Praestigiis Daemonum* (Binghamton, NY: Medieval and Renaissance Texts and Studies, 1991).

More, George, *A True Discourse Concerning the Certain Possession and Dispossession of 7 Persons in One Family in Lancashire* (London, 1600).

More, Henry, *An Antidote against Atheisme* (London, 1652).

—— *The Immortality of the Soul, so Farre forth as it is Demonstrable from the Knowledge of Nature and the Light of Reason* (London, 1659).

—— *The Immortality of the Soul*, in Henry More, *A Collection of Several Philosophical Writings* (London, 1662).

Mosher, David L. (trans.), *Saint Augustine: Eight-Three Different Questions* (Washington, DC: Catholic University of America Press, 1982).

Mumford, Joseph, *The Catholic-Scripturist: Or, The Plea of the Roman Catholics* (Edinburgh, 1687).

Murdoch, Brian, *The Apocryphal Adam and Eve in Medieval Europe* (Oxford: Oxford University Press, 2009).

Napier, John, *A Plaine Discovery of the Whole Revelation of Saint John* (Edinburgh, 1593).

Neusner, Jacob, *Genesis Rabbah: The Judaic Commentary to the Book of Genesis: A new American Translation* (Atlanta, GA: Scholars Press, 1985).

Nevinson, Charles, *Later Writings of Bishop Hooper* (Cambridge: Cambridge University Press, 1852).

Newman, William R., 'An Overview of Roger Bacon's Alchemy', in Jeremiah Hackett (ed.), *Roger Bacon and the Sciences: Commemorative Essays* (Leiden: Brill, 1997).

Newport, Kenneth G.C., *Apocalypse and Millennium: Studies in Biblical Eisegesis* (Cambridge: Cambridge University Press, 2000).

Nickelsburg, George W.E., *A Commentary on the Book of 1 Enoch, Chapters 1–36; 81–108* (Minneapolis: Fortress Press, 2001).

O'Ceallaigh, G.C., 'Dating the Commentaries of Nicodemus', *Harvard Theological Review* 56 (1963), pp. 21–58.

Pagels, Elaine, 'The Social History of Satan, the "Intimate Enemy": A Preliminary Sketch', *Harvard Theological Review* 84 (1991), pp. 105–28.

—— *The Origin of Satan* (New York: Random House, 1995).

Palmer, Philip Mason and Robert Pattison More, *The Sources of the Faust Tradition from Simon Magus to Lessing* (New York: Oxford University Press, 1936).

Patrides, C.A., 'The Salvation of Satan', *Journal of the History of Ideas* 28 (1967), pp. 467–78.

Paxia, Gaetano (trans.), *The Devil's Scourge: Exorcism during the Italian Renaissance* (Boston, MA: Weiser Books, 2002).

Perkins, William, *A Discourse of the Damned Art of Witchcraft* (Cambridge, 1608).

Pingree, David, 'The Diffusion of Arabic Magical Texts in Western Europe', in Charles S.F. Burnett et al. (eds), *La Diffusione delle Scienze Islamiche nel Medioevo Europeo* (Rome: Accademia Nazionale dei Lincei, 1987).

Potts, Thomas, *The Wonderfull Discoverie of Witches in the Countie of Lancaster* (London, 1613).

Pratten, B.P., Marcus Dods and Thomas Smith (trans.), *The Writings of Tatian and Theophilus; and the Clementine Recognitions*, Ante-Nicene Christian Library, Vol. 3 (Edinburgh: T. & T. Clark, 1883).

Pringle, William (trans.), *Commentary on a Harmony of the Evangelists, Matthew, Mark, and Luke by John Calvin* (Grand Rapids, MI: Baker Book House, 1984).

Rankin, David Ivan, *From Clement to Origen: The Social and Historical Context of the Church Fathers* (Aldershot: Ashgate, 2006).

Rashdall, Hastings, *The Idea of Atonement in Christian Theology* (London: Macmillan, 1919).

Reed, Annette Yoshiko, 'The Trickery of the Fallen Angels and the Demonic Mimesis of the Divine: Aetiology, Demonology, and Polemics in the Writings of Justin Martyr', *Journal of Early Christian Studies* 12 (2004), pp. 141–71.

Riddle, M.B. (trans.), *Acts of the Apostles Peter and Paul*, in Alexander Roberts and James Donaldson (eds), *The Ante-Nicene Fathers*, Vol. 8 (Grand Rapids, MI: Eerdmans, 1951).

Rider, Catherine, *Magic and Impotence in the Middle Ages* (Oxford: Oxford University Press, 2006).

Roberts, Alexander, *A Treatise of Witchcraft* (London, 1616).

—— and James Donaldson (eds), *Fathers of the Third Century. The Ante-Nicene Fathers*, Vol. 6 (Peabody, MA: Hendrickson Publishers, 2004).

—— —— (eds), *Latin Christianity: Its Founder, Tertullian. The Ante-Nicene Fathers*, Vol. 3 (Grand Rapids, MI: Eerdmans, 1980).

—— and W.H. Rambaut (trans.), *The Writings of Irenaeus, Vol. 2*, Ante-Nicene Christian Library, Vol. 9 (Edinburgh: T. & T. Clark, 1883).

Roper, Lyndal, *Witch Craze: Terror and Fantasy in Baroque Germany* (New Haven, CT, and London: Yale University Press, 2004).

Rusconi, Robert, 'Antichrist and Antichrists' in Bernard Mc Ginn (ed), *The Encyclopedia of Apocalypticism: Volume 2: Apocalypticism in Western History and Culture* (New York/London: Continuum, 2000), pp. 287–325.

Russell, Jeffrey Burton, *Witchcraft in the Middle Ages* (Ithaca, NY, and London: Cornell University Press, 1972).

—— *Lucifer: The Devil in the Middle Ages* (Ithaca, NY, and London: Cornell University Press, 1984).

—— *Satan: The Early Christian Tradition* (Ithaca, NY, and London: Cornell University Press, 1987).

Rust, George, *A Letter of Resolution Concerning Origen and the Chief of his Opinions* (London, 1661).

Ryan, Granger and Helmut Ripperger (trans.), *The Golden Legend of Jacobus de Voragine* (New York: Arno Press, 1969).

Schaff, Philip (ed.), *St. Augustine's City of God and Christian Doctrine* (Buffalo, NY: Christian Literature Co., 1887).

Scheck, Thomas P. (trans.), *Homilies on Numbers: Origen* (Downers Grove, IL: IVP Academic, 2009).

Schleiermacher, Friedrich, *The Christian Faith* (Edinburgh: T. & T. Clark, 1928).

Schneemelcher, Wilhelm, *New Testament Apocrypha*, Vol. 2 (Cambridge: James Clarke & Co., 1991).

—— *New Testament Apocrypha*, Vol. 2 (Cambridge: James Clarke & Co., 1991).

Schreiber, Stefan, 'The Great Opponent: The Devil in Early Jewish and Formative Christian Literature', in Friedrich V. Reiterer et al. (eds), *The Concept of Celestial Beings: Origins, Development and Reception* (Berlin: Walter de Gruyter, 2007).

Scot, Reginald, *The Discoverie of Witchcraft* (London, 1584).

Scott, H. von E. and C.C. Swinton Bland, *The Dialogue on Miracles: Caesarius of Heisterbach (1220–1235)* (London: George Routledge & Sons, 1929).

Scott, Randy A. (trans.), *On the Demon-Mania of Witches* (Toronto: Centre for Reformation and Renaissance Studies, 1995).

Sharpe, James, *The Bewitching of Anne Gunter* (London: Profile, 1999).

Sharrock, Robert, *De Finibus Virtutis Christianae* (Oxford, 1673).

Sharrock, Roger (ed.), *The Miscellaneous Works of John Bunyan* (Oxford: Clarendon Press, 1976–).

Shirley, Samuel (trans.), *Spinoza: The Letters* (Indianapolis and Cambridge: Hackett Publishing Company, 1995).

Shower, John, *Heaven and Hell: Or, The Unchangeable State of Happiness or Misery for All Mankind in Another World* (London, 1700).

Sinkewicz, Robert E., *Evagrius of Pontus: The Greek Ascetic Corpus* (Oxford: Oxford University Press, 2003).

Smith, Gregory A., 'How Thin is a Demon?', *Journal of Early Christian Studies* 16 (2008), pp. 479–512.

# Bibliography

Stephens, Walter, *Demon Lovers: Witchcraft, Sex, and the Crisis of Belief* (Chicago: University of Chicago Press, 2002).

Stearne, John, *The Discoverie of Witchcraft* (London, 1648).

Steudel, Annette, 'God and Belial', in Lawrence Schiffman, Emanuel Tov and James VanderKam (eds), *The Dead Sea Scrolls: Fifty Years After their Discovery, 1947–1997* (Jerusalem: IES, 2000).

Stone, Harriet and Gerhild Scholz Williams (trans.), *On the Inconstancy of Witches: Pierre de Lancres* Tableau de l'Inconstance des Mauvais Anges et Demons *(1612)* (Tempe, AZ: Arizona Center for Medieval and Renaissance Studies with Brepols, 2006).

Straw, Carole, *Gregory the Great: Perfection in Imperfection* (Berkeley, CA: University of California Press, c.1988).

Stubbs, William (ed.), *Gesta Regis Henrici Secundi Benedicti Abbatis: The Chronicle of the Reigns of Henry II, and Richard I. A.D. 1169–1192; Known Commonly under the Name of Benedict of Peterborough* (London: Longmans, Green, Reader and Dyer, 1867).

Stuckenbruck, Loren, 'The Origins of Evil in Jewish Apocalyptic Tradition: The Interpretation of Genesis 6: 1–4 in the Second and Third Centuries B.C.E.', in Christopher Auffarth and Loren T. Stuckenbruck (eds), *The Fall of the Angels* (Leiden and Boston, MA: Brill, 2004).

Summers, Montague (trans.), *The Malleus Maleficarum of Heinrich Kramer and James Sprenger* (New York: Dover, 1971).

—— (ed.), *Demoniality by Ludovico Maria Sinistrari Friar Minor* (New York: Benjamin Blom, 1972).

—— (ed.), *An Examen of Witches (Discours Des Sorciers) by Henri Boguet* (Warrington: Portrayer Publishers, 2002).

Swan, John, *A True and Breife Report, of Mary Glovers Vexation* (London, 1603).

Taylor, Jerome (trans.), *The* Didascalicon *of Hugh of St. Victor* (New York: Columbia University Press, 1991).

Tertullian, 'The Prescription against Heretics', in Alexander Roberts and James Donaldson (eds), *Latin Christianity: Its Founder, Tertullian. The Ante-Nicene Fathers*, Vol. 3 (Grand Rapids, MI: Eerdmans, 1980).

Thelwall, S. (trans.), *The Writings of Quintus Sept. Flor. Tertullianus, Vol. 3*, Ante-Nicene Christian Library, Vol. 18 (Edinburgh: T. & T. Clark, 1880).

—— (trans.), *The Writings of Quintus Sept. Flor. Tertullianus, Vol. 1*, Ante-Nicene Christian Library, Vol. 11 (Edinburgh: T. & T. Clark, 1882).

Thorndike, Lynn, *A History of Magic and Experimental Science* (New York: Columbia University Press, 1923–58).

—— *Michael Scot* (London: Nelson, 1965).

Thwaites, Edward, *A Marvellous Work of Late Done* (London, 1576).

Trumbower, Jeffrey A., *Rescue for the Dead: The Posthumous Salvation of Non-Christians in Early Christianity* (Oxford: Oxford University Press, 2001).

# The Devil

Tschacher, Werner, *Der Formicarius des Johannes Nider von 1437/38* (Aachen: Shaker Verlag, 2000).

Turner, Ralph V., 'Descendit ad Inferos: Medieval Views on Christ's Descent into Hell and the Salvation of the Ancient Just', *Journal of the History of Ideas* 27 (1966), pp. 173–94.

Twelftree, Graham H., *Jesus the Exorcist: A Contribution to the Study of the Historical Jesus* (Tübingen: J.C.B. Mohr (Paul Siebeck), 1993).

Van der Toorn, Karel, Bob Becking and Pieter W. van der Horst, *Dictionary of Deities and Demons in the Bible* (Leiden: Brill, 1995).

Vanderkam, James C. (trans), *The Book of Jubilees* (Louvain: E. Peeters, 1989).

—— '1 Enoch, Enochic Motifs, and Enoch in Early Christian Literature', in James C. Vanderkam, *The Jewish Apocalyptic Heritage in Early Christianity* (Assen and Minneapolis: Van Gorcum and Fortress Press, 1996).

—— *The Book of Jubilees* (Sheffield: Sheffield Academic Press, 2001).

Wakefield, Walter P. and Austin P. Evans, *Heresies of the High Middle Ages: Selected Sources Translated and Annotated* (New York and London: Columbia University Press, 1969).

Walker, Daniel P., *Unclean Spirits: Possession and Exorcism in France and England in the Late Sixteenth and Early Seventeenth Centuries* (Philadelphia: University of Pennsylvania Press, 1981).

—— 'The Cessation of Miracles', in I. Merkel and A.G. Debus (eds), *Hermeticism and the Renaissance: Intellectual History and the Occult in Early Modern Europe* (Washington, DC: Folger, 1988).

Wallis, Robert Ernest (trans.), 'On Jealousy and Envy', in Alexander Roberts and James Donaldson (eds), *The Writings of Cyprian, Bishop of Carthage, Vol. 2*, Ante-Nicene Christian Library, Vol. 13 (Edinburgh: T. & T. Clark, 1880).

Watson, Nicholas, 'John the Monk's *Book of Visions of the Blessed and Undefiled Virgin Mary*', in Claire Fanger (ed.), *Conjuring Spirits: Texts and Traditions of Medieval Ritual Magic* (Stroud: Sutton Press, 1998).

Willis, Thomas, *The London Practice of Physick* (London, 1685).

Young, Frances M., 'Insight or Incoherence? The Greek Fathers on God and Evil', *Journal of Ecclesiastical History* 24 (1973), pp. 113–26.

Zambelli, Paola, *The Speculum Astronomiae and its Enigma* (Dordrecht: Kluwer Academic, 1992).

Zimmerman, Odo John (trans.), *Saint Gregory the Great: Dialogues* (Washington, DC: Catholic University of America, 1959).

# Index

*Acts of the Apostles Peter and Paul*
    28, 75, 78–80
Adam 6, 7, 13, 15, 28, 31–4, 39–41,
    47, 50, 54, 56, 58–9, 71 *see*
    *also* Adam and Eve
Adam and Eve 6–7, 15, 29, 31–4,
    36, 39–41, 47, 71, 143, 218,
    224
Adso 176–7, 179, 190, 244–5
Africanus, Julius 13, 223
angelology 6–7, 70, 75–6, 91
Anselm of Canterbury 55, 66–7
Anthony, Saint 111–112
Antichrist 48, 244–6
    birth-place of 178
    defeat of 173, 176, 180–1, 191
    identification with the papacy
        and 174, 182–90, 200–1
    and judgement of, by God 179
    mark of 178
    power of 87, 173
    and role as persecutor 171,
        176–9
    signs and wonders of 173
    time of the 63, 168, 172–6,
        179–80, 182, 187, 190
*Apocalypse of Moses, The* 40, 226
Aquinas, Thomas 60, 64–7, 76, 84,
    106, 116–17, 129, 198, 228–30
Asael 4–5, 15, 22
astrology 12, 77, 80, 83–4, 86–7,
    133, 219, 232, 251, 256
atheism 10, 165, 211, 213, 217
Athenagoras 11
atonement, ransom theory of the
    49, 67, 74
Augustine, Saint 14–15, 45, 52–3,
    56, 66, 80, 86, 95, 111–16,
    129, 171–6, 179–80, 183–90

Bacon, Roger 85–7
Balaam 16–17
Bale, John 184–6
Bancroft, Richard 147, 165
Barnabas 28, 78
Basel, Council of 97
Baxter, Richard 148
Beaune, Jean de 68, 94
Beelzebul 15, 23, 26, 89, 133, 144
Bekker, Balthasar 117, 216–19
Belial 15, 19–22, 89
Beliar 23
Bellarmine, Robert 190–1
Benedict XI, Pope 183
Bernardino of Siena 120
Boguet, Henri 104, 107, 110, 127,
    136–7, 142
Bonaventure 60, 63, 115–17
Boniface II, Pope 185
Boniface VIII, Pope 183
Boxtel, Hugo 212
Boyle, Robert 214
Bradwell, Stephen 146
Brightman, Thomas 185, 188
Bromhall, Thomas 194
Brown, Peter 95
Browne, Thomas 148
Bunyan, John 192–3
Burgh, Alfred 21
Burton, Robert 148–9

Caesarius of Heisterbach 113–14
Calvin, John 184, 201
Calvinism 135–7, 184
cannibalism 118–20, 126
Cathars 70, 72–5, 97–9
Chrysostom, John 52–3
Clark, Stuart 209
Clement of Alexandria 56

*Commentaries in Apocalypsin ante Centum Annos Aeditus* 183
Constantine 187–8
Constantius of Lyon 124
Cotta, John 156, 166
Cranmer, Thomas 154
Cudworth, Ralph 213, 215

Dalton, Michael 139
Damned, the 59–60, 66–7, 192–5, 221
Daneau, Lambert 136, 138
Daniel 179, 189
Dante 60, 83
Daston, Lorraine 205–6
Deacon, John 144, 149–50
Dead Sea Scrolls 19, 22
Defoe, Daniel 197, 219, 220
Della Mirandola, Gianfrancesco Pico 104, 107
Della Porta, Giambattista 126–7
Della Spina, Bartolomeo 123–5
Del Rio, Martin 126
demoniac(s) 142, 155–6, 158–62, 164–70
    animal-like behaviour of 157
    and epilepsy 147–8
    fraudulence of 150–1, 166–7, 169
    Gerasene 24–5, 144, 165
    and hysteria 147
    *see also* exorcism
demonology 41, 61, 70, 75, 81, 91, 101, 103, 116, 123, 133, 140, 203–4, 206–7, 210–11, 217–18
    and Aquinas 64–5, 76, 116
    Calvinist 136–7
    Catholic 64, 102, 136
    Christian 20, 42, 53, 58, 221
    European 120
    forensic 150–6
    and James I, King of England 97, 139, 197
    Jewish 4, 6, 20

Protestant 163
    western 8, 46
demons 1, 5, 8, 10, 12, 15, 16, 26, 34–6, 38, 43–4, 47–8, 51, 64–5, 67–8, 73, 75, 80, 89–90, 96, 99, 101, 124, 129–30, 181, 197, 208–10, 213–14, 217–18
    corporeality of 76, 111–17, 207, 210–11
    location of 63, 65
    and magic 12, 68–9, 77–97, 206
    names of 89
    powers of 112–13, 122, 125, 156
    prince of 16, 22–3
    and sex and sexuality 76, 103–11, 116–17, 138, 207, 212
    and tormentors of the dead 58–61, 66, 193
Descartes, René 215, 218
Dionysius *see also* Pseudo-Dionysius
Drage, William 156
dragon (fall of the) 28–9, 172, 181
dualism, dualists 19–20, 43, 55, 70, 72, 90, 217–18

Eden, Garden of 6, 16, 28, 31–2, 34, 37, 39–41, 52, 66, 102, 143, 157, 218
    location of 32
    and paradise 39–41, 71
    river of 32
    serpent of 16, 28, 31, 34–6, 40–1, 102, 218
    and tree of knowledge 7, 33–4, 41
    and tree of life 33, 34
    envy 37, 41, 64–6, 92, 212
Epiphanes, Antiochus, emperor 177–8
*Episcopi*, canon 122–6
Erasmus (of Rotterdam) 45
Erigena, John Scotus 75
Essenes 19
Eugenius IV, Pope 94, 96, 128

Eve 6, 39–40, 71, 102 *see also*
   Adam and Eve
evil
   and God 72–4
   and good 21, 26, 33–4, 44, 47,
      142, 144
   of mankind 8
   origin of 1, 3, 13, 15, 19–20, 72
   realm of 73–4
   and spirits 1, 3, 5–9, 11, 15, 54,
      88–9, 122, 148–9, 153, 156,
      161–2, 165, 178, 197, 204
evil one, the 23–4, 27, 50
exorcism 26, 89, 120, 144–5, 147,
   149, 161–5, 167–9, 211
Eymeric, Nicholas 123

flood, the 2–3, 6–8, 12, 15
Franciscans, 'Spiritual' 182–3
free will 13, 35, 37, 43–5, 47–8, 54,
   64–5, 73, 84
Fründ, Johann 122

Garden of Eden *see* Eden, Garden
   of
Gearing, William 192–3
Géraud, Hugues 69
Gesner, Konrad 149
giants 3–8, 11, 25, 36, 111, 117 *see
   also* Nephilim
Glanvill, Joseph 197, 203–4,
   213–14, 216
Gnostic(s) 36, 43
God
   banishment of the Devil by 37,
      43, 71
   and conflict with Satan 18,
      43–4, 49, 54–5, 70, 158
   and cursing the serpent 34
   and destruction of mankind 3,
      5–6
   enemies of 6, 66
   goodness of 17, 19, 47, 52, 64,
      70, 72, 194
   judgement of 179, 181

justice of 45, 56, 194–5
Kingdom of 24–99, 182, 184,
   189
miracles worked by 76,
   198–202
providence of 56, 179, 198, 217
sons of 1–4, 7, 13–15
sovereignty of 20, 158, 218
wrath of 40, 46, 193–5
gods of the Greeks and Romans
   10, 36, 80
Goethe, Johann Wolfgang von
   133
Gog 29, 176, 181, 184, 186–7, 189,
   191
Goodwin, Thomas 194
Gratian 122
Greco-Roman religion 10, 38,
   79–80
Gregory of Nyssa 51–4
Gregory the Great, Pope 53–6, 65,
   75, 113, 143
Guazzo, Francesco Maria 130,
   143, 152
Gui, Bernard 68, 94–5, 123

Hades 30, 51
Harrowing of Hades (hell) 56–61
Harsnett, Samuel 144, 147,
   149–50, 164, 165, 167
heaven 4, 10–12, 21, 25, 27–8,
   29–30, 35–6, 39, 42, 44, 47,
   56, 59–60, 65–6, 71, 72, 79,
   88, 91, 101, 142, 154, 169,
   175, 181, 186, 189, 191, 214
hell 10, 15, 47, 55–6, 58–9, 61–3,
   65–8, 71, 73–4, 135, 154,
   169–70, 186, 193, 217, 220
   Christ's descent into 56–7, 58,
      74–5
   fire(s) of 66, 72, 187, 191–5
   harrowing of, 9, 56–7, 75
   powers of 56, 88
   torment of 45, 59–60, 169, 189,
      191–5

heresy, heretics 37–8, 69, 96, 98,
    99–100, 117, 120, 138, 181–2,
    186
Hilduin, Abbot of Saint-Denis
    75
Hobbes, Thomas 145, 199, 209–11,
    214–15, 217
Hogarth, William 196–7, 219;
Honorius of Thebes 91–2
Hugh of St Victor 82–3
Hume, David 186, 202
Hutchinson, Francis 220
Hutchinson, James 137

incubi, incubus 14, 103, 108, 117,
    209
Innocent VIII, Pope 105
Irenaeus 37, 49–50
Iscariot, Judas 27
Isidore of Seville 80–1, 113
Israel, Jonathan 216

Jacquier, Nicolas 103, 123
James VI and I, king of Scotland
    and England 97, 139, 146–7,
    155, 168, 197
Jerome, Saint 3
Jewel, John, bishop of Salisbury
    174
Joachim of Fiore 70, 179–85
John of Lugio 73–4
John of Morigny 92
John of Patmos 28
John XXII, Pope 67–9, 88, 92, 94,
    183
Johnstone, Nathan 208
Jorden, Edward 145–7, 162
Jubilees, book of 6–9, 16, 19, 25
Judas *see* Iscariot, Judas
Judgement, Day of 5, 7–10, 62–3,
    66, 169, 189

Knox, John 137
Kramer, Heinrich 102–3, 105–8,
    121–2

Lactantius 12–13, 15
Lancre, Pierre de 108–10, 118
Lemnius, Levinus 148, 158
Leo X, Pope 183
Lombard, Peter 60–3, 75, 114–15
Love, Christopher 193
Lucifer 15, 23, 31, 42, 46, 61–2,
    89, 134
Luther, Martin 45, 107, 183–4, 201

magic 79–88, 92–3, 95, 97, 100,
    129–30, 133, 200, 206, 217,
    221
    angelic 10, 92–3, 206
    demonic 12, 68–9, 77, 81, 84,
        86–9, 93–6, 206
    demonisation of 77–81
    and Devil 67, 76, 82, 87
    and divination 81–3
    and early Christianity 79
    image 69, 77, 84
    and inquisitors 95
    natural 77, 82, 84, 87, 93, 126,
        202–3, 205–6
    priestly 162–1
    ritual 78, 89, 91, 93–4, 129, 206
    and sorcerers 95
    taxonomy of 81
    *see also* necromancy, witches
magicians 69, 78–9, 85–6, 88,
    90–1, 96–7, 100, 126, 129–30,
    132–3, 176, 178, 219
Magnus, Albertus 60, 84
Magog 29, 176, 184, 186–7, 189,
    191
Magus, Simon 78–9, 133, 182
Marlowe, Christopher 133
Martyr, Justin 10, 11, 34–8
Mary, the Virgin 71, 88, 92, 131–2,
    135
Mastema 8–9, 15–16, 22, 25
Mather, Cotton 148
Mede, Joseph 185, 189
Menghi, Girolamo 161
Midelfort, Erik 142

# Index

miracles 76, 80, 198–202, 204, 217
Mohammed (Muhammad) 184,
    185–6
Montagu, Richard 46
More, Henry 193, 197, 213–16
Muslims 180, 184, 187–8

Napier, John 185–8
necromancy 77, 80, 84–5, 88–90,
    94–5, 97, 101, 133, 186, 206
Neopolitanus, Johannes Baptista
    see Della Porta, Giambattista
nephilim 1–2, 4
Nero, Emperor 79, 174, 177–8,
    180, 182, 184
Nicodemus, Gospel of 57–9
Nider, Johannes 101–2, 121, 124,
    147

Olivi, Peter 182–3
Origen 42–6, 48, 50, 56, 64, 111–12

Pagels, Elaine 4, 18
Paradise 56, 58 see also Eden,
    Garden of
Park, Katherine 205–6
Passavanti, Jacopo 198
Paul, Benedictine monk of
    Chartres 99
Paul, deacon of Naples see
    Theophilus
Paulus, Sergius 28, 78
Perkins, William 129–30, 202
Peyre Godin, Cardinal Guilhem
    de 68
Pharisees 26
Phocas, Emperor 185
Ponticus, Evagrius 112
Porphyry 111
pride 41, 43, 46–7, 54, 61, 62, 64–5,
    92, 208
Prierius, Silvestro 107
prince of darkness 20, 94
prince of demons 16, 22–3, 34
prince of lights 20–1

Pseudo-Dionysius 75
purgatory 59–61
Puritan 141, 145, 150, 164, 188,
    193, 202

Qumran 19

ransom theory of the Atonement
    49–55, 66–8
Remy, Nicholas 136
Revelation, book of 23–4, 28–31,
    61–2, 163, 168, 171–3, 178,
    180–7, 189–90
Ribera, Francisco 190
Roberts, Alexander 102
Russell, Jeffrey Burton 65
Rust, George 46, 48

sabbath 97, 100, 118–20, 123–31,
    171, 209
  sacrifices at 98
  travels to 120–3, 125–8, 131,
    204
  Devil's appearance at 98
Sacconi, Rainier 73–4
Saladin 180
San Filippo, Angelo Maria da
    194
Satan
  alternative names for 15–16,
    22–3
  army of, 181
  and beast of Revelation 172
  binding of 170–1, 174–4,
    179–89, 191
  birth of 15–17, 22
  and chief of angels 34, 54, 64
  defeat of 27–30, 176, 189, 191,
    220
  emissary of God as 17–19, 155
  fall of 27, 31–5, 37–9, 41–3, 46,
    48 49, 54, 64
  imprisonment of, in Hades 30,
    35, 55, 57–8, 61–3, 72, 170–1
  and pride 41, 43, 54

Satan (*continued*)
  and punisher of the wicked
    58–9, 66
  roles of 193
  serpent, identification with 7,
    28–9, 34–5, 40
  and superstition 196
  and temptation of Christ 25–6
  wrath of 155, 168–70
Satanism 117, 209
Schleiermacher, Friedrich 221
Scot, Michael 82–3
Scot, Reginald 117, 126, 139,
    207–9, 215, 218
Septuagint 2, 23
serpent *see* Eden, Garden of
Shakespeare, William 167
Sharrock, Robert 192
Shemihazah 4–5, 8, 15, 22
Sheol 58
Shower, John 191–2
sons of justice 20–2
sons of light 20–2
Spies, Johann 133
Spinoza, Benedict de 202, 211–12,
    214–15, 217
Sprenger, Jacob 105, 147
Stearne, John 102
Stephens, Walter 103
succubi 108
Swan, John 170
Sylvester, Pope 185

Tartarus 58
Tatian 35–7
Tertullian 37–8, 42
Theodoret, bishop of Cyrrhus 13
Theophilus (of Antioch) 36–7,
    131–3, 135
Thietland of Einsiedeln, 175–6
Tholosan, Claude 100–1
Thomas of Cantimpré 106

Ubertino of Casale 183

University of Paris, articles of
    1398 89, 90–1, 129

Virgin Mary *see* Mary, the Virgin
Voragine, Jacobus de 61, 78, 124

Walker, Daniel P. 142, 200
Walker, John 144, 149–50
watchers 3–6, 8, 11, 19, 35, 41
Weyer, Johann 126
Whiston, William 168
William of Auvergne 83–5
witchcraft 97–101, 129–30, 133,
    138, 158–9, 204, 206–7,
    220–1
  and gender 100–7
  trials 97, 100, 120, 137–9, 145,
    148, 160
witches
  and anti-mothers 121, 138
  confessions of 98, 103–5, 107,
    120
  and covenant with Satan 129,
    136–7
  and familiars 138–9, 160, 204,
    208
  and heresy 38, 98–100, 102,
    106, 128, 138
  and infanticide 118–22, 126,
    131
  of Lancashire 118–20, 158, 160,
    170
  and mark of the Devil 136–7,
    139–40
  persecution of 38, 69, 97, 105,
    138
  transport, magical of 119,
    121–8
  and witch-hunts 97, 108, 120,
    137

Young, Frances 49

Zoroastrian Persia 81